American History
A CONCISE DOCUMENTS COLLECTION
Volume 1: To 1877

American History
A CONCISE DOCUMENTS COLLECTION

Volume 1: To 1877

Douglas Bukowski

Bedford/St. Martin's
Boston/New York

For Bedford/St. Martin's
History Editor: Katherine E. Kurzman
Production Editor: Harold Chester
Production Supervisor: Dennis J. Conroy
Marketing Manager: Charles Cavaliere
Art Director: Lucy Krikorian
Text Design: Paul Agresti
Cover Art: Crocket Street Looking West by Herman Lungkwitz. Courtesy of the Witte Museum.
Composition: ComCom
Printing and Binding: Haddon Craftsmen, Inc.

President: Charles H. Christensen
Editorial Director: Joan E. Feinberg
Director of Editing, Design, and Production: Marcia Cohen
Managing Editor: Erica T. Appel

Library of Congress Catalog Card Number: 98-89220

4 3 2
f e d c b

For information, write: Bedford/St. Martin's, 75 Arlington Street, Boston, MA 02116 (617-426-7440)

ISBN: 0-312-19667-9

PREFACE

American History: A Concise Documents Collection, Volume I brings together over 100 primary source excerpts organized to parallel the chapters of *America: A Concise History, Volume I* by Henretta, Brody, and Dumenil. This collection of documents echoes the earlier, longer edition designed to accompany *America's History,* Third Edition, the full-length textbook by Henretta, Brownlee, Brody, Ware, and Johnson. Both the text and the source collection have been reduced in size by about 40 percent from their forerunners, yielding trimmer, focused volumes for courses where either less reading or simply less textbook reading is desired. The resulting package of core-text-plus-reader places less of a burden on syllabi as well as on student pocketbooks.

The *Documents Collection* follows the chapter organization of *America* to provide a streamlined set of sources chosen specifically to mirror the themes of the texts, in the order in which they are presented. In each chapter an average of five to seven sources are included, each preceded by a headnote to establish context and followed by critical thinking questions. These questions are numbered and can be assigned by instructors wishing to test students on the readings. Finally, "Further Questions" appear at the end of each chapter, encouraging students to analyze the sources as a group, reflecting on the themes emphasized in each text chapter.

As a representative collection of our political, social, economic, and cultural history, the documents reflect the diverse and balanced approach of the Henretta textbooks. Ranging from a quarter page to eight full pages in length, they present first-person accounts from the past that show the conquest, settlement, and expansion of this nation through a variety of letters, proclamations, personal narratives, sermons, and published works widely circulated at the time. Together with the textbook they accompany, these documents are meant to support a sophisticated and nuanced study of the American past.

CONTENTS

CHAPTER 15
Two Societies at War, 1861–1865

CHAPTER 16
Reconstruction, 1865–1877

CHAPTER 1

Worlds Collide:
Europe and America

Bernal Díaz del Castillo, *Discovery and Conquest of Mexico*, 1517–1521

Most of the precontact hieroglyphic writings of the Aztecs and Maya were destroyed by Spanish priests, and knowledge about these cultures has come mainly through European sources such as Bernal Díaz del Castillo (c. 1498–c. 1580). Díaz accompanied Hernando Cortés on the march to Tenochtitlan and the conquest of Mexico.

His firsthand account offers many glimpses of Mexican customs and societies and fascinating hints about Cortés's military strategies. Most subsequent histories of the conquest employ Díaz's reminiscences. Díaz wrote in his Introduction, "What I saw myself and the fighting in which I took part, with God's help I will describe quite plainly as an honest eyewitness, without twisting the facts in any way."

Cacique is a Caribbean term, adopted by the Spanish, meaning a native chief.

We slept the night in those huts, and all the caciques bore us company all the way to our quarters in their town. They were really anxious that we should not leave their country, as they were fearful that Montezuma would send his warriors against them, and they said to Cortés that as we were already their friends, they would like to have us for brothers, and that it would be well that we should take from their daughters, so as to have children by them; and to cement our friendship, they brought eight damsels, all of them daughters of caciques, and gave one of these cacicas, who was the niece of the fat cacique, to Cortés; and one who was the daughter of another great cacique was given to Alonzo Hernández Puertocarrero. All eight of them were clothed in the rich garments of the country, beautifully ornamented as is their custom. Each one of them had a golden collar around her neck and golden earrings in her ears, and they came accompanied by other Indian girls who were to serve as their maids. When the fat cacique presented them, he said to Cortés: "Tecle (which in their language means Lord) — these seven women are for your captains, and this one, who is my niece, is for you, and she is the señora of towns and vassals." Cortés received them with a cheerful countenance, and thanked the caciques for the gifts, but he said that before we could accept them and become brothers, they must get rid of those idols which they believed in and worshipped, and which kept them in darkness, and must no longer offer sacrifices to them, and that when he could see those cursed things thrown to the ground and an end put to sacrifices that then our bonds of brotherhood would be most firmly tied. He added that these damsels must become Christians before we could receive them. Every day we saw sacrificed before us three, four or five Indians whose hearts were offered to the idols and their blood plastered on the walls, and the feet, arms and legs of the victims were cut off and eaten, just as in our country we eat beef brought from the butchers. I even believe that they sell it by retail in the *tianguez* as they call their markets. Cortés told them that if they gave up these evil deeds and no longer practised them, not only would we be their friends, but we would make them lords over other provinces. All the caciques, priests and chiefs replied that it did not seem to them good to give up their idols and sacrifices and that these gods of theirs gave them health and good harvests and everything of which they had need. . . .

When the Caciques, priests, and chieftains were silenced, Cortés ordered all the idols which we had overthrown and broken to pieces to be taken out of sight and burned. Then eight priests who had charge of the idols came out of a chamber and carried them back to the house whence they had come, and burned them. These priests wore black cloaks like cassocks and long gowns reaching to their feet, and some had hoods like those worn by canons, and others had smaller hoods like those worn by Dominicans, and they wore their hair very long, down to the waist, with some even reaching down to the feet, covered with blood and so matted together that it could not be separated, and their ears were cut to pieces by way of sacrifice, and they stank like sulphur, and they had another bad smell like carrion, and as they said, and we learnt that it was true, these priests were the sons of chiefs and they abstained from women, and they fasted on certain days, and what I saw them eat was the pith of seeds of cotton when the cotton was being cleaned, but they may have eaten other things which I did not see. . . .

I remember that in the plaza where some of their oratories stood, there were piles of human skulls so regularly arranged that one could count them, and I estimated them at more than a hundred thousand. I repeat again that there were more than one hundred thousand of them. And in another part of the plaza there were so many piles of dead men's thigh bones that one could not count them; there was also a large number of skulls strung between beams of wood, and three priests who had charge of these bones and skulls were guarding them. We had occasion to see many such things later on as we penetrated into the country for the same custom we observed in all the towns, including those of Tlaxcala. . . .

Cortés then took these Caciques aside and questioned them very fully about Mexican affairs. Xicotenga, as he was the best informed and a great chieftain, took the lead in talking, and from time to time he was helped by Mase Escasi who was also a great chief.

He said that Montezuma had such great strength in warriors that when he wished to capture a great city or make a raid on a province, he could place a hundred and fifty thousand men in the field, and this they knew well from the experience of the wars and hostilities they had had with them for more than a hundred years past.

Cortés asked them how it was that with so many warriors as they said came down on them they had never been entirely conquered. They answered that although the Mexicans sometimes defeated them and killed them, and carried off many of their vassals for sacrifice, many of the enemy were also left dead on the field and others were made prisoners, and that they never could come so secretly that they did not get some warning, and that when they knew of their approach they mustered all their forces and with the help of the people of Huexotzingo they defended themselves and made counter attacks. That as all the provinces which had been raided by Montezuma and placed under his rule were ill disposed towards the Mexicans, and that as their inhabitants were carried off by force to the wars, they did not fight with good will; indeed, it was from these very men that they received warnings, and for this reason they had defended their country to the best of their ability.

The place from which the most continuous trouble came to them was a very great city a day's march distant, which is called Cholula, whose inhabitants were most treacherous. It was there that Montezuma secretly mustered his companies and, as it was near by, they made their raids by night. Moreover, Mase Escasi said that Montezuma kept garrisons of many warriors stationed in all the provinces in addition to the great force he could bring from the city, and that all the provinces paid tribute of gold and silver, feathers, stones, cloth and cotton, and Indian men and women for sacrifice and others for servants, that he [Montezuma] was such a great prince that he possessed everything he could desire, that the houses where he dwelt were full of riches and [precious] stones . . . which he had robbed and taken by force from those who would not give them willingly, and that all the wealth of the country was in his hands.

Then they spoke of the great fortifications of the city, and what the lake was like, and the depth of water, and about the causeways that gave access to the city, and the wooden bridges in each causeway, and how one can go in and out [by water] through the opening that there is in each bridge, and how when the bridges are raised one can be cut off between bridge and bridge and not be able to reach the city. How the greater part of the city was built in the lake, and that one could not pass from house to house except by draw-bridges and canoes which they had ready. That all the houses were flat-roofed and all the roofs were provided with parapets so that they could fight from them.

They brought us pictures of the battles they had fought with the Mexicans painted on large henequen cloths, showing their manner of fighting. . . .

Questions

1. What "unusual" customs or rituals did Díaz del Castillo observe?
2. Díaz del Castillo emphasizes the strange and bizarre. Can you notice any similarities between the native American and Spanish cultures?

3. Noting the relevant cultural similarities and differences, do you think Cortés and Montezuma could have avoided conflict? Why or why not?

Iroquois and Penobscot Myths of Creation

The peoples of the eastern North American woodlands recounted their origins and explained important aspects of their cultures through the oral tradition of storytelling. Some accounts of clan or language-group origins seemed strange and even unbelievable to Europeans in the sixteenth and seventeenth centuries.

Yet there were often striking similarities between Indian stories and European folklore or biblical accounts of birth, natural disasters, and the significance of certain rituals. Corn, or maize, was the central object of many eastern and southeastern peoples' sacred and secular history. It was probably domesticated in the central plains of Mexico at least 8,000 years ago and gradually transmitted and adapted to more northerly climates.

IROQUOIS ACCOUNT OF THE ORIGINS OF HUMAN LIFE

In a house in the Sky World, a man and a woman lived on opposite sides of a fireplace. The two had great spiritual power because each had been isolated from other people until the age of puberty. Every day after the housemates went out to work, the woman crossed to the other side of the fire to comb the man's hair. Through mysterious means, she became pregnant and bore a daughter. Shortly thereafter, the man fell ill and announced that he would soon die. Because no one in the Sky World knew what death was, he had to explain to the woman what would happen to him and instruct her how to preserve his body. After he died, the woman's growing daughter endured fits of weeping that, despite the best efforts of village neighbors to comfort her, could be relieved only by visits to the preserved corpse of the deceased, whose spirit told her that he was her father and taught her many things.

When the daughter, whom the Iroquois called Sky Woman, reached adulthood, her father's spirit instructed her to take a dangerous journey to the village of a man destined to become her spouse. She brought her prospective husband loaves of bread baked with berries and then, enduring great travail, cooked him a potent soup that cured him of a long-troublesome ailment. In exchange, he sent her home with a burden of venison that nearly filled her family's house. After Sky Woman returned to her husband, the pair always slept on opposite sides of the fire and refrained from sexual intercourse. Nevertheless, she, like her mother before her, inexplicably became pregnant. Stricken by jealousy, the husband again became ill and dreamed that a great tree near his house must be uprooted so that he and his spouse could look down through the resulting hole to the world below. To cure his sickness, all the people of the village worked together to pull it up. When Sky Woman looked over the edge of the abyss, her husband pushed her down.

As Sky Woman fell toward the endless waters below, the spirit birds and animals of the sea held a council to decide how to rescue her, Ducks flew up to catch her on their wings and bring her safely down, and the Turtle agreed to provide a place for her to rest on his back. Meantime, various animals tried to dive to the bottom of the lake and bring up earth on which the woman could walk; only the Muskrat succeeded. The material he placed on the Turtle's back grew, with Sky Woman's help, into the living dry land of North America. Soon the celestial visitor gave birth to a daughter, who in time became supernaturally pregnant by the spirit of the Turtle. In the younger woman's womb grew male twins, who began arguing over the best way to emerge from her body. The Good Twin (Upholder of the Heavens, or Sky Grasper) was born normally. The second, the Evil Twin, burst forth from his mother's side and thus killed her. When Sky Woman asked which of her grandsons had slain her daughter, they blamed each other, but the Evil Twin was the more persistent and persuasive. The Grandmother cherished him, and she turned the body and head of the boys' deceased mother into the sun and moon, respectively; and she threw the Good Twin out of her house, assuming he would die.

But he did not. Instead, with the aid of his father the Turtle, the Good Twin improved Iroquoia, making various animals, learning the secrets of cultivating maize and other crops, and bringing into existence mortal human beings. All of these things he did not create from nothingness; they grew through a process of transformation and infusion of supernatural power from the living earth and from a kind of spirit beings who dwelled in the Sky World and under the waters. With each new creation, however, Sky Woman and the Evil Twin partially undid the Good Twin's efforts in ways that forever after would make life difficult for humans. When the Good Twin constructed straight rivers for canoeing, with the water flowing in both ways at once, the Evil Twin threw in rocks and hills to twist the streams and make their waters fall in only one direction. When the Good Twin grew succulent ears of corn, Sky Woman threw ashes into his cooking pot and decreed that maize must be parched and ground before it could be eaten. When the Good Twin made animals readily give themselves to humans as food, the Evil Twin sealed them all in a cave, from which Sky Grasper could rescue only a portion; the rest the Evil Twin turned into enemies of humans.

Finally, the two brothers also fought, and the Good Twin won. He could not, however, undo all the evil that his brother and Grandmother had left in the world. So he taught humans how to grow corn, and how to keep harm at bay with ceremonies of thanksgiving and peacekeeping with the spirits. Sky Grasper made these ceremonies easier by designating clans named after certain animals such as Wolf, Bear, Turtle. But he knew that mortals could never keep the ritual well enough. But Sky Grasper also predicted the time would come when all peoples would fall into great dispute and destroy one another. Good Twin went home, where he never died, but instead continually passed through stages of aging and then rejuvenating himself.

CORN MOTHER: A PENOBSCOT MYTH

When Kloskurbeh, the All-maker, lived on earth, there were no people yet. But one day when the sun was high, a youth appeared and called him "Uncle, brother of my mother." This young man was born from the foam of the waves, foam quickened by the wind and warmed by the sun. It was the motion of the wind, the moistness of water, and the sun's warmth, which gave him life. . . . And the young man lived with Kloskurbeh and became his chief helper.

Now, after these two powerful beings had created all manner of things, there came to them, as the sun was shining at high noon, a beautiful girl. She was born of the wonderful earth plant, and of the dew, and of warmth. Because a drop of dew fell on a leaf and was warmed by the sun, and the warming sun is life, this girl came into being from the green living plant, from moisture, and from warmth.

"I am love," said the maiden. "I am a strength giver, I am the nourisher, I am the provider of men and animals. They all love me."

Then Kloskurbeh thanked the Great Master Above for having sent them the maiden. The youth, the Great Nephew, married her, and the girl conceived and thus became First Mother. And Kloskurbeh, the Great Uncle, who teaches humans all they need to know, taught their children how to live. Then he went away to dwell in the north, from which he will return sometime when he is needed.

Now, the people increased and became numerous. They lived by hunting, and the more people there were, the less game they found. They were hunting it out, and as the animals decreased, starvation came upon the people. And First Mother pitied them.

The little children came to First Mother and said: "We are hungry. Feed us." But she had nothing to give them, and she wept. She told them: "Be patient. I will make some food. Then your little bellies will be full." But she kept weeping.

Her husband asked: "How can I make you smile? How can I make you happy?"

"There is only one thing that will stop my tears."

"What is it?" asked her husband.

"It is this: you must kill me."

"I could never do that."

"You must, or I will go on weeping and grieving forever."

The husband traveled far, to the end of the earth, to the north he went, to ask the Great Instructor, his uncle Kloskurbeh, what he should do.

"You must do what she wants. You must kill her," said Kloskurbeh. Then the young man went back to his home, and it was his turn to weep. But First Mother said: "Tomorrow at high noon you must do it. After you have killed me, let two of our sons take hold of my hair and drag my body over that empty patch of earth. Let them drag me back and forth, back and forth, over every part of the patch, until all my flesh has been torn from my body. Afterwards, take my bones, gather them up, and bury them in the middle of this clearing. Then leave that place."

She smiled and said, "Wait seven moons and then come back, and you will find my flesh there, flesh given out of love, and it will nourish and strengthen you forever and ever."

So it was done. The husband slew his wife and her sons, praying, dragged her body to and fro as she had commanded, until her flesh covered all the earth. Then they took up her bones and buried them in the middle of it. Weeping loudly, they went away.

When the husband and his children and his children's children came back to that place after seven moons had passed, they found the earth covered with tall, green, tasseled plants. The plants' fruit — corn — was First Mother's flesh, given so that people might live and flourish. And they partook of First Mother's flesh and found it sweet beyond words. Following her instructions, they did not eat all, but put many kernels back into the earth. In this way her flesh and spirit renewed themselves every seven months, generation after generation.

And at the spot where they had burned First Mother's bones, there grew another plant, broad-leafed and fragrant. It was First Mother's breath, and they heard her spirit talking: "Burn this up and smoke it. It is sacred. It will clear your minds, help your prayers, and gladden your hearts."

And First Mother's husband called the first plant Skarmunal, corn, and the second plant utarmur-yayeh, tobacco.

"Remember," he told the people, "and take good care of First Mother's flesh, because it is her goodness become substance. Take good care of her breath, because it is her love turned into smoke. Remember her and think of her whenever you eat, whenever you smoke this sacred plant, because she has given her life that you might live. Yet she is not dead, she lives: in undying love she renews herself again and again."

Questions

1. What similarities are there between the Iroquois account of human origins and the way many Europeans understood how the world began?
2. What are the roles of women and children in these cultures?
3. In what ways is a myth, as in these two examples, both a history and a moral lesson?

Raoul Glaber, Account of Famine

Countless people starve to death even in the modern world, and their plight often goads the machinery of international relief into action. But there was a time when famine was caused almost wholly by nature and not by politics; no national or international support system existed; and people were left to fend for themselves.

The monk Raoul Glaber belonged to the Cluniac monastic order in France. While the Cluniacs looked exclusively for leadership from the pope rather than secular rulers, the issue of famine did not make for easy leadership, ecclesiastical or otherwise. Here Glaber describes the effects of the great European famine of 1032–1034.

The famine started to spread its ravages and one could fear the disappearance of the human race almost whole. The weather became so bad that none could find the right time for any sowing and that, especially because of the floods, there was no way of harvesting. . . . Continual rains had steeped the whole earth to the extent that during three years one could not dig furrows that would harbor the seed. By harvest time weeds . . . had covered all the surface of the fields. In those parts where it gave the best results, a hogshead of seed would produce a harvest of about twelve bushels [about one-fifth of the original seed], and this in turn produced hardly a handful. If by chance one found any food on sale, the seller could exact an excessive price at his will.

Meantime, when the savage beasts and the birds had been eaten, men began, under the empire of a devouring hunger, to gather in order to eat, all kinds of carrion and of things horrible to tell. Certain among them had recourse to escape from death to the roots of the forests and the weeds of the rivers. In the end one is seized by horror at the tale of perversions which then reigned over the human race. Alas! Oh, woe! A thing rarely heard of in the course of ages, a maddening hunger made that men devoured human flesh. Travellers were carried off by those stronger than they, their members cut up, cooked on the fire and devoured. Many of the people who were going from one place to another to flee the famine and who had found hospitality on the way, were slaughtered during the night and served as nourishment for those who had welcomed them. Many, by showing a fruit or an egg to children, lured them into isolated places, massacred and devoured them. The bodies of the dead were in many places torn from the earth and served equally to appease hunger.

There was then tried in the region of Macon an experiment which had not, to our knowledge, yet been attempted anywhere else. Many people drew from the ground a white soil similar to clay, mixed it with what they had of wheat or bran, and made of this mixture bread, on which they relied so as not to die of hunger. However this practice brought merely the hope of salvation and the illusion of relief. One saw only pale and emaciated faces: many presented a skin distended by swellings; the human voice itself became shrill, similar to the little cries of dying birds. The corpses of the dead, whose multitude forced the living to abandon them here and there without burial, served as pasture to wolves who continued for a long time thereafter to seek their pittance among men. And as one could not, as we said, bury everyone individually because of the great number of dead, in certain places the men, fearing God, dug what was commonly known as charnel houses, in which the bodies of the dead were thrown by the five hundreds and more as long as room remained, pell mell, half naked or without any covering. The cross roads, the edges of the fields, also served as cemeteries. If some heard say that they would be better if they moved to other regions, many were those who perished on the way for want of food.

Questions

1. What caused the famine?
2. To what extremes did people go in securing food?
3. How might famine affect a society centuries after the fact?

John Hales, Objections against Enclosure (1548)

Two economic factors challenged sixteenth-century England: a dramatic rise in population and a shortage of agricultural jobs. England's population had shrunk drastically during the Black Death of the fourteenth century. By 1550 it had made good the loss; after that time, people increased their numbers more rapidly than the economy was able to absorb them.

The shortage of agricultural jobs was caused in part by enclosure, the large-scale conversion of arable land to sheep pasturage and the consequent eviction of tenant farmers (see text p. 26). Modern scholarship has minimized the actual extent of enclosure, but to contemporaries it symbolized all the economic problems they had to endure. In 1548, John Hales conducted a commission of inquiry in the Midlands (central England). Hales left no doubt about his opposition to the practice.

As by natural experience we find it to be true that if any one part of man's body be grieved . . . it is a great pain to all the whole body . . . so ought we to consider and remember in the state of the body of the realm. If the poorest sort of the people, which be members of the same body as well as the rich, be not provided and cherished in their degree, it cannot but be a great trouble of the body and a decay of the strength of the realm. Surely, good people, methinks that if men would know how much this ungodly desire of worldly things, and the unlawful getting and heaping together of riches, were hated of God, how hurtful and dangerous for the commonwealth of the realm it is, and what a virtue the mean in all things is, these laws nor a great many more that be needed not. God's Word is full of threats and curses against these kind of greediness. . . . When men in a commonwealth go about to gather as much as they can, and to get it they care not how; not considering whether by their gain any hurt should come to their neighbors or to the commonwealth; not only others, but they themselves should shortly perish. What avails a man to have his house full of gold and be not able to keep it with his force against his enemies? So what shall all our goods avail us if we be not able to defend us from our enemies?

The force and puissance [power] of the realm consists not only in riches but chiefly in the multitude of people. But it appears, good people, that the people of this realm, our native country, is greatly decayed through the greediness of a few men in comparison, and by this ungodly means of gathering together goods, by pulling down towns and houses, which we ought all to lament. Where there were [a few years ago] ten or twelve thousand people, there be now scarce four thousand. Where there were a thousand, now scarce three hundred, and in many places, where there were very many able to defend our country from landing of our enemies, now almost none. Sheep and cattle, that were ordained to be eaten of men, has eaten up the men, not of their own nature but by the help of men. Is it not a pitiful case that there should be so little charity among men? Is it not a sorrowful hearing that one Englishman should be set to destroy his countrymen? The places where poor men dwelt clearly destroyed; lands improved to so great rents, . . . that the poor husbandman cannot live. All things at this present . . . be so dear as never they were — victual and other things that be necessary for man's use. And yet, as it is said, there was never more cattle, specially sheep, than there is at this present. But the cause of the dearth is that those have it that may choose whether they will sell it or not, and will not sell it but at their own prices. . . .

To declare unto you what is meant by this word, enclosures. It is not taken where a man does enclose and hedge in his own proper ground where no man has commons. For such enclosure is very beneficial to the commonwealth: it is a cause of great increase of wood. But it is meant thereby when any man has taken away and enclosed any other men's commons, or has pulled down houses of husbandry and converted the lands from tillage to pasture. This is the meaning of the word, and so we pray you remember it.

To defeat these statutes [laws banning enclosure] as we be informed, some have not pulled down their houses but maintain them; howbeit, no person dwells therein, or if there be it is but a shepherd or a milkmaid; and convert the lands from tillage to pasture. And some about one hundred acres of ground, or more or less, make a furrow and sow that, and the rest they till not but pasture with their sheep. And some take the lands from their houses and occupy them in husbandry, but let the houses out to beggars and old poor people. Some, to colour the multitude of their sheep father them on their children, kinsfolk and servants. All which be but only crafts and subtleties to defraud the laws, such as no man will use but rather abhor. . . .

Besides, it is not unlike but that these great fines for lands and improvement of rents shall abate, and all things wax better cheap — 20 and 30 eggs for a penny, and the rest after the rate as has been in times past. And the poor craftsmen may live and set their wares at reasonable prices. And noblemen and gentlemen that have not improved nor enhanced their rents, nor were sheepmasters nor graziers but lived like noblemen and gentlemen, shall be the better able to keep good hospitality among you, and keep servants about them, as they have done in time past. . . .

Questions

1. In Hales's opinion, was enclosure a religious or an economic problem? Why?
2. Would moral strictures alone have been sufficient to reverse the enclosure movement? Why or why not?

3. Does Hales touch on any underlying economic reasons for enclosure? If so, what are they?

The Separatists State Their Case

Two groups of Protestant dissenters were among the first English people to immigrate to the New World. The Separatists, who founded the Plymouth colony in 1620, sought total withdrawal from the Anglican Church to establish independent congregations. The non-Separatists wanted to reform the Church of England from within (see text p. 45). Non-Separatists (Puritans) founded a settlement at Massachusetts Bay in 1629.

In the 1580s a small group of Separatists left England for the Netherlands, where they could worship freely. When James I succeeded Elizabeth I in 1603, the Amsterdam Separatists (Pilgrims) petitioned the new king for permission to return to England. Their unsuccessful petition spelled out fourteen points of difference between Separatism and Anglicanism.

THE POINTS OF DIFFERENCE.

1. That Christ the Lord hath by his last Testament given to his Church, and set therein, sufficient ordinary Offices, with the manner of calling or Entrance, Works, and Maintenance, for the administration of his holy things, and for the sufficient ordinary instruction guydance and service of his Church, to the end of the world.

2. That every particular Church hath like and full interest and power to enjoy and practise all the ordinances of Christ given by him to his Church to be observed therein perpetually.

3. That every true visible Church, is a company of people called and separated from the world by the word of God, and joyned together by voluntarie profession of the faith of Christ, in the fellowship of the Gospell. And that therfore no knowne Atheist, unbelever, Heretique, or wicked liver, be received or reteined a member in the Church of Christ, which is his body; God having in all ages appointed and made a separation of his people from the world, before the Law, under the Law, and now in the tyme of the Gospell.

4. That discreet, faithfull, and able men (though not yet in office of Ministerie) may be appointed to preach the gospell and whole truth of God, that men being first brought to knowledge, and converted to the Lord, may then

be ioyned togeather in holy communion with Christ our head and one with another.

5. That being thus ioyned, every Church hath power in Christ to chuse and take unto themselves meet and sufficient persons, into the Offices and functions of Pastors, Teachers, Elders, Deacons and Helpers, as those which Christ hath appointed in his Testament, for the feeding, governing, serving, and building up of his Church. And that no Antichristia Hierarchie or Minis-terie, of Popes, Arch-bishops, Lord-bishops, Suffraganes, Deanes, Archdea-cons, Chauncellors, Parsons, Vicars, Priests, Dumb-ministers, nor any such like be set over the Spouse and Church of Christ, nor reteined therein.

6. That the Ministers aforesaid being lawfully called by the Church where they are to administer, ought to continew in their functions according to Gods ordinance, and carefully to feed the flock of Christ committed unto them, being not inioyned or suffered to beare Civill offices with-all, neither bur-thened with the execution of Civill affaires, as the celebration of marriage, burying the dead etc. which things belong as well to those without as within the Church.

7. That the due maintenance of the Officers aforesaid, should be of the free and voluntarie contribution of the Church, that according to Christs or-dinance, they which preach the Gospell may live of the Gospell: and not by Popish Lordships and Livings, or Iewish Tithes and Offerings. And that there-fore the Lands and other like revenewes of the Prelats and Clergie yet re-mayning (being still also baits to allure the Iesuites and Seminaries into the Land, and incitements unto them to plott and prosecute their woonted evill courses, in hope to enjoy them in tyme to come) may now by your Highnes be taken away, and converted to better use, as those of the Abbeyes and Nun-neries have been heretofore by your Maiestyes worthie predecessors, to the honor of God and great good of the Realme.

8. That all particular Churches ought to be so constituted, as having their owne peculiar Officers, the whole body of every Church may meet together in one place, and iointly performe their duties to God and one towards an-other. And that the censures of admonition and excommunication be in due manner executed, for sinne, convicted, and obstinatly stood in. This power also to be in the body of the Church wherof the partyes so offending and per-sisting are members.

9. That the Church be not governed by Popish Canons, Courts, Classes, Customes, or any humane inventions, but by the lawes and rules which Christ hath appointed in his Testament. That no Apocrypha writings, but only the Canonicall scriptures be used in the Church. And that the Lord be wor-shipped and called upon in spirit and truth, according to that forme of praier given by the Lord Iesus, Math. 6. and after the Leitourgie of his owne Testa-ment, not by any other framed or imposed by men, much lesse by one traslated from the Popish leitourgie, as the Book of common praier etc.

10. That the Sacraments, being seales of Gods covenant, ought to be administred only to the faithfull, and Baptisme to their seed or those under their governement. And that according to the simplicitie of the Gospell, without any Popish or other abuses, in either Sacrament.

11. That the Church be not urged to the observation of dayes and tymes, Iewish or Popish, save only to sanctify the Lords day: Neyther be laden in things indifferent, with rites and ceremonies, whatsoever invented by men; but that Christian libertie may be reteined: And what God hath left free, none to make bound.

12. That all monuments of Idolatry in garments or any other things, all Temples, Altars, Chappels, and other place, dedicated heertofore by the heathens or Antichristians to their false worship, ought by lawfull aucthoritie to be rased and abolished, not suffered to remayne, for nourishing superstition, much less imploied to the true worship of God.

13. That Popish degrees in Theologie, inforcement to single life in Colledges, abuse of the study of prophane heathen Writers, with other like corruptions in Schooles and Academies, should be remooved and redressed, that so they may be the welsprings and nurseries of true learning and godlinesse.

14. Finally that all Churches and people (without exception) are bound in Religion not only to receave and submit unto that constitution, Ministerie, Worship, and order, which Christ as Lord and King hath appointed unto his Church: and not to any other devised by Man whatsoever.

Questions

1. How do the Separatists define their religious beliefs and practices?
2. In what ways was the Church of England too Catholic for the Separatists? (Hint: Look for the term *Popish*.)
3. The Church of England was a *territorial* church; that is, all English subjects had to be members. What is the Separatist response to this practice?

Richard Hakluyt, *A Discourse Concerning Western Planting* (1584)

By the end of the sixteenth century, England's economic and imperial as-pirations had led inexorably to colonization. Explorers such as Martin Fro-bisher and Humphrey Gilbert had reconnoitered the Atlantic coast of North America. The first Roanoke voyage took place in 1584, the same year Richard Hakluyt (1552–1616) issued his Discourse Concerning Western Planting.

Hakluyt, a clergyman and travel writer (who never traveled), was an ef-fective pamphleteer and propagandist for colonization. The Discourse *was written at the request of Sir Walter Raleigh and contains virtually every pos-itive argument for settlement that would be advanced over the next century. Its purpose was to persuade Queen Elizabeth I to put the English state squarely behind American ventures.*

Chapter XX. A brief collection of certain reasons to induce her Majesty and the state to take in hand the western voyage and the planting there.

1. The soil yields and may be made to yield all the several commodities of Europe. . . .

2. The passage thither and home is neither too long nor too short, but easy, and to be made twice in the year.

3. The passage cuts not near the trade of any prince, nor near any of their countries or territories, and is a safe passage, and not easy to be annoyed by prince or potentate whatsoever.

4. The passage is to be performed at all times of the year, and in that re-spect passes our trades in the Levant Seas within the Straits of Gibraltar, and the trades in the seas within the King of Denmark's Strait, and the trades to the ports of Norway and of Russia, etc. . . .

5. And where England now for certain hundred years last passed, by the peculiar commodity of wool, and of later years, by clothing of the same, has raised itself from meaner state to greater wealth and much higher honour, might, and power than before, to the equalling of the princes of the same to the greatest potentates of this part of the world; it comes now so to pass that by the great endeavour of the increase of the trade of wool in Spain and in the West Indies, now daily more and more multiplying, that the wool of England, and the cloth made of the same, will become base, and every day more base than [the] other; which, prudently weighed it behooves this realm, if it mean not to return to former old means and baseness, but to stand in present and late former honour, glory, and force, and not negligently and sleepingly to slide into beggary . . . were it not for anything else but for the hope of the sale of our wool. . . .

6. This enterprise may stay the Spanish king from flowing over all the face of that waste firmament of America, if we seat and plant there in time. . . . And England possessing the purposed place of planting, her Majesty may, by the benefit of the seat, having won good and royal havens, have plenty of excellent trees for masts, of goodly timber to build ships and to make great navies, of pitch, tar, hemp, and all things incident for a navy royal, and that for no price, and without money or request. How easy a matter may it be to this realm, swarming at this day with valiant youths, rusting and hurtful by lack of employment, and having good makers of cable and of all sorts of cordage, and the best and most cunning shipwrights of the world, to be lords of all those seas, and to spoil Philip's Indian navy, and to deprive him of yearly passage of his treasure to Europe, and consequently to abate the pride of Spain and of the supporter of the great Anti-christ of Rome, and to pull him down in equality to his neighbour princes, and consequently to cut off the common mischiefs that come to all Europe by the peculiar abundance of his Indian treasure, and this without difficulty.

7. This voyage, albeit it may be accomplished by bark or smallest pinnace for advice or for a necessity, yet for the distance, for burden and gain in trade, the merchant will not for profit's sake use it but by ships of great burden; so as this realm shall have by that means ships of great burden and of great strength for the defence of this realm. . . .

8. This new navy of mighty new strong ships, so in trade to that Norumbega and to the coasts there, shall never be subject to arrest of any prince or potentate as the navy of this realm from time to time has been in the ports of the empire, in the ports of the Low Countries, in Spain, France, Portugal, etc., in the times of Charles the Emperor, Francis the French king, and others. . . .

9. The great mass of wealth of the realm embarked in the merchants' ships, carried out in this new course, shall not lightly, in so far distant a course from the coast of Europe, be driven by winds and tempests into ports of any foreign princes, as the Spanish ships of late years have been into our ports of the West countries, etc. . . .

10. No foreign commodity that comes into England comes without payment of custom once, twice, or thrice, before it comes into the realm, and so all foreign commodities become dearer to the subjects of this realm; and by this course to Norumbega foreign princes' customs are avoided; and the foreign commodities cheaply purchased, they become cheap to the subjects of England, to the common benefit of the people, and to the saving of great treasure in the realm; whereas now the realm becomes poor by the purchasing of foreign commodities in so great a mass at so excessive prices.

11. At the first traffic with the people of those parts, the subjects of this realm for many years shall change many cheap commodities of these parts for things of high value there not esteemed; and this to the great enriching of the realm, if common use fail not.

12. By the great plenty of those regions the merchants and their factors shall lie there cheap, buy and repair their ships cheap, and shall return at pleasure without stay or restraint of foreign prince; whereas upon stays and restraints the merchant raiseth his charge in sale over of his ware. . . .

13. By making of ships and by preparing of things for the same, by making of cables and cordage, by planting of vines and olive trees, and by making of wine and oil, by husbandry, and by thousands of things there to be done, infinite numbers of the English nation may be set on work, to the unburdening of the realm with many that now live chargeable to the state at home.

14. If the sea coast serve for making of salt, and the inland for wine, oils, oranges, lemons, figs, etc., and for making of iron, all which with much more is hoped, without sword drawn, we shall cut the comb of the French, of the Spanish, of the Portuguese, and of enemies, and of doubtful friends, to the abating of their wealth and force, and to the greater saving of the wealth of the realm.

15. The substances serving, we may out of those parts receive the mass of wrought wares that now we receive out of France, Flanders, Germany, etc.; and so we may daunt the pride of some enemies of this realm, or at the least in part purchase those wares, that now we buy dearly of the French and Flemish, better cheap; and in the end, for the part that this realm was wont to receive, drive them out of trade to idleness for the setting of our people on work.

16. We shall by planting there enlarge the glory of the gospel, and from England plant sincere religion, and provide a safe and a sure place to receive people from all parts of the world that are forced to flee for the truth of God's word.

17. If frontier wars there chance to arise, and if thereupon we shall fortify, it will occasion the training up of our youth in the discipline of war, and make a number fit for the service of the wars and for the defence of our people there and at home.

18. The Spaniards govern in the Indies with all pride and tyranny; and like as when people of contrary nature at sea enter into galleys, where men are tied as slaves, all yell and cry with one voice, *Liberta, liberta,* as desirous of liberty and freedom, so no doubt whensoever the Queen of England, a prince of such clemency, shall seat upon that firmament of America, and shall be reported throughout all that tract to use the natural people there with all humanity, courtesy, and freedom, they will yield themselves to her government, and revolt clean from the Spaniard. . . .

19. The present short trades cause the mariner to be cast off, and often to be idle, and so by poverty to fall to piracy. But this course to Norumbega being longer, and a continuance of the employment of the mariner, doth keep the mariner from idleness and from necessity; and so it cuts off the principal actions of piracy, and the rather because no rich prey for them to take comes directly in their course or anything near their course.

20. Many men of excellent wits and of diverse singular gifts, overthrown by suretyship, by sea, or by some folly of youth, that are not able to live in England, may there be raised again, and do their country good service; and many needful uses there may (to great purpose) require the saving of great numbers, that for trifles may otherwise be devoured by the gallows.

21. Many soldiers and servitors, in the end of the wars, that might be hurtful to this realm, may there be unladen, to the common profit and quiet of this realm, and to our foreign benefit there, as they may be employed.

22. The fry of the wandering beggars of England, that grow up idly, and hurtful and burdenous to this realm, may there be unladen, better bred up, and may people waste countries to the home and foreign benefit, and to their own more happy state.

23. If England cry out and affirm that there are so many in all trades that one cannot live for another, as in all places they do, this Norumbega (if it be thought so good) offers the remedy.

Questions

1. What are Hakluyt's arguments for colonization? Do they seem persuasive after 400 years? Why or why not?

2. Which of the arguments pertain to England's internal conditions? Which have an imperial cast?

3. Are Hakluyt's proposed colonies more important as sources of raw materials or markets? Why?

Connections Questions

1. To what extent, if any, do Díaz del Castillo's account and the "Iroquois and Penobscot Myths of Creation" suggest that compromise was possible between the native Americans and Europeans? What factors influenced group responses?

2. Which seems the determining motive behind English immigration — economics or religion? Why?

3. What kind of reaction would Separatists ("The Separatists State Their Case") be expected to have when encountering the creation myths of other peoples ("Iroquois and Penobscot Myths of Creation")?

CHAPTER 2

The Invasion and Settlement of North America 1550–1700

A Franciscan Monk
Refutes Las Casas (1555)

In 1542 the Dominican bishop Bartholomé de Las Casas (1474–1566) indicted his countrymen for their brutal treatment of native peoples in the New World. Las Casas charged that the Spanish acted as if the native peoples "had been the dung and filth of the earth."

Thirteen years later, a Franciscan monk admonished Las Casas for impugning the Spanish and offered an alternative explanation for the demographic decline of native Americans. The opposing viewpoints have reverberated down through the centuries. Now they often appear as bloodless arguments in history textbooks.

In the encomienda *system referred to, Indian men were required to work on Spanish lands for nine months of the year in order to enjoy even minimum civil rights under Spanish law.*

I saw and read a treatise that Las Casas composed on the subject of the Indians enslaved here in New Spain and on the islands, and another one concerning the opinion he rendered on putting the Indians in encomiendas. . . .

No human being of whatever nation, law or status could read them without feeling abhorrence and mortal hate and considering all the residents of New Spain as the most cruel, abominable and detestable people there are under the sun. . . .

May God pardon Las Casas for so gravely dishonoring and defaming, so terribly insulting and affronting these communities and the Spanish nation, its prince, councils, and all those who administer justice in your majesty's name in these realms. . . .

First I must tell your majesty that when the Spaniards entered New Spain here, it had not been ruled for very long from Mexico City, nor by the Mexica [Aztecs], and the Mexica themselves had won and usurped dominion through war. . . .

People suffered the cruelest of deaths, and our adversary the demon was very pleased with the greatest idolatries and most cruel homicides there ever were, because the predecessor of Moctezuma, lord of Mexico, called Ahuitzotzin, offered to the idols in a single temple and in one sacrifice that lasted three or four days, 80,400 men, whom they brought along four streets, in four lines, until they reached the sacrificial block before the idols. And at the time when the Christians entered New Spain, more than ever before there was sacrificing and killing of men before the idols in all the towns and provinces. . . .

Now these and many other abominations, sins, and offenses made publicly to God and neighbors have been prevented and removed, our holy Catholic faith implanted, the cross of Jesus Christ and the confession of his holy name raised everywhere, and God has brought about a great conversion of people, in which many souls have been saved and are being saved every day; and many churches and monasteries have been built, with more than fifty monasteries inhabited by Franciscan friars alone. . . .

During the last ten years the natives of this land have diminished greatly in number. The reason for it has not been bad treatment, rather the cause has been the great diseases and plagues that New Spain has had, so that the natives continue to decrease each day. God knows the cause; his judgements are many and hidden from us.

Questions

1. How could the views of both Las Casas and his critic be correct?
2. Is either view more "Christian" than the other? Why or why not?
3. To what extent is the monk writing more as an apologist for empire than as a committed clergyman?

John Smith, "A True Relation of . . . Virginia" (1608)

Governor John Smith (1580–1613) is white America's first authentic hero. A soldier of fortune in Europe, Smith arrived in Jamestown in 1607 as one of its seven councillors. Over the next two and a half years he almost single-handedly saved the colony from starvation, served as its virtual dictator, explored and mapped the area, and escaped a death sentence thanks to Pocahontas, the daughter of the Indian chief Powhatan. Smith wrote an account of events in the colony; the "True Relation" brought news of Virginia's early trials to England.

The English built a military fort at Jamestown; Smith described the log walls as "palisadoed." Aqua vitae ("water of life") is strong liquor — considered essential for good health.

Kind Sir, commendations remembered, etc. You shall understand that after many crosses in the downs by tempests, we arrived safely upon the south-west part of the great Canaries. Within four or five days after, we set sail for Dominica the 26 of April. The first land we made, we fell with Cape

Henry, the very mouth of the Bay of Chesapeake, which at that present we little expected, having by a cruel storm been put to the northward.

Anchoring in this bay, twenty or thirty went ashore with the captain, and in coming aboard [on land], they were assaulted with certain Indians, which charged them within pistol shot, in which conflict Captain Archer and Matthew Morton were shot, whereupon Captain Newport seconding them, made a shot at them, which the Indians little respected, but having spent their arrows retired without harm. And in that place was the box opened wherein the Council for Virginia was nominated, and arriving at the place [Jamestown] where we are now seated, the Council was sworn and the President elected, which for that year was Master Edmund Maria Wingfield, where was made choice for our situation, a very fit place for the erecting of a great city, about which some contention passed betwixt Captain Wingfield and Captain Gosnold. Notwithstanding, all our provision was brought ashore, and with as much speed as might be we went about our fortification.

[On 22 May, Captain Newport, Smith, and several others set forth to explore the country up the James River. They returned on 27 May.] . . . the first we heard was that 400 Indians the day before [26 May] had assaulted the fort and surprised it. Had not God (beyond all their expectations) by means of the ships (at whom they shot with their ordnances and muskets) caused them to retire, they had entered the fort with our own men, which were then busied in setting corn, their arms being then in dry fats and few ready but certain gentlemen of their own, in which conflict most of the Council was hurt, a boy slain in the pinnace, and thirteen or fourteen more hurt.

With all speed we palisadoed our fort; each other day for six or seven days we had alarms by ambuscadoes, and four or five cruelly wounded by being abroad. The Indians' loss we know not, but as they report three were slain and divers[e] hurt. . . .

The day before the ship's departure the king of Pamaunke [*i.e.*, Opechancanough] sent the Indian that had met us before in our discovery, to assure us peace, our fort being then palisadoed round, and all our men in good health and comfort, albeit that through some discontented humours it did not so long continue. For the President and Captain Gosnold, with the rest of the Council, being for the most part discontented with one another, in so much that things were neither carried with that discretion nor any business effected in such good sort as wisdom would, nor our own good and safety required, whereby, and through the hard dealing of our President, the rest of the Council being diversely affected through his audacious command; and for Captain Martin, albeit very honest and wishing the best good, yet so sick and weak, and myself so disgraced through others' malice, through which disorder God (being angry with us) plagued us with such famine and sickness that the living were scarce able to bury the dead; our want of sufficient and good victuals, with continual watching four or five each night at three bulwarks, being the chief cause. Only of sturgeon we had great store, whereon our men would so greedily surfeit as it cost many their lives; the sack, *aqua vitae,* and other preservatives for our health being kept only in the President's hands, for his own diet, and his few associates.

Shortly after Captain Gosnold fell sick, and within three weeks died. Captain Ratcliffe being then also very sick and weak, and myself having also tasted of the extremity thereof, but by God's assistance being well recovered. Kendall about this time, for divers reasons, deposed from being of the Council, and shortly after it pleased God in our extremity to move the Indians to bring us corn ere it was half ripe, to refresh us, when we rather expected when they would destroy us.

About the tenth of September there was about 46 of our men dead, at which time Captain Wingfield having ordered the affairs in such sort that he was generally hated of all, in which respect with one consent he was deposed from his presidency, and Captain Ratcliffe according to his course was elected.

Our provision being now within twenty days spent, the Indians brought us great store both of corn and bread ready made, and also there came such abundance of fowls into the rivers as greatly refreshed our weak estates, whereupon many of our weak men were presently able to go abroad.

As yet we had no houses to cover us, our tents were rotten, and our cabins worse than nought. Our best commodity was iron, which we made into little chisels.

The President's and Captain Martin's sickness constrained me to be cape merchant and yet to spare no pains in making houses for the company, who notwithstanding our misery, little ceased their malice, grudging, and muttering.

As at this time were most of our chiefest men either sick or discontented, the rest being in such despair as they would rather starve and rot with idleness than be persuaded to do anything for their own relief without constraint. Our victuals being now within eighteen days spent, and the Indian trade decreasing, I was sent to the mouth of the river to Kegquouhtan, an Indian town, to trade for corn, and try the river for fish, but our fishing we could not effect by reason of the stormy weather. The Indians, thinking us near famished, with careless kindness offered us little pieces of bread and small handfuls of beans or wheat for a hatchet or a piece of copper. In like manner I entertained their kindness and in like scorn offered them like commodities, but the children, or any that showed extraordinary kindness, I liberally contented with free gift of such trifles as well contented them. . . .

[In January 1608], by a mischance our fort was burned and the most of our apparel, lodging, and private provision. Many of our old men [became] diseased, and [many] of our new for want of lodging perished. . . .

[O]ur men being all or the most part well recovered, and we not willing to trifle away more time than necessity enforced us unto, we thought good for the better content of the adventurers, in some reasonable sort to freight home

Master Nelson [of the ship *Phenix,* which had arrived on 20 April] with cedar wood. About which, our men going with willing minds, [it] was in very good time effected and the ship sent for England [on 2 June 1608]. We now remaining being in good health, all our men well contented, free from mutinies, in love one with another, and as we hope, in a continual peace with the Indians. Where we doubt not but by God's gracious assistance, and the adventurers' willing minds and speedy furtherance to so honourable an action, in after times to see our nation to enjoy a country not only exceeding pleasant for habitation, but also very profitable for commerce in general; no doubt pleasing to Almighty God, honourable to our gracious sovereign, and commodious generally to the whole kingdom.

Questions

1. Does the early experience of Jamestown support the arguments for colonization made by Richard Hakluyt (Chapter 1, "A Discourse Concerning Western Planting")? Why or why not?
2. Was there any discernible economic base in Smith's Virginia? Explain.
3. What does Smith say about Indian–white relations in the first year of the Jamestown colony?
4. Why does Smith believe the settlers "would rather starve and rot with idleness than be persuaded to do anything for their own relief"?

Nathaniel Bacon, "Manifesto Concerning the Troubles in Virginia" (1676)

Who was Nathaniel Bacon (1647–1676)? Early twentieth-century historiography depicted Bacon as a popular democratic leader who headed a revolt of have-nots against the privileged few. The historian Wilcomb Washburn later dismissed him as an Indian killer, whereas Edmund S. Morgan saw Bacon's rebellion as a war of plunder. Evidence for all these views can be found in Bacon's own words. The troubled young fop who was exiled from England by his own father may not deserve his heroic reputation, but his "Manifesto" tells of problems in Governor William Berkeley's Virginia.

If virtue be a sin, if piety be guilt, all the principles of morality, goodness and justice be perverted, we must confess that those who are now called rebels may be in danger of those high imputations. Those loud and several bulls would affright innocents and render the defence of our brethren and the inquiry into our sad and heavy oppressions, treason. But if there be, as sure there is, a just God to appeal to; if religion and justice be a sanctuary here; if to plead the cause of the oppressed; if sincerely to aim at his Majesty's honour and the public good without any reservation or by interest; if to stand in the gap after so much blood of our dear brethren bought and sold; if after the loss of a great part of his Majesty's colony deserted and dispeopled, freely with our lives and estates to endeavour to save the remainders be treason; God Almighty judge and let guilty die. But since we cannot in our hearts find one single spot of rebellion or treason, or that we have in any manner aimed at the subverting of the settled government or attempting of the person of any either magistrate or private man, notwithstanding the several reproaches and threats of some who for sinister ends were disaffected to us and censured our innocent and honest designs, and since all people in all places where we have yet been can attest our civil, quiet, peaceable behaviour far different from that of rebellion and tumultuous persons, let truth be told and all the world know the real foundations of pretended guilt. We appeal to the country itself what and of what nature their oppressions have been, or by what cabal and mystery the designs of many of those whom we call great men have been transacted and carried on; but let us trace these men in authority and favour to whose hands the dispensation of the country's wealth has been committed. Let us observe the sudden rise of their estates composed with the quality in which they first entered this country, or the reputation they have held here amongst wise and discerning men. And let us see whether their extractions and education have not been vile, and by what pretence of learning and virtue they could so soon [come] into employments of so great trust and consequence. Let us consider their sudden advancement and let us also consider whether any public work for our safety and defence or for the advancement and propagation of trade, liberal arts, or sciences is here extant in any way adequate to our vast charge. Now let us compare these things together and see what sponges have sucked up the public treasure, and whether it has not been privately contrived away by unworthy favourites and juggling parasites whose tottering fortunes have been repaired and supported at the public charge. Now if it be so, judge what greater guilt can be than to offer to pry into these and to unriddle the mysterious wiles of a powerful cabal; let all people judge what can be of more dangerous import than to suspect the so long safe proceedings of some of our grandees, and whether people may with safety open their eyes in so nice a concern.

Another main article of our guilt is our open and manifest aversion of all, not only the foreign but the protected and darling Indians. This, we are informed, is rebellion of a deep dye for that both the governor and council are by Colonel Cole's assertion bound to defend the queen and the Appamatocks with their blood. Now, whereas we do declare and can prove that they have been for these many years enemies to the king and country, robbers and thieves and invaders of his Majesty's right and our interest and estates, but yet have by persons in authority been defended and protected even against his Majesty's loyal subjects, and that in so high a nature that even the complaints and oaths of his Majesty's most loyal subjects in a lawful manner proffered by them against those barbarous outlaws, have been by the right honourable governor rejected and the delinquents from his presence dismissed, not only with pardon and indemnity, but with all encouragement and favour; their firearms so destructful to us and by our laws prohibited, commanded to be restored them, and open declaration before witness made that they must have ammunition, although directly contrary to our law. Now what greater guilt can be than to oppose and endeavour the destruction of these honest, quiet neighbors of ours? . . .

THE DECLARATION OF THE PEOPLE

For having upon specious pretences of public works, raised unjust taxes upon the commonalty for the advancement of private favourites and other sinister ends, but no visible effects in any measure adequate.

For not having during the long time of his government in any measure advanced his hopeful colony, either by fortification, towns or trade.

For having abused and rendered contemptible the majesty of justice, of advancing to places of judicature scandalous and ignorant favourites.

For having wronged his Majesty's prerogative and interest by assuming the monopoly of the beaver trade.

By having in that unjust gain bartered and sold his Majesty's country and the lives of his loyal subjects to the barbarous heathen.

For having protected, favoured and emboldened the Indians against his Majesty's most loyal subjects, never contriving, requiring, or appointing any due or proper means of satisfaction for their many invasions, murders, and robberies committed upon us.

For having, when the army of the English was just upon the track of the Indians, which now in all places burn, spoil, and murder, and when we might with ease have destroyed them who then were in open hostility, for having expressly countermanded and sent back our army by passing his word for the peaceable demeanour of the said Indians, who immediately prosecuted their evil intentions, committing horrid murders and robberies in all places, being protected by the said engagement and word passed of him, the said Sir William Berkeley, having ruined and made desolate a great part of his Majesty's country, have now drawn themselves into such obscure and remote places and are by their successes so emboldened and confirmed, and by their confederacy so strengthened that the cries of blood are in all places, and the terror and consternation of the people so great, that they are now become not only a difficult, but a very formidable enemy who might with ease have been destroyed, etc. When upon the loud outcries of blood, the Assembly had with all care raised and framed an army for the prevention of future mischiefs and safeguard of his Majesty's colony.

For having with only the privacy of some few favourites, without acquainting the people, only by the alteration of a figure, forged a commission by we know not what hand, not only without but against the consent of the people, for raising and effecting of civil wars and distractions, which being happily and without bloodshed prevented.

For having the second time attempted the same thereby calling down our forces from the defence of the frontiers, and most weak exposed places, for the prevention of civil mischief and ruin amongst ourselves, whilst the barbarous enemy in all places did invade, murder, and spoil us, his Majesty's most faithful subjects.

Of these, the aforesaid articles, we accuse Sir William Berkeley, as guilty of each and every one of the same, and as one who has traitorously attempted, violated and injured his Majesty's interest here, by the loss of a great part of his colony, and many of his faithful and loyal subjects by him betrayed, and in a barbarous and shameful manner exposed to the incursions and murders of the heathen.

And we further declare these, the ensuing persons in this list, to have been his wicked, and pernicious counsellors, aiders and assisters against the commonalty in these our cruel commotions:

Sir Henry Chicherly, Knt.	Jos. Bridger
Col. Charles Wormley	Wm. Clabourne
Phil. Dalowell	Thos. Hawkins, Jr.
Robert Beverly	William Sherwood
Robert Lee	Jos. Page, Clerk
Thos. Ballard	Jo. Cliffe, "
William Cole	Hubberd Farrell
Richard Whitacre	John West
Nicholas Spencer	Thos. Reade

Mathew Kemp

And we do further demand, that the said Sir William Berkeley, with all the persons in this list, be forthwith delivered up, or surrender themselves, within four days after the notice hereof, or otherwise we declare as followeth: that in whatsoever house, place, or ship any of the said persons shall reside, be hid, or protected, we do declare that the owners, masters, or inhabitants of the said places, to be confederates and traitors to the people, and the estates of them, as also of all the aforesaid persons, to be confiscated. This we, the commons of Virginia, do declare desiring a prime union amongst ourselves, that we may jointly, and with one accord defend ourselves against the common enemy. And let not the faults of the guilty be the reproach of the innocent, or the faults or crimes of the oppressors divide and separate us, who have suffered by their oppressions.

These are therefore in his Majesty's name, to command you forthwith to seize the persons above mentioned as traitors to the king and country, and them to bring to Middle Plantation, and there to secure them, till further order, and in case of opposition, if you want any other assistance, you are forthwith to demand it in the name of the people of all the counties of Virginia.

[signed]

NATH BACON, Gen'l.
By the Consent of the People.

Questions

1. Bacon's rebellion was the first serious tax revolt in American history. What evidence is there to support this statement in Bacon's "Manifesto"?
2. Did Indian assaults trigger the rebellion? Were the native Americans pawns in a larger dispute between Bacon and Governor Berkeley? Explain why or why not.
3. Is there evidence of "democracy" in Bacon's "Manifesto" and Declaration? To what extent was Bacon a democrat?

The Examination of Anne Hutchinson (1637)

Anne Hutchinson (1591–1643) caused the worst internal crisis in the early theological history of Massachusetts by rejecting the Puritan belief that good works are a sign of God's grace. Instead, Hutchinson believed in salvation by faith alone, a heresy the Puritans called antinomianism.

Her "subversive" teachings undermined the authority of magistrates and ministers alike and called into question the traditional submissiveness of women. Tried in court for her opinions, Hutchinson admitted her differences with mainstream theology. Although she might have won a theological battle, Hutchinson lost the political war and was expelled from Massachusetts.

Note: Among Protestants, the Jesuits were hated and feared for the subtlety of their theological arguments.

NOVEMBER 1637.
The Examination of Mrs. Anne Hutchinson at the court at Newtown.

Mr. Winthrop, governor. Mrs. Hutchinson, you are called here as one of those that have troubled the peace of the commonwealth and the churches here; you are known to be a woman that hath had a great share in the promoting and divulging of those opinions that are causes of this trouble, and to be nearly joined not only in affinity and affection with some of those the court had taken notice of and passed censure upon, but you have spoken divers things as we have been informed very prejudicial to the honour of the churches and ministers thereof, and you have maintained a meeting and an assembly in your house that hath been condemned by the general assembly as a thing not tolerable nor comely in the sight of God nor fitting for your sex, and notwithstanding that was cried down you have continued the same, therefore we have thought good to send for you to understand how things are, that if you be in an erroneous way we may reduce you that so you may become a profitable member here among us, otherwise if you be obstinate in your course that then the court may take such course that you may trouble us no further, therefore I would intreat you to express whether you do not hold and assent in practice to those opinions and factions that have been handled in court already, that is to say, whether you do not justify Mr. Wheelwright's sermon and the petition. . . .

Mrs. H. . . . I shall not equivocate, there is a meeting of men and women, and there is a meeting only for women. . . .

Mr. Endicot. Who teaches in the men's meetings, none but men? Do not women sometimes?

Mrs. H. Never as I heard, not one. . . .

Deputy Gov. Now it appears by this woman's meeting that Mrs. Hutchinson hath so forestalled the minds of many by their resort to her meeting that now she hath a potent party in the country. Now if all these things have endangered us as from that foundation, and if she in particular hath disparaged all our ministers in the land that they have preached a covenant of works, . . . why this is not to be suffered. And therefore being driven to the foundation, and it being found that Mrs. Hutchinson is she that hath depraved all the ministers and hath been the cause of what is fallen out, why we must take away the foundation and the building will fall.

Mrs. H. I pray Sir prove it that I said they preached nothing but a covenant of works.

Deputy Gov. Nothing but a covenant of works, why a Jesuit may preach truth sometimes.

Mrs. H. Did I ever say they preached a covenant of works then?

Deputy Gov. If they do not preach a covenant of grace clearly, then they preach a covenant of works.

Mrs. H. No Sir, one may preach a covenant of grace more clearly than another, so I said.

Deputy Gov. We are not upon that now but upon position.

Mrs. H. Prove this then Sir that you say I said.

Deputy Gov. When they do preach a covenant of works do they preach truth?

Mrs. H. Yes Sir, but when they preach a covenant of works for salvation, that is not truth.

Deputy Gov. I do but ask you this, when the ministers do preach a covenant of works do they preach a way of salvation?

Mrs. H. I did not come hither to answer to questions of that sort.

Deputy Gov. Because you will deny the thing.

Mrs. H. Ey [Aye], but that is to be proved first.

Deputy Gov. I will make it plain that you did say that the ministers did preach a covenant of works.

Mrs. H. I deny that. . . . Now if you do condemn me for speaking what in my conscience I know to be truth I must commit myself unto the Lord.

Mr. Nowell. How do you know that that was the spirit?

Mrs. H. How did Abraham know that it was God that bid him offer his son, being a breach of the sixth commandment [Thou shalt not kill]?

Deputy Gov. By an immediate voice.

Mrs. H. So to me by an immediate revelation.

Deputy Gov. How! an immediate revelation.

Mrs. H. By the voice of his own spirit to my soul. . . .

Gov. The court hath already declared themselves satisfied concerning the things you hear, and concerning the troublesomeness of her spirit and the danger of her course amongst us, which is not to be suffered. Therefore if it be the mind of the court that Mrs. Hutchinson for these things that appear before us is unfit for our society, and if it be the mind of the court that she shall be banished out of our liberties and imprisoned till she be sent away, let them hold up their hands.

All but three. . . .

Mrs. Hutchinson, the sentence of the court you hear is that you are banished from out of our jurisdiction as being a woman not fit for our society, and are to be imprisoned till the court shall send you away.

Mrs. H. I desire to know[,] wherefore I am banished?

Gov. Say no more, the court knows wherefore and is satisfied.

Questions

1. Why is Hutchinson's "immediate revelation" considered subversive?
2. Is this court stacked against Anne Hutchinson? Is there any way she could have won?

3. Is there evidence of sexism in this document? Why didn't Governor Winthrop move to have Hutchinson hanged?

The Mayflower Compact (1620)

The Mayflower Compact of 1620 (see text p. 44) is one of the most important political statements in American history as a wellspring for constitutional government. In the Compact, a small group of Separatists agreed to govern themselves. The Separatists honored the king of England but not the Church of England, which he headed; these dissenters came to America (greater Virginia) to effect a complete withdrawal from Anglicanism. They were the Pilgrims, who settled Plymouth about a decade before the Massachusetts Bay Colony was established. Plymouth continued as a separate colony until it was absorbed into Massachusetts in 1691.

In the name of God, amen. We, whose names are underwritten, the Loyal Subjects of our dread Sovereign Lord King *James,* by the Grace of God, of *Great Britain, France,* and *Ireland,* King, *Defender of the Faith,* &c. Having undertaken for the Glory of God, and Advancement of the Christian Faith, and Honour of our King and Country, a Voyage to plant the first Colony in the northern Parts of *Virginia;* Do by these Presents, solemnly and mutually, in the Presence of God and one another, covenant and combine ourselves together into a civil Body Politick, for our better Ordering and Preservation, and Furtherance of the Ends aforesaid: And by Virtue hereof do enact, constitute, and frame, such just and equal Laws, Ordinances, Acts, Constitutions, and Officers, from time to time, as shall be thought most meet and convenient for the general Good of the Colony; unto which we promise all due Submission and Obedience. IN WITNESS whereof we have hereunto subscribed our names at *Cape-Cod* the eleventh of *November,* in the Reign of our Sovereign Lord King *James,* of *England, France,* and *Ireland,* the eighteenth, and of *Scotland,* the fifty-fourth, *Anno Domini,* 1620.

Questions
1. Is this a civil or religious document, or both? Why?
2. How does the Compact suggest that the Pilgrims will clash with native Americans?

3. Should the authors of the Mayflower Compact have recognized the concept of the separation of church and state? Why or why not?

Metacom's War: A Puritan Explanation (1675)

In June 1675 Metacom, a Wampanoag Indian whom the English called King Philip, launched the most devastating Indian uprising in American colonial history (see text pp. 53–55). Lasting almost two years and threatening the very survival of New England, the rebellion called into question the colonies' religious underpinnings. The Massachusetts General Court responded with a mixture of piety and military preparation. On the one hand, the Puritans blamed themselves for straying from God's ways and thus calling down divine wrath. On the other hand, they intensified their military response.

WHEREAS the most wise & holy God, for severall yeares past, hath not only warned us by his word, but chastized us with his rods, inflicting upon us many generall (though lesser) judgments, but we have neither heard the word nor rod as wee ought, so as to be effectually humbled for our sinns to repent of them, reforme, and amend our wayes; hence it is the righteous God hath heightened our calamity, and given commission to the barbarous heathen to rise up against us, and to become a smart rod and severe scourge to us, in burning & depopulating severall hopefull plantations, murdering many of our people of all sorts, and seeming as it were to cast us off, and putting us to shame, and not going forth with our armies, heereby speaking aloud to us to search and try our wayes, and turne againe unto the Lord our God, from whom wee have departed with a great backsliding.

1. The Court, apprehending there is too great a neglect of discipline in the churches, and especially respecting those that are their children, through the non acknowledgment of them according to the order of the gospell; in watching over them, as well as chattechising of them, inquireing into theire spirituall estates, that, being brought to take hold of the covenant, they may acknowledge & be acknowledged according to theire relations to God & to his church, and theire obligations to be the Lords, and to approve themselves so to be by a suitable profession & conversation; and doe therefore solemnly recommend it unto the respective elders and brethren of the severall churches throughout this jurisdiction to take effectuall course for reformation herein.

2. Whereas there is manifest pride openly appearing amongst us in that long haire, like weomens haire, is worne by some men, either their owne or others haire made into perewiggs, and by some weomen wearing borders of haire, and theire cutting, curling, & immodest laying out theire haire, which practise doeth prevayle & increase, especially amongst the younger sort, —

This Court doeth declare against this ill custome as offencive to them, and divers sober christians amongst us, and therefore doe hereby exhort and advise all persons to use moderation in this respect; and further, doe impower all grand juries to present to the County Court such persons, whither male or female, whom they shall judge to exceede in the premisses; and the County Courts are hereby authorized to proceed against such delinquents either by admonition, fine, or correction, according to theire good discretion.

3. Notwithstanding the wholesome lawes already made by this Court for restreyning excesse in apparrell, yet through corruption in many, and neglect of due execution of those lawes, the evill of pride in apparrell, both for costlines in the poorer sort, & vaine, new, strainge fashions, both in poore & rich, with naked breasts and armes, or, as it were, pinioned with the addition of superstitious ribbons both on haire & apparrell; for redresse whereof, it is ordered by this Court, that the County Courts, from time to time, doe give strict charge to present all such persons as they shall judge to exceede in that kinde, and if the grand jury shall neglect theire duty herein, the County Court shall impose a fine upon them at their discretion.

And it is further ordered, that the County Court, single magistrate, Commissioners Court in Boston, have heereby power to summon all such persons so offending before them, and for the first offence to admonish them, and for each offence of that kinde afterwards to impose a fine of tenn shillings upon them, or, if unable to pay, to inflict such punishment as shall be by them thought most suiteable to the nature of the offence; and the same judges above named are heereby impowred to judge of and execute the laws already extant against such excesse. . . .

5. Whereas there is so mutch profanes amongst us in persons turning their backs upon the publick worship before it be finished and the blessing pronounced, —

It is ordered by this Court, that the officers of the churches, or selectmen, shall take care to prevent such disorders, by appointing persons to shutt the meeting house doores, or any other meete way to attaine the end.

6. Whereas there is much disorder & rudenes in youth in many congregations in time of the worship of God, whereby sin & prophaness is greatly increased, for reformation whereof, —

It is ordered by this Court, that the select men doe appoint such place or places in the meeting house for children or youth to sit in where they may be most together and in publick veiw, and that the officers of the churches, or selectmen, doe appoint some grave & sober person or persons to take a particcular care of and inspection over them, who are heereby required to present a list of the names of such, who, by their owne observance or the information of others, shall be found delinquent, to the next magistrate or Court, who are impowred for the first offence to admonish them, for the second offence to impose a fine of five shillings on theire parents or governors, or order the children to be whipt, and if incorrigible, to be whipt with ten stripes, or sent to the house of correction for three dayes.

7. Whereas the name of God is prophaned by common swearing and cursing in ordinary communication, which is a sin that growes amongst us, and many heare such oathes and curses, and conceales the same from authority, for reformation whereof, it is ordered by this Court, that the lawes already in force against this sin be vigorously prosecuted; and, as addition thereunto, it is further ordered, that all such persons who shall at any time heare prophane oathes and curses spoken by any person or persons, and shall neglect to disclose the same to some magistrate, commissioner, or constable, such persons shall incurr the same poenalty provided in that law against swearers.

8. Whereas the shamefull and scandelous sin of excessive drinking, tipling, & company keeping in tavernes, &c, ordinarys, grows upon us, for reformation whereof, —

It is commended to the care of the respective County Courts not to license any more publick houses then are absolutely necessary in any toune, and to take care that none be licenst but persons of approoved sobriety and fidelity to law and good order; and that licensed houses be regulated in theire improovement for the refreshing & enterteynment of travailers & strangers only, and all toune dwellers are heereby strictly enjoyned & required to forebeare spending their time or estates in such common houses of enterteynment, to drincke & tiple, upon poenalty of five shillings for every offence, or, if poore, to be whipt, at the discretion of the judge, not exceeding five stripes; and every ordinary keeper, permitting persons to transgress as above said, shall incurr the poenalty of five shillings for each offence in that kinde; and any magistrate, commissioner, or selectmen are impowred & required vigorously to putt the abovesaid law in execution.

And, ffurther, it is ordered, that all private, unlicensed houses of enterteinment be diligently searched out, and the poenalty of this law strictly imposed; and that all such houses may be the better discovered, the selectmen of every toune shall choose some sober and discreete persons, to be authorized from the County Court, each of whom shall take the charge of ten or twelve families of his neighbourhood, and shall diligently inspect them, and present the names of such persons so transgressing to the magistrate, commissioners, or selectmen of the toune, who shall returne the same to be proceeded with by the next County Court as the law directs; and the persons so chosen and authorized, and attending theire duty ffaithfully therein, shall have one third of the fines allowed them; but, if neglect of their duty, and shall be so judged by authority, they shall incurr the same poenalty provided against unlicensed houses.

9. Whereas there is a wofull breach of the fifth commandment [Honor thy father and thy mother] to be found amongst us, in contempt of authority, civil, ecclesiasticall, and domesticall, this Court doeth declare, that sin is highly provoaking to the Lord, against which he hath borne severe testimony in his word, . . . and therefore doe strictly require & comand all persons under this government to reforme so great an evil, least God from heaven punish offenders heerin by some remarkeable judgments. And it is further ordered, that all County Courts, magistrates, commissioners, selectmen, and grand jurors, according to theire severall capacities, doe take strict care that the lawes already made & provided in this case be duely executed, and particcularly that evil of inferiours absenting themselves out of the families whereunto they belong in the night, and meeting with corrupt company without leave, and against the minde & to the great greife of theire superiours, which evil practise is of a very perrillous nature, and the roote of much disorder.

It is therefore ordered by this Court, that whatever inferiour shall be legally convicted of such an evil practise, such persons shall be punished with admonition for the first offence, with fine not exceeding ten shillings, or whipping not exceeding five stripes, for all offences of like nature afterwards.

10. Whereas the sin of idlenes (which is a sin of Sodom) doeth greatly increase, notwithstanding the wholesome lawes in force against the same, as an addition to that law, —

This Court doeth order, that the constable, with such other person or persons whom the selectmen shall appoint, shall inspect particcular families, and present a lyst of the names of all idle persons to the selectmen, who are heereby strictly required to proceed with them as already the law directs, and in case of obstinacy, by charging the constable with them, who shall convey them to some magistrate, by him to be committed to the house of correction. . . .

12. Whereas there is a loose & sinfull custome of going or riding from toune to toune, and that oft times men & weomen together, upon pretence of going to lecture, but it appears to be meerely to drincke & revell in ordinarys & tavernes, which is in itself scandalous, and it is to be feared a notable meanes to debauch our youth and hazard the chastity of such as are draune forth thereunto, for prevention whereof, —

It is ordered by this Court, that all single persons who, meerly for their pleasure, take such journeys, & frequent such ordinaryes, shall be reputed and accounted riotous & unsober persons, and of ill behaviour, and shall be liable to be summoned to appear before any County Court, magistrate, or commissioner, & being therof convicted, shall give bond & sufficient sureties for the good behaviour in twenty pounds, and upon refusall so to doe, shall be committed to prison for ten days, or pay a fine of forty shillings for each offence.

It is ordered by this Court, that every toune in this jurisdiction shall provide, as an addition to their toune stocke of ammunition, six hundred of flints for one hundred of lysted souldiers, and so proportionably for a lesser or greater number, to be constantly mainteyned & fitted for publick service. . . .

14. This Court, considering the great abuse & scandall that hath arisen by the license of trading houses with the Indians, whereby drunkenes and other crimes have binn, as it were, sold unto them, —

It is ordered by this Court, that all such trading houses, from the publication hereof, shall wholly cease, and none to presume to make any sale unto them, except in open shops and tounes where goods are sold unto the English, upon the poenalty of ten pounds for every conviction before laufall authority, one third to the informers, the remainder to the country, any law, usage, or costume to the contrary notwithstanding. . . .

Questions

1. List the causes of Metacom's War as indicated in this document. Do they make sense to you? Was there a direct relationship between Metacom's resistance and Puritan permissiveness?
2. How are the Indians viewed — as an instrument of God's will or as a community with grievances against the colonists? Why do the colonists regard the situation from this particular perspective?
3. Do the Puritans show any generational differences in this lament?

Connections Questions

1. Compare the views of John Smith ("A True Relation") and Nathaniel Bacon ("Nathaniel Bacon, 'Manifesto' ") on native Americans. How different are they and why?
2. How might the Franciscan monk ("A Franciscan Monk Refutes") have viewed the Puritan explanation of war with Metacom ("Metacom's War")?
3. How would you assess life for newcomers to North America in the period 1565–1675? For native Americans? Is there anything to suggest the excitement of frontier life? Why or why not?

CHAPTER 3

The British Empire in America 1660–1750

William Penn, Preface to the Frame of Government for Pennsylvania (1682)

The charter for the settlement of Pennsylvania as a Quaker colony was granted in 1681 to William Penn (1644–1718) by Charles II, "having regard to the memory and merits of his late father." The preface, a bold statement of intent, was enacted in the 1682 Charter of Privileges and its subsequent revisions. Penn regarded the founding of the colony as an opportunity to carry out a "Holy Experiment": a colony devoted to the ideal of religious toleration. The development of the colony's government was an experimental process in which Penn showed no fixed convictions but one — the principle of political participation by the governed. . . .

. . . Government seems to me a part of religion itself, a thing sacred in its institution and end. For, if it does not directly remove the cause, it crushes the effects of evil, and is as such an emanation of the same Divine Power that is both author and object of pure religion; the difference being that the one is more free and mental, the other more corporal and compulsive in its operations. But that is only to evildoers; government itself being otherwise as capable of kindness, goodness, and charity as a more private society. . . .

I know what is said by the several admirers of monarchy, aristocracy, and democracy, which are the rule of one, a few, and many, and are the three common ideas of government. But I choose to solve the controversy with this small distinction, and it applies to all three: Any government is free to the people under it (whatever be the frame) where the laws rule, and the people participate in making those laws, and more than this is tyranny, oligarchy, or confusion. . . .

I know some say let us have good laws, and no matter for the men that execute them; but let them consider that though good laws do well, good men do better; for good men will never lack good laws, nor submit to ill ones. That, therefore, which makes a good constitution must keep it, namely: men of wisdom and virtue, qualities that — because they descend not with worldly inheritances — must be carefully propagated by a virtuous education of youth. . . . The great end of all government, namely: to support power in reverence with the people, and to secure the people from the abuse of power; that they may be free by their just obedience, and the magistrates honorable, for their just administration; for liberty without obedience is confusion, and obedience without liberty is slavery. To carry this balance is partly owing to the constitution, and partly to the magistracy. Where either of these fail, government will be subject to convulsions; but where both are lacking, it must be totally subverted; then where both meet, the government is likely to endure. Which I humbly pray and hope God will please to make the destiny of Pennsylvania. Amen.

Questions

1. To what extent is the Preface a modern document? a traditional document?
2. How does Penn's religious faith compare to that expressed in the Puritan explanation for Metacom's War (Chapter 2, "Metacom's War")?
3. Why are good laws not enough to guarantee good government? What else is needed?

James Albert Ukawsaw Gronniosaw, An African Prince Sold into Slavery

James Albert Ukawsaw Gronniosaw was sold into slavery when he was about fifteen years old. The narrative of his enslavement provides some insight into the intrigue and culture shock produced in West Africa by the slave trade (see text pp. 65–69). Eventually, Gronniosaw was freed when his master died. After serving as a sailor in the French and Indian War, he left New York, where he had settled after gaining his freedom, and went to England. There he and his family fell on hard times. One purpose of this narrative was to raise money to help him get out of debt.

I was born in the city of Bournou; my mother was the eldest daughter of the reigning King there. . . . I had, from my infancy, a curious turn of mind; was more grave and reserved, in my disposition, than either of my brothers and sisters. . . . 'Twas certain that I was, at times, very unhappy in myself: It being strongly impressed on my mind that there was some GREAT MAN of power, which resided above the sun, moon and stars, the objects of our worship. My dear indulgent mother would bear more with me than any of my friends beside. I often raised my hands to heaven, and asked her who lived there? . . . I was frequently lost in wonder at the works of the creation: Was afraid, and uneasy, and restless, but could not tell for what. I wanted to be informed of things that no person could tell me; and was always dissatisfied. . . .

To this moment I grew more and more uneasy every day, insomuch that one Saturday (which is the day on which we keep our sabbath) I labored under anxieties and fears that cannot be expressed; and, what is more extra-ordinary, I could not give a reason for it. I rose, as our custom is, about three o'clock (as we are obliged to be at our place of worship an hour before the sunrise). We say nothing in our worship, but continue on our knees with our hands held up, observing a strict silence till the sun is at a certain height. . . . When, at a certain sign made by the Priest, we get Up (our duty being over) and disperse to our different houses. Our place of meeting is under a large palm tree; we divide ourselves into many congregations. . . .

About this time there came a merchant from the Gold Coast (the third city in GUINEA). He traded with the inhabitants of our country in ivory, etc. He took great notice of my unhappy situation, and inquired into the cause; he ex-pressed vast concern for me, and said, if my parents would part with me for a little while, and let him take me home with him, it would be of more ser-vice to me than any thing they could do for me. He told me that if I would go with him, I should see houses with Wings to them walk upon the water, and should also see the white folks; and that he had many sons of my age, which should be my companions; and he added to all this that he would bring me safe back again soon. I was highly pleased with the account of this strange place, and was very desirous of going. I seemed sensible of a secret impulse upon my mind, which I could not resist, that seemed to tell me I must go. When my dear mother saw that I was willing to leave them, she spoke to my father and grandfather and the rest of my relations, who all agreed that I should accompany the merchant to the Gold Coast. . . . Indeed if I could have known when I left my friends and country, that I should never return to them again my misery on that occasion would have been inexpressible. . . .

I had a very unhappy and discontented journey, being in continual fear that the people I was with would murder me. I often reflected with extreme re-gret on the kind friends I had left, and the idea of my dear mother frequently drew tears from my eyes. I cannot recollect how long we were in going from Bournou to the Gold Coast; but as there is no shipping nearer to Bournou than that city, it was tedious in travelling so far by land, being upwards of a thousand miles. I was heartily rejoiced when we arrived at the end of our jour-ney: I now vainly imagined that all my troubles and inquietudes would ter-minate here; but could I have looked into futurity, I should have perceived that I had much more to suffer than I had before experienced, and that they had as yet but barely commenced.

I was now more than a thousand miles from home, without a friend or means to procure one. . . . I was mightily pleased with sounds so entirely new to me, and was very inquisitive to know the cause of this rejoicing, and asked many questions concerning it; I was answered that it was meant as a compli-ment to me, because I was grandson to the King of Bournou.

This account gave me a secret pleasure; but I was not suffered long to enjoy this satisfaction, for, in the evening of the same day, two of the merchant's sons (boys about my own age) came running to me, and told me, that the next day I was to die, for the King intended to behead me. I reply'd that I was sure it could not be true, for that I came there to play with them, and to see houses walk upon the water with wings to them, and the white folks; but I was soon informed that their King imagined I was sent by my father as a spy, and would make such discoveries, at my return home, that would enable them to make war with greater advantage to ourselves; and for these reasons he had resolved I should never return to my native country. When I heard this, I suffered misery that cannot be described. I wished, a thousand times, that I had never left my friends and country, but still the Almighty was pleased to work miracles for me.

The morning I was to die, I was washed and all my gold ornaments made bright and shining, and then carried to the palace, where the King was to behead me himself (as is the custom of the place). . . . I went with an undaunted courage, and it pleased God to melt the heart of the King, who sat with his scymitar in his hand ready to behead me; yet, being himself so affected, he dropped it out of his hand, and took me upon his knee and wept over me. I put my right hand round his neck, and prest him to my heart. He set me down and blest me; and added, that he would not kill me, and that I should not go home, but be sold for a slave, so then I was conducted back again to the merchant's house. . . .

A few days after a Dutch ship came into the harbour, and they carried me on board, in hopes that the captain would purchase me. As they went, I heard them agree, that, if they could not sell me then, they would throw me overboard. I was in extreme agonies when I heard this; and as soon as ever I saw the Dutch Captain, I ran to him, and put my arms round him, and said, "Father save me;" (for I knew that if he did not buy me, I should be treated very ill, or, possibly murdered.) And though he did not understand my language, yet it pleased the Almighty to influence him in my behalf, and he bought me for two yards of check [checkered cloth], which is of more value there, than in England. . . .

I was now washed and clothed in the Dutch or English manner. My master grew very fond of me, and I loved him exceedingly. . . . He used to read prayers in public to the ship's crew every sabbath day; and when first I saw him read, I was never so surprised in my whole life as when I saw the book talk to my master; for I thought it did, as I observed him to look upon it, and move his lips. I wished it would do so to me. As soon as my master had done reading I follow'd him to the place where he put the book, being mightily delighted with it, and when nobody saw me, I open'd it and put my ear down close upon it, in great hope that it would say something to me; but was very sorry and greatly disappointed when I found it would not speak, this thought immediately presented itself to me, that every body and every thing despised me because I was black.

Questions

1. How did Gronniosaw come to the Gold Coast?
2. Was the king moved by mercy or profit to save the young man's life? Explain.
3. What was one of Gronniosaw's first realizations about slavery?

"An Act for the Better Order and Government of Negroes and Slaves" (1712)

Until the early 1700s most legislation involving African-Americans concerned the personal status of slaves and was motivated primarily by racial prejudice. In time another element appeared — fear of their growing numbers. The presence of a servile but potentially rebellious population made it seem necessary to adopt measures of control. The act passed by South Carolina served as a model for slave codes in the colonial South and later in southern states.

WHEREAS, the plantations and estates of this Province cannot be well and sufficiently managed and brought into use, without the labor and service of negroes and other slaves [i.e., Indians]; and forasmuch as the said negroes and other slaves brought unto the people of this Province for that purpose, are of barbarous, wild, savage natures, and such as renders them wholly unqualified to be governed by the laws, customs, and practices of this Province; but that it is absolutely necessary, that such other constitutions, laws and orders, should in this Province be made and enacted, for the good regulating and ordering of them, as may restrain the disorders, rapines and inhumanity, to which they are naturally prone and inclined, and may also tend to the safety and security of the people of this Province and their estates; to which purpose, . . .

II. . . . That no master, mistress, overseer, or other person whatsoever . . . shall give their negroes and other slaves leave . . . to go out of their plantations, except such negro or other slave as usually wait upon them at home or abroad, or wearing a livery; and every other negro or slave that shall be taken hereafter out of his master's plantation, without a ticket, or leave in writing, from his master or mistress, or some other person by his or her appointment, or some white person in the company of such slave, to give an account of his business, shall be whipped; and every person who shall not (when in his power) apprehend every negro or other slave which he shall see out of his master's plantation, without leave as aforesaid, and after apprehended, shall neglect to punish him by moderate whipping, shall forfeit twenty shillings. . . . And for the better security of all such persons that shall endeavor to take any run-away, or shall examine any slave for his ticket, passing to and from his master's plantation, it is hereby declared lawful for any white person to beat, maim or assault, and if such negro or slave cannot otherwise be taken, to kill him, who shall refuse to shew his ticket, or, by running away or resistance, shall endeavor to avoid being apprehended or taken.

III. And be it further enacted by the authority aforesaid, That every master, mistress or overseer of a family in this Province, shall cause all his negro houses to be searched diligently and effectually, once every fourteen days, for fugitive and runaway slaves, guns, swords, clubs, and any other mischievous weapons, and finding any, to take them away, and cause them to be secured. . . .

VI. And be it further enacted . . . That every master or head of any family, shall keep all his guns and other arms, when out of use, in the most private and least frequented room in the house, upon the penalty of being convicted of neglect therein, to forfeit three pounds. . . .

IX. And be it further enacted by the authority aforesaid, That upon complaint made to any justice of the peace, of any heinous or grievous crime, committed by any slave or slaves, as murder, burglary, robbery, burning of houses, or any lesser crimes, as killing or stealing any meat or other cattle, maiming one the other, stealing of fowls, provisions, or such like trespasses or injuries, the said justice shall issue out his warrant for apprehending the offender or offenders, . . . he shall commit him or them to prison, or immediately proceed to tryal of the said slave or slaves . . . [and if] they shall find such negro or other slave or slaves guilty thereof, they shall give sentence of death, if the crime by law deserve the same. . . .

X. And in regard great mischiefs daily happen by petty larcenies committed by negroes and slaves of this Province, Be it further enacted by the authority aforesaid, That if any negro or other slave shall hereafter steal or destroy any goods, chattels, or provisions whatsoever, of any other person than his master or mistress . . . [if] adjudged [guilty is] to be publicly and severely whipped, not exceeding forty lashes; and if such negro or other slave punished as aforesaid, be afterwards, by two justices of the peace, found guilty of the like crimes, he or they, for such his or their second offence, shall either have one of his ears cut off, or be branded in the forehead with a hot iron, that the mark thereof may remain; and if after such punishment, such negro or slave for his third offence, shall have his nose slit; and if such negro or other slave, after the third time as aforesaid, be accused of petty larceny, or of any of the offences before mentioned, such negro or other slave shall be tried in such manner as those accused of murder, burglary, etc. are before by this Act provided for to be tried, and in case they shall be found guilty a fourth time of any the offences before mentioned, then such negro or other slave shall be adjudged to suffer death, or other punishment, as the said justices shall think fitting. . . .

XII. And It is Further enacted by the authority aforesaid, That if any negroes or other slaves shall make mutiny or insurrection . . . the offenders shall be tried by two justices of the peace and three freeholders . . . who are hereby empowered and required to . . . inflict death, or any other punishment, upon the offenders . . . if the Governor and council of this Province shall think fitting . . . that only one or more of the said criminals should suffer death as exemplary, and the rest to be returned to the owners. . . .

Questions

1. What does this act assume about the cultural level of the slave population?
2. What are the responsibilities and duties of slave owners in regard to governing their slaves?
3. What does the statute suggest about the role of government in slavery?

Early Protests against Slavery: The Mennonites (1688)

As laws began to define the condition of African servants and slaves and to distinguish slavery from other forms of labor in the colonies, a few voices were raised against the institution. Among the earliest protesters were Quakers and Mennonites. The following document is a Mennonite statement that dates from 1688, about the time of the Glorious Revolution in England and the beginning of the extensive importation of slaves into the Chesapeake area.

This is to the monthly meeting held at Richard Worrell's:

These are the reasons why we are against the traffic of men-body, as followeth: Is there any that would be done or handled in this manner? viz., to be sold or made a slave for all the time of his life? How fearful and faint-hearted are many at sea, when they see a strange vessel, being afraid it should be a Turk, and they should be taken, and sold for slaves into Turkey. Now, what is *this* better done, than Turks do? Yea, rather it is worse for them, which say they are Christians; for we hear that the most part of such negers are brought hither against their will and consent, and that many of them are stolen. Now, though they are black, we cannot conceive there is more liberty to have them slaves, as it is to have other white ones. There is a saying, that we should do to all men like as we will be done ourselves; making no difference of what generation, descent, or colour they are. And those who steal or rob men, and those who buy or purchase them, are they not all alike? Here is liberty of conscience, which is right and reasonable; here ought to be likewise liberty of the body, except of evil-doers, which is another case. But to bring men hither, or to rob and sell them against their will, we stand against. In Europe there are many oppressed for conscience-sake; and here there are those oppressed which are of a black colour. . . . Ah! do consider well this thing, you who do it, if you would be done at this manner — and if it is done according to Christianity! You surpass Holland and Germany in this thing. This makes an ill report in all those countries of Europe, where they hear of [it], that the Quakers do here handel men as they handel there the cattle. And for that reason some have no mind or inclination to come hither. And who shall maintain this your cause, or plead for it? Truly, we cannot do so, except you shall inform us better hereof, viz.: that Christians have liberty to practice these things. Pray, what thing in the world can be done worse towards us, than if men should rob or steal us away and sell us for slaves to strange countries; separating husbands from their wives and children. Being now this is not done in the manner we would be done at; therefore, we contradict, and are against this traffic of men-body. . . .

If once these slaves (which they say are so wicked and stubborn men) should join themselves — fight for their freedom, and handel their masters and mistresses, as they did handel them before; will these masters and mistresses take the sword at hand and war against these poor slaves, like, as we are able to believe, some will not refuse to do? Or, have these poor negers not as much right to fight for their freedom, as you have to keep them slaves? . . .

Questions

1. What is the "saying" that the Mennonite statement cites as a reason to oppose slavery?
2. How are slaves described? Why should that be important?
3. Why is the last sentence especially powerful?

Conflicts between Masters and Slaves: Maryland in the Mid-Seventeenth Century (1658)

Almost from the beginning of Maryland and Virginia's slave history, the first legislation defined the lifelong condition of slavery. Colonists also imposed harsher punishments against laborers of African descent than against white servants. Masters could, for example, whip a naked slave without breaking the law, and they were not legally required to provide their slaves with food and clothing.

But there were limits to punishment and daily mistreatment of slaves, as the following case outlines. In the end, however, the case was referred to a higher court, where testimony portrayed the slave Tony as a rogue and consistent runaway. At that point the court acquitted Mr. Overzee of cruelty against the slave.

ATT A PROVINCIAL COURT HELD ATT ST. CLEMENT'S MANOR DECEMBER 2, 1658
Attorney General v. [Symon] Overzee

Mr. William Barton informes the court against Mr. Symon Overzee, for that the said Overzee correcting his negro servant the said negro dyed under his said correction.

The examination of Hannah Littleworth aged 27 yeares or thereabouts taken the 27th of November 1658, before Philip Calvert, Esq.

This Examinant sayth that sometime (as shee conseives) in September was two years, Mr. Overzee commanded a negro (commonly called Tony) formerly chayned up for some misdemeanors by the command of Mr. Overzee (Mr. Overzee being then abroad) to be lett loose, and ordered him to goe to worke, but instead of goeing to worke the said negro layd himselfe downe and would not stirre. Whereupon Mr. Overzee beate him with some peare tree wands or tweiggs to the bigness of man's finger att the biggest end, which hee held in his hand, and uppon the stubberness of the negro caused his dublett to be taken of, and whip'd him uppon his bare back, and the negro still remayned in his stubbernes, and feyned himselfe in fitts, as hee used att former times to doe. Whereupon Mr. Overzee commanded this examinant to heate a fyre shovel, and to bring him some lard, which shee did and sayth that the said fyre shovel was hott enough to melt the lard, but not soe hot as to blister anyone, and that it did not blister the negro, on whom Mr. Overzee powr'd it. Immediately thereuppon the negro rose up, and Mr. Overzee commanded him to be tyed to a Ladder standing on the foreside of the dwelling howse, which was accordingly done by an Indian slve, who tyed him by the wrist, with a piece of dryed hide, and (as she remembers but cannot justly say) that hee did stand uppong the grownd. And still the negro remayned mute or stubborne, and made noe signs of conforming himselfe to his masters will or command. And about a quarter of an howre after, or less, Mr. Overzee and Mrs. Overzee went from home, and [she] doth not know of any order Mr. Overzee gave concerning the said negro. And that while Mr. Overzee beate the negro and powred the lard on him, there was nobody by, save only Mr. Mathew Stone, and Mrs. Overzee now deceased. And that from the time of Mr. Overzee and his wife going from hime, till the negro was dead, there was nobody about the howse but only the said Mr. Mathew Stone, William Hewes, and this examinant, and a negro woman in the quartering house, who never stir'd out. And that after Mr. Overzee was gone, uppon the relation of Mr. Mathew Stone, in the presence of William Hewes that the negro was dying, this examinant desyred Mr. Mathew Stone to cutt the negro downe, and hee refused to doe it, William Hewes allso bidding him let him alone and within lesse then halfe a howre after the negro dyed, the wind comming up att northwest soone after hee was soe tyed, and hee was tyed up betweene three and fowre o'clock in the afternoone, and dyed about six or seaven. . . .

William Hewes sworne in upon court sayth that hee was present, att the time when Mr. Overzee beate the negro, and saw him allso powre lard uppon him, and that as hee conceaves and remembers, he saw noe blood drawne of the negro, and this deponent being willing to help the negro from the grownd, Mr. Overzee haveing his knife in his hand, cutting the twigs, threatened him to runne his knife in him (or words to that effect) if he molested him, and that the negro (as he think, but cannot justly say) stood uppon the grownd, and sayth further that the negro did commonly use to runne away, and absent himselfe from his Mr. Overzees service. . . .

Questions

1. What was Symon Overzee tried for? What excuses did he give, according to the witnesses?
2. Do the witnesses offer unambiguous testimony, or did you develop doubts about their memories of details?
3. What is the connection between the South Carolina legislation ("An Act for the Better Order and Government of Negroes and Slaves") and the kind of situation described here?

Phillis Wheatley, *Poems on Various Subjects, Religious and Moral* (1773)

Born in Africa around 1753, Phillis Wheatley was brought as a young girl to Boston. She became the property of Susannah Wheatley, the wife of a prosperous tailor, who took her into the family. There Wheatley learned to read and write, showing a remarkable aptitude for study and reflection. She was freed after her mistress's death.

Although Wheatley was already published in Boston, her fame spread with the publication of a volume of her poems in London when she was twenty years old; it was only the third book of verse published by a woman in colonial America. On the eve of the Revolution, Wheatley wrote to George Washington, who responded that he would like to meet her; however, revolution or circumstance got in the way. Wheatley died impoverished in 1784.

ON BEING BROUGHT FROM AFRICA TO AMERICA

'Twas mercy brought me from my Pagan land,
Taught my benighted soul to understand
That there's a God, that there's a Saviour too:
Once I redemption neither sought nor knew.

Some view our sable race with scornful eye,
"Their colour is a diabolic die."
Remember, Christians, Negroes, black as Cain,
May be refin'd, and join th'angelic train.

TO THE RIGHT HONORABLE WILLIAM, EARL OF DARTMOUTH, HIS MAJESTY'S SECRETARY OF STATE FOR NORTH AMERICA, ETC.

Hail, Happy day, when, smiling like the morn,
Fair Freedom rose New-England to adorn.
No more America, in mournful strain
Of wrongs, and grievance unredress'd complain,
No longer shall thou dread the iron chain,
Which wanton Tyranny with lawless hand
Had made, and with it meant t'enslave the land.
Should you, my lord, while you peruse my song,

Wonder from whence my love of Freedom sprung,
Whence flow these wishes for the common good,
By feeling hearts alone best understood,
I, young in life, by seeming cruel fate
Was snatch'd from Afric's fancy'd happy seat:
What pangs excruciating must molest,
What sorrows labour in my parent's breast?
Steel'd was that soul and by no misery mov'd
That from a father seiz'd his babe belov'd:
Such, such my case. And can I then but pray
Others may never feel tyrannic sway?

Questions

1. In the first poem, how does Wheatley regard her enslavement?
2. Is that same viewpoint evident in the second poem? Why or why not?
3. Does Wheatley see herself as an American? Where does she comment about this, one way or another?

William Penn, A New Plan of Government (1701)

From 1682 to 1692 Pennsylvanians lived under a cumbersome Frame of Government worked out by William Penn ("Preface to the Frame of Government"). In 1692 Parliament placed the colony under the authority of New York's governor, Benjamin Fletcher, thereby making it a royal colony.

Over the following years, however, Pennsylvanians demanded more privileges than this relationship allowed, and they slowly increased the powers of the colonial Assembly. The Assembly's powers grew at the expense of the governor's council, until the latter became no more than an advisory body. Finally the colonists adopted a new plan of government in 1701, also worked out by Penn; this became the basis for embodying Assembly privileges and lasted until the American Revolution.

. . . for the further Well-being and good Government of the said Province, and Territories and in Pursuance of the Rights and Powers before-mentioned, I the said William Penn do declare, grant and confirm, unto all the Freemen, Planters and Adventurers, and other Inhabitants of this Province and Territories, these following Liberties, Franchises and Privileges. . . .

First

Because no People can be truly happy, though under the greatest Enjoyment of Civil Liberties, if abridged of the Freedom of their Consciences, as to their Religious Profession and Worship: And Almighty God being the only Lord of Conscience, Father of Lights and Spirits; and the Author as well as Object of all divine Knowledge, Faith and Worship, who only doth enlighten the Minds, and persuade and convince the Understandings of People, I do hereby grant and declare, That no Person or Persons, inhabiting in this province or Territories, who shall confess and acknowledge *One* almighty God, the Creator, Upholder and Ruler of the World; and profess him or themselves obliged to live quietly under the Civil Government, shall be in any Case molested or prejudiced, in his or their Person or Estate, because of his or their conscientious Persuasion or Practice, nor be compelled to frequent or maintain any religious Worship, Place or Ministry, contrary to his or their Mind, or to do or suffer any other Act or Thing, contrary to their religious Persuasion.

And that all Persons who also profess to believe in *Jesus Christ,* the Saviour of the World, shall be capable . . . to serve this Government in any Capacity, both legislatively and executively, he or they solemnly promising, when lawfully required, Allegiance to the King as Sovereign, and Fidelity to the Proprietary and Governor. . . .

For the well government of this Province and Territories, there shall be an Assembly yearly chosen, by the Freemen thereof, to consist of Four Persons out of each County, of most Note for Virtue, Wisdom and Ability . . . Which Assembly shall have Power to chuse a Speaker and other their Officers; and shall be Judges of the Qualifications and Elections of their own Members; sit upon their own Adjournments; appoint Committees; prepare Bills in order to pass into Laws; impeach Criminals, and redress Grievances; and shall have all other Powers and Privileges of an Assembly, according to the Rights of the free-born Subjects of *England,* and as is usual in any of the King's Plantations in *America.* . . .

That the Freemen in each respective County, at the Time and Place of Meeting for Electing their Representatives to serve in Assembly, may as often as there shall be Occasions, chuse a double Number of Persons to present to the Governor for Sheriffs and Coroners to serve for *Three* Years, if so long they behave themselves well. . . .

And that the Justices of the respective Counties shall or may nominate and present to the Governor *Three* Persons, to serve for Clerk of the Peace for the said County, when there is a Vacancy, one of which the Governor shall commissionate within *Ten* Days after such Presentment, or else the *First* nominated shall serve in the said Office during good Behavior.

That the Laws of this Government shall be in the Stile, viz. *By the Governor, with the Consent and Approbation of the Freemen in General Assembly met;* and shall be, after Confirmation by the Governor, forthwith recorded in the Rolls Office, and kept at *Philadelphia,* unless the Governor and Assembly shall agree to appoint another Place.

That all Criminals shall have the same Privileges of Witnesses and Council as their Prosecutors.

That no Person or Persons shall or may, at any Time hereafter, be obliged to answer any Complaint, matter or Thing whatsoever, relating to Property, before the Governor and Council, or in any other Place, but in ordinary Course of Justice, unless Appeals thereunto shall be hereafter by Law appointed.

That no person within this Government, shall be licensed by the Governor to keep an Ordinary, Tavern or House of Public Entertainment, but such who are first recommended to him, . . . [and] Justices are and shall be hereby impowered, to suppress and forbid any Person, keeping such Public-House as aforesaid, upon their Misbehavior, on such Penalties as the Law doth or shall direct. . . .

Questions

1. What different offices does this charter create, and what powers are conferred on the major branches of the government?
2. Are the privileges and obligations discussed in this charter similar to those you recognize in American government today? In what ways?
3. The liberty of conscience professed in this document applied to a great number of Pennsylvanians, but some groups would be permitted to live in the colony and yet be excluded from officeholding. Who is included and who is excluded?

Connections Questions

1. Use four documents — "An African Prince," "An Act for the Better Order and Government of Negroes and Slaves," "Early Protests against Slavery," and "Conflicts between Masters and Slaves" — to explain the differences between establishing the institution of slavery and making it work.
2. What, if any, is the contradiction between using government to promote slavery ("An Act for the Better Order and Government of Negroes and Slaves") and to promote civil liberties (William Penn, "Preface" and "A New Plan of Government")? Explain.
3. Do the documents in this chapter show colonial society as more interested in slavery or in civil liberties? In answering, keep in mind such factors as regional economics, geography, and religion.

CHAPTER 4

Growth and Crisis in American Society 1720–1765

Benjamin Wadsworth, *The Well-Ordered Family, or Relative Duties* (1712)

When the Reverend Benjamin Wadsworth of Boston wrote about families in 1712, he advocated beliefs that colonial life was drawing into question. In this selection from his Puritan marriage manual, Wadsworth attempts to define the duties and obligations of each member of the family, particularly the husband and wife.

Wives are part of the House and Family, and ought to be under the Husband's Government: they should Obey their own Husbands. Though the Husband is to rule his Family and his Wife yet his Government of his Wife should not be with rigour, haughtiness, harshness, severity; but with the greatest love, gentleness, kindness, tenderness that may be. Though he governs her, he must not treat her as a Servant, but as his own flesh: he must love her as himself. He should make his government of her, as easie and gentle as possible; and strive more to be lov'd than fear'd; though neither is to be excluded. On the other hand, Wives ought readily and cheerfully to obey their Husbands. Wives submit your selves to your own Husbands, be in subjection to them.

Those Husbands are much to blame, who dont carry it [behave] lovingly and kindly to their Wives. O man, if thy Wife be not so young, beautiful, healthy, well temper'd and qualify'd as thou couldst wish; if she brought not so much Estate to thee, or cannot do so much for thee, as some other women brought to or have done for their Husbands; nay, if she does not carry it so well to thee as she should yet she is thy Wife, and the Great God Commands thee to love her, not to be bitter, but kind to her. What can be more plain and express than that? Let every one of you in particular, so love his Wife even as himself. . . . Those Wives are much to blame who dont carry it lovingly and obediently to their own Husbands. O Woman, if thy Husband be not so young, beautiful, healthy, so well temper'd and qualified as thee couldst wish; if he has not such abilities, riches, honours, as some others have; if he does not carry it so well as he should; yet he's thy Husband, and the Great God Commands thee to love, honour and obey him. Yea, though possibly thou hast greater abilities of mind than he has, wast of some high birth, and he of a more mean Extract, or didst bring more Estate at Marriage than he did; yet since he is thy Husband, God has made him thy Head, and set him above thee, and made it thy duty to love and reverence him. . . .

Questions

1. How is a husband expected to behave toward his wife?
2. How is a wife expected to behave toward her husband?
3. Does any factor such as intelligence or estate alter a wife's obligation to her husband? Why or why not?

Esther Edwards Burr, Letter on the Birth of Her Son (1756)

Esther Edwards Burr (1732–1758) was the daughter of the famed Great Awakening minister Jonathan Edwards (see text p. 100) and the wife of the Reverend Aaron Burr, a Presbyterian minister and the president of the College of New Jersey (Princeton). Here she describes the trials of childbirth faced by all colonial women regardless of wealth or social position. Her son was Aaron Burr Jr., who later became the vice-president of the United States.

I am my dear Fidelia yet alive and allowed to tell you so. . . . I was unexpectedly delivered of a Son the sixth of Febry. Had a fine time altho' it pleased God in infinite wisdome so to order it that Mr Burr was from home. . . . It seemed very gloomy when I found I was actually in Labour to think that I was, as it were, destitute of Earthly friends — No Mother — No Husband and none of my petecular [*sic*] friends that belong to this Town, they happening to be out of Town — but O my dear God was all these relations and more than [*sic*] all to me in the Hour of my distre[ss]. . . . I had a very quick and good time — A very good laying in till about 3 weeks, then I had the Canker [an infection of the mouth] very bad, and before I had recovered of that my little Aaron (for so we call him) was taken very sick so that for some days we did not expect his life — he has never been so well since tho' he is comfortable at present. I have my self got a very bad Cold and very soar Eyes which makes it very diffecult [*sic*] for me to write atall. Some times I am almost blind.

Questions

1. Given this description, why does Burr describe the birth as a "fine time"?
2. What does she seem to regard as the most serious problems in the process?
3. Why do you think she refers to her husband as "Mr. Burr"?

Peter Kalm, A Description of
Philadelphia (1748)

*Probably the most striking features of the British middle colonies of North
America were their prosperity as well as their diverse ethnic and religious
makeup. The following selection consists of the observations of Peter Kalm, a
Swedish naturalist who toured the colonies from 1748 to 1751. While visiting
Philadelphia in 1748, Kalm was struck by all the features mentioned above.*

The town is now quite filled with inhabitants, which in regard to their
country, religion, and trade, are very different from each other. You meet
with excellent masters in all trades, and many things are made here full as well
as in England. Yet no manufactures, especially for making fine cloth, are established. Perhaps the reason is, that it can be got with so little difficulty from
England, and that the breed of sheep which is brought over, degenerates in
process of time, and affords but a coarse wool.

Here is great plenty of provisions, and their prices are very moderate.
There are no examples of an extraordinary dearth. Every one who acknowledges God to be the Creator, preserver, and ruler of all things, and teaches or
undertakes nothing against the state, or against the common peace, is at liberty to settle, stay, and carry on his trade here, be his religious principles ever
so strange. No one is here molested on account of the erroneous principles
of the doctrine which he follows, if he does not exceed the above-mentioned
bounds. And he is so well secured by the laws in his person and property, and
enjoys such liberties, that a citizen of Philadelphia may in a manner be said
to live in his house like a king.

On a careful consideration of what I have already said, it will be easy to
conceive how this city should rise so suddenly from nothing, into such
grandeur and perfection, without supposing any powerful monarch's contributing to it, either by punishing the wicked, or by giving great supplies in
money. And yet its fine appearance, good regulations, agreeable situation,
natural advantages, trade, riches and power, are by no means inferior to those
of any, even of the most ancient towns in Europe. It has not been necessary
to force people to come and settle here; on the contrary, foreigners of different languages have left their country, houses, property, and relations, and
ventured over wide and stormy seas, in order to come hither. Other countries,
which have been peopled for a long space of time, complain of the small
number of their inhabitants. But Pennsylvania, which was no better than a
desert in the year 1681, and hardly contained five hundred people, now vies
with several kingdoms in Europe in number of inhabitants. It has received

numbers of people, which other countries, to their infinite loss, have either neglected or expelled.

Questions

1. What factors does Kalm believe are the most significant in accounting for Philadelphia's rapid rise to prominence?
2. How does Kalm perceive Philadelphia's religious environment?
3. Does Kalm approve of how Philadelphia has attracted diverse people from other colonies and countries? How can you tell?

Cadwallader Colden, "State of the Province of New York" (1765)

Cadwallader Colden, lieutenant governor of New York from 1761 to 1776, lived in America for fifty-six years. Merchant, writer, philosopher, and politician, Colden proved to be a perceptive observer of colonial life. His attitudes can be discerned in this description of the class structure in New York. Unlike other observers, Colden did not view America as a classless society.

The people of New York are properly Distinguished into different Ranks.

1. The Proprietors of the large Tracts of Land, who include within their claims from 100,000 acres to above one Million of acres under one Grant. Some of these remain in one single Family. Others are, by Devises and Purchases claim'd in common by considerable numbers of Persons.

2. The Gentlemen of the Law make the second class in which properly are included both the Bench and the Bar. Both of them act on the same Principles, and are of the most distinguished Rank in the Policy of the Province.

3. The Merchants make the third class. Many of them have rose suddenly from the lowest Rank of the People to considerable Fortunes, and chiefly by illicit Trade in the last War [French and Indian War]. They abhor every limitation of Trade and Duty on it, and therefore gladly go into every Measure whereby they hope to have Trade free.

4. In the last Rank may be placed the Farmers and Mechanics. Tho' the Farmers hold their Lands in fee simple, they are as to condition of Life in no way superior to the common Farmers in England; and the Mechanics such only as are necessary in Domestic Life. This last Rank comprehends the bulk

of the People, and in them consists the strength of the Province. They are the most useful and the most Morall, but allwise made the Dupes of the former; and often are ignorantly made their Tools for the worst purposes.

Questions

1. According to Colden, what class predominates? Does he say how they achieved their status?
2. Does he detect class conflict?
3. What exactly is "the strength of the Province"? Why?

George Whitefield, *A Continuation of the Reverend Mr. Whitefield's Journal* (1740)

The Anglican cleric George Whitefield (1714–1770) was a leading participant in the Great Awakening and its most celebrated itinerant preacher (see text pp. 100–101). In this document Whitefield recounts his visit to and work in Charles Town (as it was called before the Revolution), then famous as a wealthy playground for South Carolina's planter and merchant aristocracy. Whitefield went there to spread the gospel and raise funds for his orphanage in Georgia.

Friday, March 14
Arrived last night at Charles Town. . . . Waited on the Commissary [official representative of the Bishop of London]. . . . He charged me with Enthusiasm and Pride [i.e., with being too harsh], for speaking against the Generality of the Clergy. . . . I told him, I thought I had already; but, as yet, I had scarce begun with them. He then asked me, Wherein were the Clergy so much to blame? I answered, they did not preach up Justification by Faith alone. . . . He charged me with breaking the Canons and Ordination vow; . . . in a great rage he told me, if I preached in any publick church in that Province, he would suspend me. I replied, "I shall regard that as much as I would a Pope's Bull [papal decree].["] . . . [I said to him,] "But if you will make an application to yourself, be pleased, Sir, to let me ask you one Question: have you delivered your Soul by exclaiming against the Assemblies and Balls here?" "What, Sir," says he, "must you come to catechise me? No, I have not exclaim'd against them; I think there is no Harm in them." "Then, Sir," said I, "I shall think it my Duty to exclaim against you." "Then, Sir," replied he, (in

a very great Rage) "get you out of my House." Upon which I made my Bow, and, with my Friends took my leave, pitying the Commissary, who I really tho't was more noble than to give such Treatment. . . .

Saturday, March 15
Preached in the Baptist Meeting-House. . . . I was led out to shew the utter Inability of Man to save himself, and the absolute Necessity of his depending on the rich and sovereign Grace of God in Christ Jesus, in order to be restored to his primitive Dignity. Some, I observ'd, were put under concern, and most seem'd willing to know, whether those Things were so. In the Evening I preach'd again in the Independent Meeting-House, to a more attentive Auditory [audience] than ever; And had the Pleasure afterwards of Finding that a Gentlewoman, whose Family has been carried away for some time with Deistical Principles, began now to be unhinged, and to see that there was no Rest in such a Scheme, for a fallen Creature to rely on. . . .

Sunday, March 16
Preached at Eight in the Morning at the Scotch Meeting-House, . . . heard the Commissary represent me under the Character of the Pharisee, who came to the Temple, saying, "God, I thank thee that I am not as other Men are." But whether I do what I do out of a Principle of Pride, or Duty, the Searcher of Hearts will discover 'ere long, before Men and Angels. . . .

Monday, March 17
Preach'd in the Morning at the Independent Meeting-House, and was more explicit than ever, in exclaiming against Balls and Assemblies, to which the People seem'd to hearken with much Attention.

Preached again in the Evening, and being excited thereto by some of the Inhabitants, spoke on Behalf of my poor Orphans. God was pleased to give it his Blessing, and I collected upwards of Seventy Pounds Sterling for them, the largest Collection I ever yet made on that Occasion. . . .

Tuesday, March 18
Preached twice again today, and took an affectionate Leave of, and gave Thanks to, my Hearers for their great Liberality. Many wept, and my own Heart yearn'd much towards them. For I believe a good Work is begun in many Souls. . . . The Congregations grew larger on the Week Days, and many Things concurred to induce us to think that God intended to visit some in Charlestown with his Salvation.

Questions
1. In what ways does the Great Awakening echo Puritan beliefs?
2. How does George Whitefield threaten the status quo of Charles Town?

3. Where in this account does Whitefield demonstrate his own religious prejudice?

Charles Chauncy, *Enthusiasm Describ'd and Caution'd Against* (1742)

Though at first they welcomed the Great Awakening, Old Light ministers began denouncing a movement that in their eyes threatened reason and order (see text p. 101). One Old Light leader was Charles Chauncy, a Congregational minister of the First Church in Boston. Chauncy's religious views, as revealed in the following excerpt from one of his sermons, were strongly influenced by the Enlightenment and in many respects resembled those of Benjamin Franklin.

Chauncy's views reflect an educated gentleman's disgust at the New Light's attacks on the rational teachings of the orthodox clergy. They also show an intellectual conservative's suspicion of the emotional outpouring of the lower classes, the divisive effect of revivalism on churches and communities, and challenges to authority.

[The] Enthusiast is one who has a conceit of himself as a person favored with the extraordinary presence of the Deity. He mistakes the workings of his own passions for divine communications, and fancies himself immediately inspired by the Spirit of God, when all the while, he is under no other influence than that of an overheated imagination.

The cause of this enthusiasm is a bad temperament of the blood and spirits; 'tis properly a disease, a sort of madness, and there are few, perhaps none at all, but are subject to it; though none are so much in danger of it as those in whom melancholy is the prevailing ingredient in their constitution. . . .

And various are the ways in which their enthusiasm discovers itself. Sometimes, it may be seen in their countenance. A certain wildness is discernable in their look and air, especially when their imaginations are moved and fired. Sometimes, it strangely loosens their tongues and gives them such an energy, as well as fluency and volubility in speaking, as they themselves, by their utmost efforts, can't so much as imitate, when they are not under the enthusiastic influence. . . . Sometimes, it appears in their imaginary peculiar intimacy with heaven. They are, in their own opinion, the special favorites of God, have more familiar converse with Him than other good men, and receive immediate, extraordinary communications from Him. . . . And what extravagances, in this temper of mind, are they not capable of, and under the specious pretext, too, of paying obedience to the authority of God? . . . But in nothing does the enthusiasm of these persons discover itself more than in the disregard they express to the dictates of reason. They are above the force of argument. . . . And in vain will you endeavor to convince such persons of any mistakes they are fallen into. . . .

Questions

1. To what degree are Chauncy's criticisms class-influenced?
2. Is he more concerned with religious doctrine or practice? Explain.
3. Why does Chauncy think reason should matter in worship? Do you agree?

The Regulators, "To the Inhabitants of the Province of North-Carolina" (1769)

Settlers were spreading far into the wilderness even before the French and Indian War. By war's end, when the Proclamation Line of 1763 defined the extent of English jurisdiction on the frontier, thousands of new farms and villages dotted the countryside of Pennsylvania, Virginia, and the Carolinas. Many newcomers had just arrived from Scotland, Wales, and Germany; others came looking for land from the older coastal settlements.

Everywhere on this developing frontier people struggled to define political institutions or challenged the dominant elites of the coastline. Sometimes this strife erupted into violence between the judges, sheriffs, and tax collectors who attempted to enforce imperial laws, and the frontier settlers who resisted. For example, the Regulators fought against North Carolina authorities for many years over representation in colonial government. When the Revolution occurred, most Regulators fought with the British or remained neutral because their former enemies on the coastline had become Patriot leaders.

"To the INHABITANTS of the Province of North-Carolina"

Dear Brethren,
    Nothing is more common than for Persons who look upon themselves to be injured than to resent and complain. These are sounded aloud, and plain in Proportion to the Apprehension of it. Our Fearfulness too, frequently aug-

ment our real as well as apparent Dangers. Let us adjust our Complaints or Resentments to the Reality as well as the Nature of the Injury received.

Excess in any Matter breeds Contempt; whereas strict Propriety obtains the Suffrage of every Class. The Oppression of inferior Individuals must only demand Tutelage of superiors; and in civil Matters our Cries should reach the authorative Ear, when the Weight that crusheth from the higher Powers. — But when imposed by the Populace, to the Populace our complaints must extend. — When therefore the Cry of any City, Province or Nation is general, it must be generally directed to the Source from whence the Cry is caused.

The late Commotions and crying Dissatisfactions among the common People of this Province, is not unknown nor unfelt by any thinking Person. — No Person among you could be at a Loss to find out the true Cause. — I dare venture to assert you [are] all advised to the Application of the Public Money; — these you saw misapplied to the enriching of Individuals, or at least embezzled in some way without defraying the publick Expenses. Have not your Purses been pillaged by the exorbitant and unlawful Fees taken by Officers, Clerks, &c.? — I need not mention the intolerable expensive Method of Recovery by Law, occasioned by the narrow Limits of the inferior Court's Jurisdiction. — Have you not been grieved to find the Power of our County Courts so curtailed, that scarce the Shadow of Power is left? This Body, however respectable, is intrusted with little more than might pertain to the Jurisdiction of a single Magistrate, or at least two or three Justices of the Peace in Conjunction. — In Consequence of this, very small Sums drags us to Superior Courts. — These must be attended with all our Evidences, altho many at the Distance of 150 Miles. Add to this a double Fee to all Officers; Hence we are made feelingly sensible, that our necessary Expenses, with the additional Costs, are equal, if not surpass the original Sum.

For what End was the Jurisdiction of the Courts reduced to such narrow Limits? Is it not to fill the Superior Houses with Business? Why has the Authority fallen upon this wonderful Expedient? Is it not evident, that this was calculated for the Emolument of Lawyers, Clerks, &c.? What other Reason can be assigned for this amazing Scheme? — none Brethren, none! . . .

The Exorbitant, not to say unlawful Fees, required and assumed by Officers, — the unnecessary, not to say destructive Abridgement of a Court's Jurisdiction, — the enormous Encrease of the provincial tax unnecessary; these are Evils of which no Person can be insensible, and which I doubt not has been lamented by each of you. It must have obliged you to examine from what Quarter Relief might be found against these sad Calamities. — In Vain will you search for a Remedy until you find out the Disease.

Many are accusing the Legislative Body as the Source of all those woeful Calamities. — These, it must be confessed, are the instrumental Cause; they can, yea do impose some of these heavy Burdens. — But whence received they this Power? Is not their Power delegated from the Populace? The original principal Cause is our own blind stupid Conduct.

If it be queried, How doth our Conduct contribute to this? Answer presents itself — we have chosen Persons to represent us to make Laws, &c. whose former Conduct and Circumstance might have given us the highest Reason to expect they would sacrifice the true Interest of their Country to Avarice, or Ambition, or both.

I need not inform you, that a Majority of our Assembly is composed of Lawyers, Clerks, and others in Connection with them, while by our own Voice we have excluded the Planter. — It is not evident their own private Interest is, designed in the whole Train of our Laws? — We have not the least Reason to expect the Good of the Farmer, and consequently of the Community, will be consulted, by those who hang on Favour, or depend on the Intricacies of the Laws. — What can be expected from those who have ever discovered a Want of good Principles, and whose highest Study is the Promotion of their Wealth; and with whom the Interest of the Publick, when it comes in Competition with their private Advantages, is suffered to sink? — nothing less than the Ruin of the Publick. . . . Doth not Reason declare we might expect such cringing Vassals would readily sacrifice the Interest of the Community to the Idol Self? . . .

But you will say, what is the Remedy against this malignant Disease?

I will venture to prescribe a sovereign one if duly applied; that is, as you have now a fit Opportunity, choose for your Representatives or Burgesses such Men as have given you the strongest Reason to believe they are truly honest: Such as are disinterested, publick spirited, who will not allow their private Advantage once to stand in Competition with the Publick Good. . . . Let your Judgment be formed on their past Conduct; let them be such as have been unblamable in Life, independent in their Fortunes, without Expectations from others; let them be such as enjoy no Places of Benefit under the Government; such as do not depend upon Favour for their Living, nor do derive Profit or Advantage from the intricate Perplexity of the Law. In short, let them be Men whose private Interest neither doth nor can clash with the Interest or special Good of their Country.

Are you not sensible, Brethren, that we have too long groaned in Secret under the Weight of these crushing Mischiefs? How long will ye in this servile Manner subject yourselves to Slavery? Now shew yourselves to be Freemen, and for once assert your Liberty and maintain your Rights. — This, this Election let us exert ourselves, and show, that we will not through Fear, Favour or Affection, bow and subject ourselves to those who, under the Mask of Friendship, have long drawn Calamities upon us. . . .

Have they not monopolized your Properties; and what is wanting but Time to draw from you the last Farthing? Who that has the Spirit of a Man could endure this? Who that has the least Spark of Love to his Country or to himself would bear the Delusion?

In a special Manner then, let us, at this Election, rose all our Powers to act like free publick spirited Men, knowing that he that betrays the Cause now betrays his Country, and must sink in the general Ruin. . . .

Salisbury [North Carolina], September 14, 1769

Questions

1. Summarize the Regulators' main grievances. Who do they blame for their problems?
2. What is their proposed solution?
3. Who is missing in this protest as a victim of mistreatment? Why are they ignored?

Connections Questions

1. Does Esther Edwards Burr ("Letter on the Birth") seem to be the kind of wife Benjamin Wadsworth (*"The Well-Ordered Family"*) would approve of? Why or why not?
2. Which argument do you find more compelling — the argument for or against the Great Awakening (Whitefield, *"The Reverend Mr. Whitefield's Journal"*; Chauncy, *"Enthusiasm Describ'd"*)? Explain.
3. How does the protest of the Regulators ("The Regulators, 'To the Inhabitants of North-Carolina'") compare to that of Nathaniel Bacon (Chapter 2, "Nathaniel Bacon, 'Manifesto' ")? Are there more similarities or differences?

CHAPTER 5

Toward Independence: Years of Decision 1763–1775

Thomas Hutchinson, Account of a
Crowd Action (1765)

Thomas Hutchinson, a descendant of Anne Hutchinson, was born in Boston in 1711. By 1765, Hutchinson held a number of appointed political offices. In addition to serving on the Governor's Council, he was both the chief justice and lieutenant governor of Massachusetts. He also served as the colony's acting governor from 1769 to 1771 and then as governor until he moved in 1774 to Great Britain, where he died six years later.

Because Hutchinson was a wealthy, leading conservative, many colonists regarded him as a symbol of British imperial rule. These factors made him an appealing target during the Stamp Act controversy; indeed, as the letter he wrote on August 30, 1765, indicates, Hutchinson personally experienced the fury of the crowds in Boston (see text p. 122). Ironically, he opposed the Stamp Act and had tried to convince the Grenville administration that its enactment would be a mistake.

Boston, August 30, 1765

My Dear Sir

I came from my [country] house at Milton with my family the 26th in the morning. After dinner it was whispered in town there would be a mob at night and that Paxtons Hallowell, and the custom-house and admiralty officers houses would be attacked but my friends assured me the rabble were satisfied with the insult I had received and that I was become rather Popular. In the evening whilst I was at supper and my children round me somebody ran in and said the mob were coming. I directed my children to fly to a secure Place and shut up my house as I had done before intending not to quit it but my eldest daughter repented her leaving me and hastened back and protested she would not quit the house unless I did. I could not stand against this and withdrew with her to a neighbouring house where I had been but a few minutes before the hellish crew fell upon my house with the Rage of devils and in a moment with axes split down the doors and entered my son being in the great entry heard them cry damn him he is upstairs we'll have him. Some ran immediately as high as the top of the house others filled the rooms below and cellars and others Remained without the house to be employed there. Messages soon came one after another to the house where I was to inform me the mob were coming in Pursuit of me and I was obliged to retire thro yards and gardens to a house more remote where I remained until 4 o'clock by which time one of the best finished houses in the Province had nothing remaining but the bare walls and floors. Not contented with tearing off all the wainscot and hangings and splitting the doors to pieces they beat down the Partition walls and altho that alone cost them near two hours they cut down the cupola or lanthern and they began to take the slate and boards from the roof and were prevented only by the approaching daylight from a total demolition of the building. The garden fence was laid flat and all my trees etc. broke down to the ground. Such ruins were never seen in America. Besides my Plate and family Pictures household furniture of every kind my own my children and servants apparel they carried off about £900 sterling in money and emptied the house of every thing whatsoever except a part of the kitchen furniture not leaving a single book or paper in it and have scattered or destroyed all the manuscripts and other papers I had been collecting for 30 years together besides a great number of Publick Papers in my custody. The evening being warm I had undressed me and slipt on a thin camlet surtout over my wastcoat, the next morning the weather being changed I had not cloaths enough in my possession to defend me from the cold and was obliged to borrow from my host. Many articles of clothing and good part of my Plate have since been picked up in different quarters of the town but the Furniture in general was cut to pieces before it was thrown out of the house and most of the beds cut open and the feathers thrown out of the windows. The next evening I intended with my children to Milton but meeting two or three small Parties of the Ruffians who I suppose had concealed themselves in the country and my coachman hearing one of them say there he is, my daughters were terrified and said they should never be safe and I was forced to shelter them that night at the castle.

The encouragers of the first mob never intended matters should go this length and the people in general express the utmost detestation of this unparalleled outrage and I wish they could be convinced what infinite hazard there is of the most terrible consequences from such daemons where they are let loose in a government where there is not constant authority at hand sufficient to suppress them.

I am told the government here will make me a compensation for my own and my family's loss which I think cannot be much less than £3000 sterling. I am not sure that they will. If they should not it will be too heavy for me and I must humbly apply to his Majesty in whose service I am a sufferer but this and a much greater sum would be an insufficient compensation for the constant distress and anxiety of mind I have felt for some time past and must feel for months to come. You cannot conceive the wretched state we are in. Such is the resentment of the people against the stamp duty that there can be no dependence upon the general court to take any steps to enforce or rather advise the payment of it. On the other hand, such will be the effects of not submitting to it that all trade must cease all courts fall and all authority be at an end. Must not the ministry be extremely embarrassed. On the one hand it will be said if concessions be made the Parliament endanger the loss of their authority over the colonies on the other hand if external force should be used there seems to be danger of a total lasting alienation of affection. Is there no alternative? May the infinitely wise God direct you. I am with the greatest esteem

Sir Your most faithful humble servant

Questions

1. Did Hutchinson merit the treatment he and his family received? Why or why not?
2. How does he assess the political situation? How accurate is he?
3. What does the incident described here suggest about the nature of mass protests? What is their value? their danger?

New York Merchant
Boycott Agreement (1765)

Crowd actions kept the Stamp Act from being enforced as scheduled on November 1, 1765 (see text pp. 123–125). Members of Parliament were outraged by the protests. Thus it seemed unlikely that crowds alone could achieve the colonists' ultimate goal of getting the Stamp Act repealed.

Realizing that economic pressure might be more effective, Patriots in many locations entered into formal agreements to boycott British goods. The article reprinted here is from the Pennsylvania Gazette *of November 7, 1765. It describes an agreement that more than 200 "principal Merchants" of New York entered into and signed.*

At a general Meeting of the Merchants of the City of New-York, trading to Great-Britain, at the House of Mr. George Burns, of the said City, Innholder, to consider what was necessary to be done in the present Situation of Affairs, with respect to the STAMP ACT, and the melancholy State of the North-American Commerce, so greatly restricted by the Impositions and Duties established by the late Acts of Trade: They came to the following Resolutions, viz.

FIRST, That in all Orders they send out to Great-Britain, for Goods or Merchandize, of any Nature, Kind or Quality whatsoever, usually imported from Great-Britain, they will direct their Correspondents not to ship them, unless the STAMP ACT be repealed: It is nevertheless agreed, that all such Merchants as are Owners of, and have Vessels already gone, and now cleared out for Great-Britain, shall be at Liberty to bring back in them, on their own Accounts, Crates and Casks of Earthen Ware, Grindstones, Pipes, and such other bulky Articles, as Owners usually fill up their Vessels with.

SECONDLY, It is further unanimously agreed, that all Orders already sent Home, shall be countermanded by the very first Conveyance; and the Goods and Merchandize thereby ordered, not to be sent, unless upon the Condition mentioned in the foregoing Resolution.

THIRDLY, It is further unanimously agreed, that no Merchant will vend any Goods or Merchandize sent upon Commission from Great-Britain, that shall be shipped from thence after the first Day of January next, unless upon the Condition mentioned in the first Resolution.

FOURTHLY, It is further unanimously agreed, that the foregoing Resolutions shall be binding until the same are abrogated at a general Meeting hereafter to be held for that Purpose.

In Witness whereof we have hereunto respectively subscribed our Names. [*This was subscribed by upwards of Two Hundred principal Merchants.*]

Questions

1. In what ways is the agreement firmly rooted both in British and colonial history?
2. How sophisticated is the agreement as a protest policy? Why?
3. What elements are necessary for the agreement's success?

Norfolk Sons of Liberty Pronouncement (1766)

Patriots understood that the success of the boycott movement depended on some kind of enforcement mechanism. Hence the Sons of Liberty were organized, with the name taken from a speech by Colonel Barre protesting the Stamp Act. But even in protest, the Patriots routinely emphasized their loyalty to George III and their commitment to the rule of law. The statement issued by the Norfolk, Virginia, Sons of Liberty — reprinted from the Pennsylvania Journal *of April 17, 1766 — describes both the philosophy and the enforcement measures typically espoused by the Sons of Liberty.*

At a meeting of a considerable number of inhabitants of the town and county of Norfolk, *and others,* SONS OF LIBERTY, *at the Court House of the said county, in the colony of* Virginia, *on* Monday *the 31st of* March, 1766.

Having taken into consideration the evil tendency of that oppressive and unconstitutional act of parliament commonly called the Stamp Act, and being desirous that our sentiments should be known to posterity, and recollecting that we are a part of the colony, who first, in General Assembly, openly expressed their detestation to the said act, which is pregnant with ruin, and productive of the most pernicious consequences; and unwilling to rivet the shackles of slavery and oppression on ourselves, and millions yet unborn, have unanimously come to the following resolutions:

I. Resolved, That we acknowledge our sovereign Lord King George III to be our rightful and lawful King, and that we will at all times, to the utmost of our power and ability, support and defend his most sacred person, crown, and dignity; and will be always ready, when constitutionally called upon, to assist his Majesty with our lives and fortunes, and defend all his just rights and prerogatives.

II. Resolved, That we will by all lawful ways and means, which divine providence hath put into our hands, defend ourselves in the full enjoyment of, and preserve inviolate to posterity, those inestimable privileges of all free-born British subjects, of being taxed by none but representatives of their own choosing, and of being tried only by a jury of their own Peers; for, if we quietly submit to the execution of the said Stamp Act, all our claims to civil liberty will be lost, and we and our posterity become absolute slaves.

III. Resolved, That we will, on any future occasion, sacrifice our lives and fortunes, in concurrence with the other Sons of Liberty in the American provinces, to defend and preserve those invaluable blessings transmitted us by our ancestors.

IV. Resolved, That whoever is concerned, directly or indirectly, in using, or causing to be used, in any way or manner whatever, within this colony, unless authorized by the General Assembly thereof, those detestable papers called the Stamps, shall be deemed, to all intents and purposes, an enemy to his country, and by the Sons of Liberty treated accordingly.

V. Resolved, That a committee be appointed to present the thanks of the Sons of Liberty to Colonel Richard Bland, for his treatise entitled "An Inquiry into the Rights of the British Colonies."

VI. Resolved, That a committee be appointed, who shall make public the above resolutions, and correspond as they shall see occasion, with the associated Sons and Friends of Liberty in the other British colonies in America.

Questions

1. Is this a radical or conservative pronouncement? Explain.
2. What appears to be the chief motivation behind the document?
3. How does the pronouncement mix statements of loyalty with threats?

Congress at New-York, "Declarations . . . of the Colonists" (1765)

The first major reactions against the Stamp Act took place in Boston, where protests succeeded in blocking the act's implementation. Meanwhile, the Massachusetts colonial leaders suggested that the colonies send delegates to a special intercolonial congress to formulate a unified response to the detested legislation. Representatives from Virginia, North Carolina, and Georgia could not attend because their governors refused to convene their respective assemblies; New Hampshire chose not to participate.

But twenty-seven delegates from the other colonies met in New York on October 7, 1765. During twelve days of deliberation, the members of this Stamp Act Congress prepared a petition to the king, a memorial to the House of Lords, a petition to the House of Commons, and a series of "Declarations . . . respecting the most Essential Rights and Liberties of the Colonists." The "Declarations" of the Stamp Act Congress provide a clear statement of the pragmatic and philosophical positions of the colonists on both the Stamp Act and the efforts of the British government to institute general imperial reform.

The Members of this Congress, sincerely devoted, with the warmest Sentiments of Affection and Duty to his Majesty's Person and Government, inviolably attached to the present happy Establishment of the Protestant Succession, and with Minds deeply impressed by a Sense of the present and impending Misfortunes of the *British* Colonies on this Continent; having considered as maturely as Time will permit, the Circumstances of the said Colonies, esteem it our indispensable Duty, to make the following Declarations of our humble Opinion, respecting the most Essential Rights and Liberties of the Colonists, and of the Grievances under which they labour, by Reason of several late Acts of Parliament.

I. That his Majesty's Subjects in these Colonies, owe the same Allegiance to the Crown of *Great-Britain,* that is owing from his Subjects born within the Realm, and all due Subordination to that August Body the Parliament of *Great-Britain.*

II. That his Majesty's Liege Subjects in these Colonies, are entitled to all the inherent Rights and Liberties of his Natural born Subjects, within the Kingdom of *Great-Britain.*

III. That it is inseparably essential to the Freedom of a People, and the undoubted Right of *Englishmen,* that no Taxes be imposed on them, but with their own Consent, given personally, or by their Representatives.

IV. That the People of these Colonies are not, and from their local Circumstances cannot be, Represented in the House of Commons in *Great-Britain.*

V. That the only Representatives of the People of these Colonies, are Persons chosen therein by themselves, and that no Taxes ever have been, or can be Constitutionally imposed on them, but by their respective Legislature.

VI. That all Supplies to the Crown, being free Gifts of the People, it is unreasonable and inconsistent with the Principles and Spirit of the *British* Constitution, for the People of *Great-Britain,* to grant to his Majesty the Property of the Colonists.

VII. That Trial by Jury, is the inherent and invaluable Right of every *British* Subject in these Colonies.

VIII. That the late Act of Parliament, entitled, *An Act for granting and applying certain Stamp Duties, and other Duties, in the* British *Colonies and Plantations* in America, etc. by imposing Taxes on the Inhabitants of these Colonies, and the said Act, and several other Acts, by extending the Jurisdiction of the Courts of Admiralty beyond its ancient Limits, have a manifest Tendency to subvert the Rights and Liberties of the Colonists.

IX. That the Duties imposed by several late Acts of Parliament, from the peculiar Circumstances of these Colonies, will be extremely Burthensome and Grievous; and from the scarcity of Specie, the Payment of them absolutely impracticable.

X. That as the Profits of the Trade of these Colonies ultimately center in *Great-Britain,* to pay for the Manufactures which they are obliged to take from thence, they eventually contribute very largely to all Supplies granted there to the Crown.

XI. That the Restrictions imposed by several late Acts of Parliament, on the Trade of these Colonies, will render them unable to purchase the Manufactures of *Great-Britain.*

XII. That the Increase, Prosperity, and Happiness of these Colonies, depend on the full and free Enjoyment of their Rights and Liberties, and an Intercourse with *Great-Britain* mutually Affectionate and Advantageous.

XIII. That it is the Right of the *British* Subjects in these Colonies, to Petition the King, or either House of Parliament.

Lastly, That it is the indispensable Duty of these Colonies, to the best of Sovereigns, to the Mother Country, and to themselves, to endeavour by a loyal and dutiful Address to his Majesty, and humble Applications to both Houses of Parliament, to procure the Repeal of the Act for granting and applying certain Stamp Duties, of all Clauses of any other Acts of Parliament, whereby the Jurisdiction of the Admiralty is extended as aforesaid, and of the other late Acts for the Restriction of *American* Commerce.

Questions

1. Are the delegates stressing their rights as British subjects or as Americans? Why does it make a difference?
2. What is the essence of the protest in this declaration?
3. In making their declarations, what are the delegates assuming about George III?

The Boycott Agreements of Women in Boston (1770)

Colonial women were not permitted to vote and were traditionally excluded from the hurly-burly of politics. But their role as household manager made them a crucial element in the boycott against the Townshend duties. Although never intending to allow women to participate in electoral politics, the men who organized the boycott urged them to support liberty by joining forces. As the following reports show, women demonstrated their ability to organize in support of the boycott.

Boston, January 31, 1770.

The following Agreement has lately been come into by upwards of 300 Mistresses of Families in this Town; in which Number the Ladies of the highest Rank and Influence, that could be waited upon in so short a Time, are included.

["]At a Time when our invaluable Rights and Privileges are attacked in an unconstitutional and most alarming Manner, and as we find we are reproached for not being so ready as could be desired, to lend our Assistance, we think it our Duty perfectly to concur with the true Friends of Liberty, in all the Measures they have taken to save this abused Country from Ruin and Slavery: And particularly, we join with the very respectable Body of Merchants, and other Inhabitants of this Town, who met in Faneuil-Hall the 23d of this Instant, in their Resolutions, *totally* to abstain from the Use of TEA: And as the greatest Part of the Revenue arising by Virtue of the late Acts, is produced from the Duty paid upon Tea, which Revenue is wholly expended to support the American Board of Commissioners, We the Subscribers do strictly engage, that we will *totally* abstain from the Use of that Article (Sickness excepted) not only in our respective Families; but that we will absolutely refuse it, if it should be offered to us upon any Occasion whatsoever. This Agreement we chearfully come into, as we believe the very distressed Situation of our Country requires it, and we do hereby oblige ourselves religiously to observe it, till the late Revenue Acts are repealed."

The following is a Copy of the Agreement of the young Ladies of this Town against drinking foreign TEA.

Boston, February 12, 1770.

["]We the Daughters of those Patriots who have, and now do appear for the public Interest, and in *that* principally for *us* their Posterity; *we,* as such, do with Pleasure engage with them, in denying ourselves the drinking of foreign *Tea,* in Hopes to frustrate a Plan that tends to deprive the whole Community of their *All* that is valuable in Life."

To the above Agreement 126 young Ladies have already signed. In Addition to the List of Mistresses of Families, who signed the Agreement against drinking foreign Tea, 110 have been added the Week past.

Questions

1. Do the women who made these agreements appear to be leaders or followers of the boycott movement? Explain the difference.
2. To what extent, if any, do the signers of the agreements spell out the basic rights they believe they are supporting?
3. Does it appear that the specifics of the agreements, including any provisions for enforcement, will help make the tea boycott effective? Why or why not?

Joseph Galloway, Plan of Union (1774)

Despite a British administration that was both clumsy and arrogant, Americans moved toward independence reluctantly and cautiously. Only a minority of the population was ready to follow the Patriot cause.

Joseph Galloway (c. 1731–1803) of Pennsylvania took a leading role among those members of the Continental Congress who, as the text notes, considered themselves men of "loyal principles" (see text p. 137). Galloway offered the following plan in the hope of averting rebellion. But the Congress rejected Galloway's effort. When the colonists declared their independence, Galloway cast

*his lot with Great Britain, moved to England in 1778, and lived out his life as
an exile from his native land.*

[28 September, 1774]
Resolution submitted by Joseph Galloway:

Resolved, That the Congress will apply to his Majesty for a redress of grievances under which his faithful subjects in America labour; and assure him, that
the Colonies hold in abhorrence the idea of being considered independent
communities on the British government, and most ardently desire the establishment of a Political Union, not only among themselves, but with the Mother
State, upon those principles of safety and freedom which are essential in the constitution of all free governments, and particularly that of the British Legislature;
and as the Colonies from their local circumstances, cannot be represented in the
Parliament of Great-Britain, they will humbly propose to his Majesty and his two
Houses of Parliament, the following plan, under which the strength of the whole
Empire may be drawn together on any emergency, the interest of both countries
advanced, and the rights and liberties of America secured.

*A Plan of a proposed Union between
Great-Britain and the Colonies.*

That a British and American legislature, for regulating the administration
of the general affairs of America, be proposed and established in America, including all the said colonies; within, and under which government, each
colony shall retain its present constitution, and powers of regulating and governing its own internal police, in all cases what[so]ever.

That the said government be administered by a President General, to be
appointed by the King, and a grand Council, to be chosen by the Representatives of the people of the several colonies, in their respective assemblies,
once in every three years.

That the several assemblies shall choose members for the grand council. . . .

Who shall meet at the city of   for the first time, being called by
the President-General, as soon as conveniently may be after his appointment.

That there shall be a new election of members for the Grand Council
every three years; and on the death, removal or resignation of any member,
his place shall be supplied by a new choice, at the next sitting of Assembly of
the Colony he represented.

That the Grand Council shall meet once in every year, if they shall think it
necessary, and oftener, if occasions shall require, at such time and place as
they shall adjourn to, at the last preceding meeting, or as they shall be called
to meet at, by the President-General, on any emergency.

That the grand Council shall have power to choose their Speaker, and shall hold and exercise all the like rights, liberties and privileges, as are held and exercised by and in the House of Commons of Great-Britain.

That the President-General shall hold his office during the pleasure of the King, and his assent shall be requisite to all acts of the Grand Council, and it shall be his office and duty to cause them to be carried into execution.

That the President-General, by and with the advice and consent of the Grand-Council, hold and exercise all the legislative rights, powers, and authorities, necessary for regulating and administering all the general police and affairs of the colonies, in which Great-Britain and the colonies, or any of them, the colonies in general, or more than one colony, are in any manner concerned, as well civil and criminal as commercial.

That the said President-General and the Grand Council, be an inferior and distinct branch of the British legislature, united and incorporated with it, for the aforesaid general purposes; and that any of the said general regulations may originate and be formed and digested, either in the Parliament of Great Britain, or in the said Grand Council, and being prepared, transmitted to the other for their approbation or dissent; and that the assent of both shall be requisite to the validity of all such general acts or statutes.

That in time of war, all bills for granting aid to the crown, prepared by the Grand Council, and approved by the President-General, shall be valid and passed into a law, without the assent of the British Parliament.

Questions

1. How detailed a plan is this? How realistic is it? Why?
2. What sources and ideas is Galloway drawing on?
3. Why does the timing of Galloway's plan ensure its fate?

Connections Questions

1. What do the various documents in this chapter indicate about American views on protest?
2. Both the "Norfolk Sons of Liberty Pronouncement" and "Boycott Agreements of Women in Boston" use the term *slavery*. Why would the authors do so? Why is such usage ironic? How does it reveal certain beliefs?
3. Imagine yourself as a colonial official loyal to the crown yet aware of local conditions. How would you interpret the documents in this chapter in a report to your superiors in London? What would be your recommendations?

CHAPTER 6

War and Revolution 1775–1783

The Dangers of Race War within a War for Independence (1775)

Approximately one-fifth of the residents of the British mainland colonies in 1775 were African-American slaves. Lord Dunmore, the royal governor of Virginia, realized the slaves might help defeat the rebels. So in November 1775 he issued a proclamation addressed to every slave or indentured servant belonging to a rebel. Dunmore offered them their freedom if they joined the loyalist cause and fought for the king (see text p. 146).

By December 1, Dunmore had 300 slaves in uniforms bearing the inscription "Liberty to Slaves." The governor called them "Lord Dunmore's Ethiopian Regiment." The following excerpt from the Pennsylvania Evening Post *of December 14, 1775, shows the proclamation could have a powerful effect.*

PHILADELPHIA, December 14, 1775
Late last night a gentlewoman, going along Second-street, was insulted by a Negro, near Christ church. And upon her reprimanding him for his rude behaviour, the fellow replied, "Stay, you d—d white bitch, till Lord Dunmore and his black regiment come, and then we will see who is to take the wall." Two gentlemen coming up, and hearing his reply, they endeavoured to secure him, but the fellow escaped, the lamps not being lighted.

Questions
1. What attitude does this newspaper account reveal unintentionally?
2. Given racial conditions in colonial America, which is more likely — that a black man spoke this way, or that a white writer exaggerated the story for effect?
3. How might the British use the account in their own propaganda efforts?

Thomas Paine, *Common Sense* (1776)

Throughout the long movement toward independence, the Patriots emphasized their loyalty to the British monarchy. Members of Parliament seemed to be the villains; they were the ones who supposedly wanted to strip the colonies of fundamental rights. Reverence for the king had to be undermined if independence was to be won. Thomas Paine (1737–1809) did that and more through his powerful and broadly popular Common Sense *(see text p. 147), which was first published on January 9, 1776. The selections reprinted here come from the expanded "NEW EDITION," dated a month later.*

OF MONARCHY AND HEREDITARY SUCCESSION

There is something exceedingly ridiculous in the composition of monarchy; it first excludes a man from the means of information, yet empowers him to act in cases where the highest judgment is required. The state of a king shuts him from the world, yet the business of a king requires him to know it thoroughly; wherefore the different parts, by unnaturally opposing and destroying each other, prove the whole character to be absurd and useless. . . .

In the early ages of the world, according to the scripture chronology, there were no kings; the consequence of which was, there were no wars; it is the pride of kings which throw mankind into confusion. . . .

As the exalting one man so greatly above the rest cannot be justified on the equal rights of nature, so neither can it be defended on the authority of scripture; for the will of the Almighty, as declared by Gideon and the prophet Samuel, expressly disapproves of government by kings. All antimonarchical parts of scripture have been very smoothly glossed over in monarchical governments. . . .

To the evil of monarchy we have added that of hereditary succession; and as the first is a degradation and lessening of ourselves, so the second, claimed as a matter of right, is an insult and an imposition on posterity. For all men being originally equals, no *one* by *birth* could have a right to set up his own family in perpetual preference to all others for ever, and though himself might deserve *some* decent degree of honors of his contemporaries, yet his descendants might be far too unworthy to inherit them. One of the strongest *natural* proofs of the folly of hereditary right in kings, is, that nature disapproves it, otherwise she would not so frequently turn it into ridicule by giving mankind an *Ass for a Lion*. . . .

Most wise men, in their private sentiments, have ever treated hereditary right with contempt; yet it is one of those evils, which when once established is not easily removed; many submit from fear, others from superstition, and the more powerful part shares with the king the plunder of the rest. . . .

In short, monarchy and succession have laid (not this or that kingdom only) but the world in blood and ashes. 'Tis a form of government which the word of God bears testimony against, and blood will attend it.

In England a king hath little more to do than to make war and give away places; which in plain terms, is to impoverish the nation and set it together by the ears. A pretty business indeed for a man to be allowed eight hundred thousand sterling a year for, and worshipped into the bargain! Of more worth is one honest man to society and in the sight of God, than all the crowned ruffians that ever lived.

THOUGHTS ON THE PRESENT STATE OF AMERICAN AFFAIRS

In the following pages I offer nothing more than simple facts, plain arguments, and common sense; and have no other preliminaries to settle with the reader, than that he will divest himself of prejudice and prepossession, and suffer his reason and his feelings to determine for themselves; that he will put *on*, or rather that he will not put *off* the true character of a man, and generously enlarge his views beyond the present day.

Volumes have been written on the subject of the struggle between England and America. Men of all ranks have embarked in the controversy, from different motives, and with various designs; but all have been ineffectual, and the period of debate is closed. Arms, as the last resource, decide the contest; the appeal was the choice of the king, and the continent hath accepted the challenge. . . .

The sun never shined on a cause of greater worth. 'Tis not the affair of a city, a county, a province, or a kingdom, but of a continent —of at least one eighth part of the habitable globe. 'Tis not the concern of a day, a year, or an age; posterity are virtually involved in the contest, and will be more or less affected, even to the end of time, by the proceedings now. Now is the seed-time of continental union, faith and honor. The least fracture now will be like a name engraved with the point of a pin on the tender rind of a young oak; the wound will enlarge with the tree, and posterity read it in full grown characters.

By referring the matter from argument to arms, a new æra for politics is struck; a new method of thinking hath arisen. . . .

As much hath been said of the advantages of reconciliation, which, like an agreeable dream, hath passed away and left us as we were, it is but right, that we should examine the contrary side of the argument, and inquire into some of the many material injuries which these colonies sustain, and always will sustain, by being connected with, and dependant on Great-Britain: To examine that connexion and dependance, on the principles of nature and common sense, to see what we have to trust to, if separated, and what we are to expect, if dependant.

I have heard it asserted by some, that as America hath flourished under her former connexion with Great-Britain, that the same connexion is necessary towards her future happiness, and will always have the same effect. Nothing can be more fallacious than this kind of argument. We may as well assert that because a child has thrived upon milk, that it is never to have meat, or that the first twenty years of our lives is to become a precedent for the next twenty. But even this is admitting more than is true, for I answer roundly, that America would have flourished as much, and probably much more, had no European power had any thing to do with her. The commerce, by which she hath enriched herself, are the necessaries of life, and will always have a market while eating is the custom of Europe.

But she has protected us, say some. That she has engrossed us is true, and defended the continent at our expence as well as her own is admitted, and she would have defended Turkey from the same motive, viz. the sake of trade and dominion.

Alas, we have been long led away by ancient prejudices, and made large sacrifices to superstition. We have boasted the protection of Great-Britain, without considering, that her motive was *interest* not *attachment;* that she did not protect us from *our enemies* on *our account,* but from *her enemies* on *her own account,* from those who had no quarrel with us on any *other account,* and who will always be our enemies on the *same account.* . . .

France and Spain never were, nor perhaps ever will be our enemies as *Americans,* but as our being the *subjects of Great-Britain.*

But Britain is the parent country, say some. Then the more shame upon her conduct. Even brutes do not devour their young, nor savages make war upon their families; wherefore the assertion, if true, turns to her reproach; but it happens not to be true, or only partly so, and the phrase *parent* or *mother country* hath been jesuitically adopted by the king and his parasites, with a low papistical design of gaining an unfair bias on the credulous weakness of our minds. Europe, and not England, is the parent country of America. This new world hath been the asylum for the persecuted lovers of civil and religious liberty from *every part* of Europe. Hither have they fled, not from the tender embraces of the mother, but from the cruelty of the monster; and it is so far true of England, that the same tyranny which drove the first emigrants from home, pursues their descendants still.

In this extensive quarter of the globe, we forget the narrow limits of three hundred and sixty miles (the extent of England) and carry our friendship on a larger scale; we claim brotherhood with every European Christian, and triumph in the generosity of the sentiment.

It is pleasant to observe by what regular gradations we surmount the force of local prejudice, as we enlarge our acquaintance with the world. A man born in any town in England divided into parishes, will naturally associate most with his fellow-parishioners (because their interests in many cases will be common) and distinguish him by the name of *neighbour;* if he meet him but a few miles from home, he drops the narrow idea of a street, and salutes him by the name of *townsman;* if he travel out of the county, and meet him in any other, he forgets the minor divisions of street and town, and calls him *countryman,* i. e. *county-man;* but if in their foreign excursions they should associate in France or any other part of *Europe,* their local remembrance would be enlarged into that of *Englishmen.* And by a just parity of reasoning, all Europeans meeting in America, or any other quarter of the globe, are *country-men;* for England, Holland, Germany, or Sweden, when compared with the whole, stand in the same places on the larger scale, which the divisions of street, town, and county do on the smaller ones; distinctions too limited for continental minds. Not one third of the inhabitants, even of this province, are of English descent. Wherefore I reprobate the phrase of parent or mother country applied to England only, as being false, selfish, narrow and ungenerous. . . .

As to government matters, it is not in the power of Britain to do this continent justice: The business of it will soon be too weighty, and intricate, to be managed with any tolerable degree of convenience, by a power so distant from us, and so very ignorant of us; for if they cannot conquer us, they cannot govern us. To be always running three or four thousand miles with a tale or a petition, waiting four or five months for an answer, which when obtained requires five or six more to explain it in, will in a few years be looked upon as folly and childishness — There was a time when it was proper, and there is a proper time for it to cease.

Small islands not capable of protecting themselves, are the proper objects for kingdoms to take under their care; but there is something very absurd, in supposing a continent to be perpetually governed by an island. In no instance hath nature made the satellite larger than its primary planet, and as England and America, with respect to each other, reverses the common order of nature, it is evident they belong to different systems; England to Europe, America to itself. . . .

But where, says some, is the King of America? I'll tell you. Friend, he reigns above, and doth not make havoc of mankind like the Royal Brute of Britain. Yet that we may not appear to be defective even in earthly honors, let a day be solemnly set apart for proclaiming the charter; let it be brought forth placed on the divine law, the word of God; let a crown be placed thereon, by which the world may know, that so far we approve of monarchy, that in America THE LAW IS KING. For as in absolute governments the King is law, so in free countries the law *ought* to be King; and there ought to be no other. But lest any ill use should afterwards arise, let the crown at the conclusion of the ceremony, be demolished, and scattered among the people whose right it is.

A government of our own is our natural right: And when a man seriously reflects on the precariousness of human affairs, he will become convinced, that it is infinitely wiser and safer, to form a constitution of our own in a cool deliberate manner, while we have it in our power, than to trust such an interesting event to time and chance. . . .

O ye that love mankind! Ye that dare oppose, not only the tyranny, but the tyrant, stand forth! Every spot of the old world is overrun with oppression. Freedom hath been hunted round the globe. Asia, and Africa, have long expelled her — Europe regards her like a stranger, and England hath given her warning to depart. O! receive the fugitive, and prepare in time an asylum for mankind.

Questions

1. Why is Paine's use of language so important? Cite examples.
2. Why did *Common Sense* strike such a popular chord?
3. What does Paine say about the mission or role of an independent America?

Thomas Jefferson Attacks the King on the Issue of Slavery (1776)

As the full text of the Declaration of Independence reveals, Thomas Jefferson, its principal author, prepared a lengthy and varied bill of indictment against George III (see text p. 148). But the Continental Congress did not approve of all the charges Jefferson drew up. Indeed, the Congress expunged from its records the longest section in Jefferson's list of charges against the king. Congress took that extraordinary action when the Georgia and South Carolina delegations threatened not to sign the Declaration unless that section was eliminated. The "missing" section is reprinted here.

He [the king] has waged cruel war against human nature itself, violating its most sacred rights of life & liberty in the persons of a distant people who never offended him, captivating & carrying them into slavery in another hemisphere, or to incur miserable death in their transportation thither. this piratical warfare, the opprobrium of *infidel* powers, is the warfare of the CHRISTIAN king of Great Britain. determined to keep open a market where MEN should be bought & sold, he has prostituted his negative for suppressing every legislative attempt to prohibit or to restrain this execrable commerce: and that this assemblage of horrors might want no fact of distinguished die, he is now exciting those very people to rise in arms among us, and to purchase that liberty of which *he* has deprived them, by murdering the people upon whom *he* also obtruded them; thus paying off former crimes committed against the *liberties* of one people, with crimes which he urges them to commit against the *lives* of another.

Questions

1. How does Jefferson personalize the king's responsibility for slavery? Why does that matter?
2. Why would the Georgia and South Carolina delegations object to a passage written by a fellow Southerner and slaveholder?
3. What does the passage suggest about Jefferson's opinions concerning slavery?

Nicholas Cresswell, The Importance of the American Victory at Trenton (1776–1777)

Nicholas Cresswell was the twenty-six-year-old son of a prosperous English landowner. Cresswell journeyed to Virginia in 1774 to seek good, inexpensive land to, as he said, begin life with. He arrived just in time to get caught up in the rush toward revolution. Cresswell adamantly opposed the Patriots and began describing the most ardent ones as Slebers. The following entries from his journal reveal the impact the Patriot victory at Trenton had on his thinking. Cresswell returned to Britain in 1777.

Saturday, December 14th, 1776. News that General Howe is at Trenton in the Jerseys, from Philadelphia. It is certain the Congress has left Philadelphia and are now at Baltimore. Great numbers of recruiting parties are out to raise men, but can scarcely get a man by any means, tho' their bounty is 12£. None will enlist that can avoid it. They get some servants and convicts which are purchased from their Masters, these will desert the first opportunity. The violent *Slebers* are much dispirited. The Politicians (or rather timid Whigs) give all up for lost. And the Torys begin to exult. The time is out that the Flying Camp was enlisted for, and it is said that they refuse to serve any longer, tho' they have been solicited in the strongest terms. This will make a great deficiency in their Army, the loss of Ten Thousand men. I am convinced that if General Howe will push to Philadelphia the day is his own. . . .

Monday, Jan. 6th, 1777. News that Washington had taken 760 Hessian prisoners at Trenton in the Jerseys. Hope it is a lie. This afternoon hear he has likewise taken six pieces of Brass Cannon.

Tuesday, Jan. 7th, 1777. The news is confirmed. The minds of the people are much altered. A few days ago they had given up the cause for lost. Their late successes have turned the scale and now they are all liberty mad again. Their Recruiting parties could not get a man (except he bought him from his master) no longer since than last week, and now the men are coming in by companies. Confound the turncoat scoundrels and the cowardly Hessians together. This has given them new spirits, got them fresh succours and will prolong the War, perhaps for two years. They have recovered their panic and it will not be an easy matter to throw them into that confusion again. Volunteer Companies are collecting in every County on the Continent and in a few months the rascals will be stronger than ever. Even the parsons, some of them, have turned out as Volunteers and Pulpit Drums or Thunder, which you please to call it, summoning all to arms in this cursed babble. D—them all.

Questions

1. How does Cresswell reveal his own biases?
2. What causes the situation he describes to change so dramatically?
3. Is there anything in these passages to indicate Cresswell's own political views? If so, identify and explain.

Sarah Osborn, Account of Life with the Army

Women in colonial America were all but excluded from any meaningful role in public politics. But the exigencies of revolution changed that, however fitfully.

Sarah Osborn was one of the women who traveled with the army. We know about her activities because in 1832 Congress passed what the historian John C. Dann describes as the first comprehensive pension act for veterans and the widows of veterans of the American Revolution. Under that and subsequent legislation, applicants had to provide a statement or prove their right to a pension. Osborn prepared her account in 1837.

It was given in the legal deposition form, which is why Osborn is referred to as "deponent." She was eighty-one years old at the time, but her memory had not dimmed; her account, as far as it can be verified, is accurate. The section reprinted here describes her activities as the spouse of Aaron Osborn, a soldier whom she married in January 1780. Professor Dann, whose work with the pension records led him to edit the collection of accounts entitled The Revolution Remembered *(Chicago: University of Chicago Press, 1980), notes that the deposition may be the only extant autobiographical account of a woman who traveled with the army* (The Revolution Remembered, *p. 240).*

After deponent had married said [Aaron] Osborn, he informed her that he was returned during the war, and that he desired deponent to go with him. Deponent declined until she was informed by Captain Gregg that her husband should be put on the commissary guard, and that she should have the means of conveyance either in a wagon or on horseback. That deponent then in the same winter season in sleighs accompanied her husband and the forces under command of Captain Gregg on the east side of the Hudson river to Fishkill, then crossed the river and went down to West Point. There remained till the river opened in the spring, when they returned to Albany. Captain Gregg's company was along, and she thinks Captain Parsons, Lieutenant Forman, and Colonel Van Schaick, but is not positive.

Deponent, accompanied by her said husband and the same forces, returned during the same season to West Point. Deponent recollects no other females in company but the wives of Lieutenant Forman and of Sergeant Lamberson. . . .

Deponent further says that she and her husband remained at West Point till the departure of the army for the South, a term of perhaps one year and a half, but she cannot be positive as to the length of time. While at West Point, deponent lived at Lieutenant Foot's, who kept a boardinghouse. Deponent was employed in washing and sewing for the soldiers. Her said husband was employed about the camp. . . .

When the army were about to leave West Point and go south, they crossed over the river to Robinson's Farms and remained there for a length of time to induce the belief, as deponent understood, that they were going to take up quarters there, whereas they recrossed the river in the nighttime into the Jerseys and traveled all night in a direct course for Philadelphia. Deponent was part of the time on horseback and part of the time in a wagon. Deponent's said husband was still serving as one of the commissary's guard. . . . They continued their march to Philadelphia, deponent on horseback through the streets, and arrived at a place towards the Schuylkill where the British had burnt some houses, where they encamped for the afternoon and night. Being out of bread, deponent was employed in baking the afternoon and evening. Deponent recollects no females but Sergeant Lamberson's and Lieutenant Forman's wives and a colored woman by the name of Letta. The Quaker ladies who came round urged deponent to stay, but her said husband said, "No, he could not leave her behind." Accordingly, next day they continued their march from day to day till they arrived at Baltimore, where deponent and her said husband and the forces under command of General Clinton, Captain Gregg, and several other officers, all of whom she does not recollect, embarked on board a vessel and sailed down the Chesapeake. . . . They continued sail until they had got up the St. James River as far as the tide would carry them, about twelve miles from the mouth, and then landed, and the tide being spent, they had a fine time catching sea lobsters, which they ate.

They, however, marched immediately for a place called Williamsburg, as she thinks, deponent alternately on horseback and on foot. There arrived, they remained two days till the army all came in by land and then marched for Yorktown, or Little York as it was then called. The York troops were posted at the right, the Connecticut troops next, and the French to the left. In about one day or less than a day, they reached the place of encampment about one mile from Yorktown. Deponent was on foot and the other females above named and her said husband still on the commissary's guard. . . . Deponent took her stand just back of the American tents, say about a mile from the town, and busied herself washing, mending, and cooking for the soldiers, in which she was assisted by the other females; some men washed their own clothing. She heard the roar of the artillery for a number of days, and the last night the Americans threw up entrenchments, it was a misty, foggy night, rather wet but not rainy. Every soldier threw up for himself, as she understood, and she afterwards saw and went into the entrenchments. Deponent's said husband was there throwing up entrenchments, and deponent cooked and carried in beef, and bread, and coffee (in a gallon pot) to the soldiers in the entrenchment.

On one occasion when deponent was thus employed carrying in provisions, she met General Washington, who asked her if she "was not afraid of the cannonballs?"

She replied, "No, the bullets would not cheat the gallows," that "It would not do for the men to fight and starve too."

They dug entrenchments nearer and nearer to Yorktown every night or two till the last. While digging that, the enemy fired very heavy till about nine o'clock next morning, then stopped, and the drums from the enemy beat excessively. Deponent was a little way off in Colonel Van Schaick's or the officers' marquee and a number of officers were present, among whom was Captain Gregg, who, on account of infirmities, did not go out much to do duty.

The drums continued beating, and all at once the officers hurrahed and swung their hats, and deponent asked them, "What is the matter now?"

One of them replied, "Are not you soldier enough to know what it means?"

Deponent replied, "No."

They then replied, "The British have surrendered."

Deponent, having provisions ready, carried the same down to the entrenchments that morning, and four of the soldiers whom she was in the habit of cooking for ate their breakfasts.

Deponent stood on one side of the road and the American officers upon the other side when the British officers came out of the town and rode up to the American officers and delivered up [their swords, which the deponent] thinks were returned again, and the British officers rode right on before the army, who marched out beating and playing a melancholy tune, their drums covered with black handkerchiefs and their fifes with black ribbands tied around them, into an old field and there grounded their arms and then returned into town again to await their destiny. Deponent recollects seeing a great many American officers, some on horseback and some on foot, but cannot call them all by name. Washington, Lafayette, And Clinton were among the number. The British general at the head of the army was a large, portly man, full face, and the tears rolled down his cheeks as he passed along. She does not recollect his name, but it was not Cornwallis. She saw the latter afterwards and noticed his being a man of diminutive appearance and having cross eyes. . . .

After two or three days, deponent and her husband, Captain Gregg, and others who were sick or complaining embarked on board a vessel from Yorktown, not the same they came down in, and set sail up the Chesapeake Bay and continued to the Head of Elk, where they landed. The main body of the army remained behind but came on soon afterwards. Deponent and her husband proceeded with the commissary's teams from the Head of Elk, leaving Philadelphia to the right, and continued day after day till they arrived at Pompton Plains in New Jersey. Deponent does not recollect the county. They were joined by the main body of the army under General Clinton's command, and they set down for winter quarters. Deponent and her husband lived a part of the time in a tent made of logs but covered with cloth, and a part of the time at a Mr. Manuel's near Pompton Meetinghouse. She busied herself during the winter in cooking and sewing as usual. Her said husband was on duty among the rest of the army and held the station of corporal from the time he left West Point.

In the opening of spring, they marched to West Point and remained there during the summer, her said husband still with her. In the fall they came up a little back of Newburgh to a place called New Windsor and put up huts on Ellis's lands and again sat down for winter quarters, her said husband still along and on duty. The York troops and Connecticut troops were there. In the following spring or autumn they were all discharged. Deponent and her said husband remained in New Windsor in a log house built by the army until the spring following. Some of the soldiers boarded at their house and worked round among the farmers, as did her said husband also.

Deponent and her said husband spent certainly more than three years in the service, for she recollects a part of one winter at West Point and the whole of another winter there, another winter at Pompton Plains, and another at New Windsor. And her husband was the whole time under the command of Captain Gregg as an enlisted soldier holding the station of corporal to the best of her knowledge.

In the winter before the army were disbanded at New Windsor, on the twentieth of February, deponent had a child by the name of Phebe Osborn, of whom the said Aaron Osborn was the father. A year and five months afterwards, on the ninth day of August at the same place, she had another child by the name of Aaron Osborn, Jr., of whom the said husband was the father. . . .

About three months after the birth of her last child, Aaron Osborn, Jr., she last saw her said husband, who then left her at New Windsor and never returned. He had been absent at intervals before this from deponent, and at one time deponent understood he was married again to a girl by the name of Polly Sloat above Newburgh about fifteen or sixteen miles. Deponent got a horse and rode up to inquire into the truth of the story. She arrived at the girl's father's and there found her said husband, and Polly Sloat, and her parents. Deponent was kindly treated by the inmates of the house but ascertained for a truth that her husband was married to said girl. After remaining overnight, deponent determined to return home and abandon her said husband forever, as she found he had conducted in such a way as to leave no hope of reclaiming him. About two weeks afterwards, her said husband came to see deponent in New Windsor and offered to take deponent and her children to the northward, but deponent declined going, under a firm belief that he would conduct no better, and her said husband the same night absconded with two others, crossed the river at Newburgh, and she never saw him afterwards. This was about a year and a half after his discharge. . . .

After deponent was thus left by Osborn, she removed from New Windsor to Blooming Grove, Orange County, New York, about fifty years ago, where she had been born and brought up, and, having married Mr. [John] Benjamin . . . she continued to reside there perhaps thirty-five years, when she and her husband Benjamin removed to Pleasant Mount, Wayne County, Pennsylvania, and there she has resided to this day. Her said husband, John Benjamin, died there ten years ago last April, from which time she has continued to be and is now a widow.

Questions

1. What motivated Sarah Osborn to serve in a quasi-military capacity?
2. Does it appear that the officers and enlisted men understood the value of Osborn's support of the war effort? Why or why not?
3. Does her account strike you as believable? Why or why not?

Charles Herbert, Prisoner of War Diary (1847)

Americans captured in land battles during the Revolution often met a horrible fate; rebel seamen captured at sea and taken to Great Britain usually fared better. However, the British considered them pirates, not prisoners of war (POWs). They were incarcerated to await trial —and possible execution—on the charge of piracy.

The following passages from Charles Herbert's prison diary show how POWs responded to their situation. Herbert, who was born in Massachusetts in 1757, was serving on the American ship Dolton *when the British captured it on December 24, 1776. He spent nearly two years at Mill Prison, Plymouth, until he was released in a prisoner exchange.*

MILL PRISON AT PLYMOUTH, ENGLAND
1777

[October] 18. We learn by those who came to prison last, that Dr. Franklin has written to the English ambassador, concerning an exchange of prisoners.

[October] 19. Sunday. This morning we found out that one of our company, confederate with a black man, had stolen, last night, an allowance of bread and cheese from those who came last to prison, — for which they made him run the gantlet up one side of the prison and down the other, one hundred and thirty feet, through a double file of men armed each with a nettle.

[October] 27. Last night two prisoners, Cutter and Morris, made their escape from the prison hospital; also to-day another prisoner ran the gantlet for stealing a penny loaf from one of the prisoners.

[November] 15. It is twelve months to-day since we sailed from Newburyport. I hope the Lord in whom we ought to trust, will, in his own good time, deliver us out of the hands of our enemies, and return us to a free country, —which would be a day of good fortune, a day of agreeable surprise and great joy. Then would I say —

Thrice happy youth, though destitute and poor,
These are my restoration days;
The Lord, who brought me out, I'm sure
Can teach me how his name to praise.

[December] 3. This morning the guard discovered another hole which we begun to dig yesterday. I think we have been very diligent and careful to improve every opportunity to make our escape, but the guard is so very strict with us, that I think it almost impossible to succeed, and we have reason to think that there are some traitors amongst us, who give information of every thing of the kind which we undertake.

[December] 8. To-day we were all mustered, and after this was over, the [British] agent informed us that he had received a letter . . . to put all in this prison on half allowance, for breaking orders and attempting to make our escape, until the transgressor should be found out. But as we all, with one voice joined in one cause, we thought it inhuman to pitch upon any one man; therefore, by way of contribution, we raised money enough to hire one man to own the same and suffer for all, so that we are obliged to support him while on half allowance and make him amends for his sufferings.

[December] 9. To-day the man delivered himself up, to go to the Blackhole, and the agent allows him every indulgence consistent with his orders, which is a very uncommon thing for him.

[December] 11. There have been various reports for several days past, but I thought them not worthy of observation, because they did not come from so good authority as I could wish they might; but to-day [we] have a very authentic account from Captain Henry Johnston's brother, who is lately from London, that General Burgoyne and his army are totally routed, many killed, and taken to a man; and as I do not doubt the truth of it, it gives me more satisfaction than any news I have heard since I have been a prisoner. . . .

[December] 12. I purchased a book called the "American Crisis," on purpose to lend it to a friend without. We are told that the generality of the people in England are very much disaffected at the proceedings of the ministry.

[December] 25. Christmas. . . . I must confess I have a very agreeable expectation, if my life is spared and the Lord pleases to permit me, to sit down at my father's table next Christmas.

1778

[January] 24. I have heard little or no news, for this week past, and indeed no news is the best news for us; for if there is any thing against us, they are ready enough to tell us.

[March] 12. We are informed that General Howe has written home for a reinforcement immediately, or he must inevitably share the fate of Burgoyne; this inspires us with fresh courage. . . . I hope our days of trouble are nearly at an end, and after we have borne them with a spirit of manly fortitude, we shall be returned to a free country to enjoy our just rights and privileges, for which we have been so long contending. This will make ample satisfaction for all our sufferings.

[June] 5. . . . It is twelve months to-day since I came to prison. I believe four months ago it was the opinion of every one within these walls, that we should be out before this day, but I believe now, most of us despair of being exchanged this summer, unless General Burgoyne's coming home should be of advantage to us. He is able to represent the case as it is, for we hear that the Congress told him, before he left America, to go home and take his seat in Parliament, and speak the truth, for the truth could not hurt them.

> Twelve months in prison we have spent, —
> This judgment for our sins was sent,
> To awake us from our carnal sleep,
> And teach us God's commands to keep.

[June] 25. According to the newspapers, General Burgoyne gives the American troops a brave name; he says that the troops he had at his command were as good as double the number of any other troops the King has, and that the American troops were as good as his, and would fight as well.

[July] 3. As it is two years to-morrow since the Declaration of Independence in America, we are resolved, although we are prisoners, to bear it in remembrance; and for that end, several of us have employed ourselves to-day in making cockades. They were drawn on a piece of paper, cut in the form of a half-moon, with the thirteen stripes, a union, and thirteen stars, painted out, and upon the top is printed in large capital letters, "Independence," and at the bottom "Liberty or Death," or some appeal to Heaven.

[July] 4. This morning when we were let out, we all hoisted the American flag upon our hats, except about five or six, who did not choose to wear them. The agent, seeing us all with those papers on our hats, asked for one to look at, which was sent him, and it happened to be one which had "Independence" written upon the top, and at the bottom, "Liberty or Death." He, not knowing the meaning of it, and thinking we were going to force the guard, directly ordered a double sentry at the gate. Nothing happened till one o'clock; we then drew up in thirteen divisions, and each division gave three cheers, till it came to the last, when we all cheered together, all of which was conducted with the greatest regularity. We kept our colors hoisted till sunset, and then took them down.

[July] 17. There are a number of very quarrelsome, lawless men in prison, who have been the occasion of a great deal of mutiny and disturbance amongst us, which has obtained for us the ill-will of our friends; and we have been informed that unless there is an alteration among us, our donations [from kindly Britons] will be stopped; so that we thought it proper to have Articles among ourselves. These were drawn up to-day; they forbid all gambling, and blackguarding, which have caused great disturbance in the yard, and occasioned much fighting. They also forbid any improper language to any officer or soldier, who are now, or may hereafter be, appointed to preside over us. These articles were read in the yard before all the prisoners, and then stuck up in prison, and two men out of each ship's company were appointed to see them put into execution.

[July] 23. Most of this day the prison has been in an uproar, occasioned by a few men that will not be conformable to the rules and articles that we have amongst ourselves, but threaten to take them down and destroy them.

[July] 24. This morning we found that our articles were abused, and we took three of the before-mentioned men and tied them up to a post in the prison, and poured cold water down their arms and neck, for the space of half an hour. One of the three was afterwards complained of to the agent, who ordered him to be put in irons, and separated from us.

[August] 18. This afternoon there were five Americans brought to prison. They were all taken in different vessels. Some of them belonged to armed ships, others to merchantmen. Some of them have been taken this six months, and have been hurried about from ship to ship, and used scandalously. They had a bounty offered them to go on board this fleet, now lying in the Sound, but they, like brave Americans, refused, and chose rather to come to prison. They were sent here without being examined, or committed by any justice of the peace.

[October] 4. Sunday. This forenoon a gentleman came with a pardon for thirty-three men that petitioned to go on board the men-of-war, which was nearly as follows:

"His Majesty has been graciously pleased to grant a free pardon to thirty-three men, by name —, resident in this prison, upon condition that they will serve, and continue to serve in His Majesty's Navy." This gentleman said that these men are to be taken out of prison to-morrow, but one of the thirty-three has lately made his escape, and we have heard since that he is on board a man-of-war. He also said that those whose names are not on the list, but wish to enter on board the men-of-war, if they would petition, the same course would be taken, and he had no doubt it would be answered to their satisfaction. Accordingly, this afternoon a petition was written, and about fourteen signed it.

[October] 6. Last night there was but very little sleep in this prison, for the men who went on board the men-of-war this morning, were so overjoyed at the thought of being released from prison, that they could not, or would not, sleep the fore part of the night, but ran about the prison, hallooing, and stamping, and singing, like mad-men, till they were tired out, and then went to bed; but the rest in prison were resolved, as they would not let us sleep the first part of the night, we would not let them sleep the latter; accordingly, we all turned out, and had an Indian Pow-wow, and as solid as the prison is, we made it shake. In this manner we spent the night, and in the morning early the men were called out, twenty of whom were immediately carried on board the Russel ship-of-war, now lying in the Sound. The other twelve were taken out about eleven o'clock, and sent on board the Royal George, now lying in Plymouth dock. As they went out, they gave us three cheers; we returned it, for in joy we parted. Among those who went to-day were about a dozen Americans, but they were chiefly inconsiderate youths. This is a move that I have long wished to see, but it came now very unexpectedly. For my own part, to enter on board a ship of war is the last thing I would do. I would undergo every thing but death before I would think of such a thing. This prison has been a little hell upon earth, but I prefer it as much before a man-of-war, as I would a palace before a dungeon. Ten days ago there were 330 prisoners here, now there are only 294.

[October] 6. There is a great alteration to be seen in this prison since those men went away, and I make no doubt that after another draft, we shall have peace and tranquility, and live in harmony, and make ourselves happy, considering our situation, to what we have been for months past.

Questions

1. What is the worst part of Herbert's incarceration?
2. How does he receive news? Is it accurate?
3. Under what conditions will the British release prisoners? Why doesn't Herbert take advantage of this chance for freedom?

Abigail Adams, Boston Women Support Price Control (1777)

Financing the Patriots' war effort produced a range of problems, including disagreements over how to control prices and prevent profiteering. Given the active role women had played in earlier economic boycotts and were taking in the war effort, it seems logical they would have participated in any program to regulate prices. Such an effort occurred in Massachusetts in 1777. As the following letter from Abigail Adams to her husband, John, shows, Boston women were capable of some intriguing methods to achieve price regulation.

31 July, 1777
I have nothing new to entertain you with, unless it is an account of a new set of mobility, which has lately taken the lead in Boston. You must know that there is a great scarcity of sugar and coffee, articles which the female part of the state is very loth to give up, especially whilst they consider the scarcity occasioned by the merchants having secreted a large quantity. There had been much rout and noise in the town for several weeks. Some stores had been opened by a number of people, and the coffee and sugar carried into the market, and dealt out by pounds. It was rumored that an eminent, wealthy, stingy merchant (who is a bachelor) had a hogshead of coffee in his store, which he refused to sell to the committee under six shillings per pound. A number of females, some say a hundred, some say more, assembled with a cart and trucks, marched down to the warehouse, and demanded the keys, which he refused to deliver. Upon which, one of them seized him by his neck, and tossed him into the cart. Upon his finding no quarter, he delivered the keys, when they tipped up the cart and discharged him; then opened the warehouse, hoisted out the coffee themselves, put it into the truck, and drove off.

It was reported, that he had personal chastisement among them; but this, I believe was not true. A large concourse of men stood amazed, silent spectators of the whole transaction.

Questions
1. What actions do the women take?
2. How does this account suggest the danger inherent in a time of revolution?
3. What matters more in a revolution — issues or prices? Explain.

Virginia Statute of Religious Freedom (1786)

The Patriots wanted not only freedom from Britain but greater freedom at home as well; this was especially clear in terms of religion. One of the landmarks on the way to true religious freedom in the republic was the Virginia statute of religious liberty, reprinted here in full. Thomas Jefferson, who authored the law, considered its enactment one of the three principal achievements of his life.

I. WHEREAS Almighty God hath created the mind free; that all attempts to influence it by temporal punishments or burthens, or by civil incapacitations, tend only to beget habits of hypocrisy and meanness, and are a departure from the plan of the Holy author of our religion, who being Lord both of body and mind, yet chose not to propagate it by coercions on either, as was in his Almighty power to do; that the impious presumption of legislators and rulers, civil as well as ecclesiastical, who being themselves but fallible and uninspired men, have assumed dominion over the faith of others, setting up their own opinions and modes of thinking as the only true and infallible, and as such endeavouring to impose them on others, hath established and maintained false religions over the greatest part of the world, and through all time; that to compel a man to furnish contributions of money for the propagation of opinions which he disbelieves, is sinful and tyrannical; that even the forcing him to support this or that teacher of his own religious persuasion, is depriving him of the comfortable liberty of giving his contributions to the particular pastor, whose morals he would make his pattern, and whose powers he feels most persuasive to righteousness, and is withdrawing from the ministry those temporary rewards, which proceeding from an approbation of their personal conduct, are all additional incitement to earnest and unremitting labours for the instruction of mankind; that our civil rights have no dependence on our religious opinions, any more than our opinions in physics or geometry; that therefore the proscribing any citizen as unworthy the public confidence by laying upon him an incapacity of being called to offices of trust and emolument, unless he profess or renounce this or that religious opinion, is depriving him injuriously of those privileges and advantages to which in common with his fellow-citizens he has a natural right; that it tends only to corrupt the principles of that religion it is meant to encourage, by bribing with a monopoly of worldly honours and emoluments, those who will externally profess and conform to it; that though indeed these are criminals who do not withstand such temptation, yet neither are those innocent who lay the bait in their way; that to suffer the civil magistrate to intrude his powers into the field of opinion, and to restrain the profession or propagation of principles on supposition of their ill tendency, is a dangerous fallacy, which at once destroys all religious liberty, because he being of course judge of that tendency will make his opinions the rule of judgment, and approve or condemn the sentiments of others only as they shall square with or differ from his own; that it is time enough for the rightful purposes of civil government, for its officers to interfere when principles break out into overt acts against peace and good order; and finally, that truth is great and will prevail if left to herself, that she is the proper and sufficient antagonist to error, and has nothing to fear from the conflict, unless by human interposition disarmed of her natural weapons, free argument and debate, errors ceasing to be dangerous when it is permitted freely to contradict them:

II. *Be it enacted by the General Assembly,* That no man shall be compelled to frequent or support any religious worship, place, or ministry whatsoever, nor shall be enforced, restrained, molested, or burthened in his body or goods, nor shall otherwise suffer on account of his religious opinions or belief; but that all men shall be free to profess, and by argument to maintain, their opinion in matters of religion, and that the same shall in no wise diminish, enlarge, or affect their civil capacities.

III. And though we well know that this assembly elected by the people for the ordinary purposes of legislation only, have no power to restrain the acts of succeeding assemblies, constituted with powers equal to our own, and that therefore to declare this act to be irrevocable would be of no effect in law; yet we are free to declare, and do declare, that the rights hereby asserted are of the natural rights of mankind, and that if any act shall be hereafter passed to repeal the present, or to narrow its operation, such act will be an infringement on natural right.

Questions

1. Does the statute's wording truly guarantee absolute religious freedom? Why or why not?
2. Does the statute echo the Declaration of Independence in any important ways? If so, how?
3. How might George Whitefield (Chapter 4, "The Reverend Mr. Whitefield's Journal") react to the statute? Why?

Connections Questions

1. How do the documents in this section trace the stages that a revolution is likely to take?

2. Reflecting on Thomas Paine *("Common Sense")* and Thomas Jefferson ("Thomas Jefferson Attacks the King"), assess the role of propaganda in furthering a revolutionary cause. What are the dangers? Can a revolution be conducted without propaganda? Why or why not?

3. The documents in Chapters 5 and 6 suggest that the Revolutionary experience changed the status of women in society. In what way? To what extent was it intentional? To what extent was it unintentional?

CHAPTER 7

The New Political Order 1776–1800

Virginia Declaration of Rights (1776)

The people of Great Britain and its colonies regarded the Magna Carta of 1215 as an example of a written guarantee of basic political rights. Moreover, England adopted a bill of rights in 1689, and many of the colonies passed laws that amounted to bills of rights.

Thus, it was logical that a number of the new Patriot-led governments would address the matter of enumerating basic rights. Virginia acted first. Its Declaration of Rights, written principally by George Mason, was issued in June 1776 and offered a bold vision of Virginia's — and America's — political system. The democratically inclined men among those who drafted new state constitutions (see text p. 174) often copied sections of this declaration verbatim.

A declaration of rights made by the representatives of the good people of Virginia, assembled in full and free convention; which rights do pertain to them and their posterity, as the basis and foundation of government.

SECTION 1. That all men are by nature equally free and independent, and have certain inherent rights, of which, when they enter into a state of society, they cannot, by any compact, deprive or divest their posterity; namely, the enjoyment of life and liberty, with the means of acquiring and possessing property, and pursuing and obtaining happiness and safety.

SEC. 2. That all power is vested in, and consequently derived from, the people; that magistrates are their trustees and servants, and at all times amenable to them.

SEC. 3. That government is, or ought to be, instituted for the common benefit, protection, and security of the people, nation, or community; of all the various modes and forms of government, that is best which is capable of producing the greatest degree of happiness and safety, and is most effectually secured against the danger of maladministration; and that, when any government shall be found inadequate or contrary to these purposes, a majority of the community hath an indubitable, inalienable, and indefeasible right to reform, alter, or abolish it, in such manner as shall be judged most conducive to the public weal.

SEC. 4. That no man, or set of men, are entitled to exclusive or separate emoluments or privileges from the community, but in consideration of public services; which, not being descendible, neither ought the offices of magistrate, legislator, or judge to be hereditary.

SEC. 5. That the legislative and executive powers of the State should be separate and distinct from the judiciary; and that the members of the two first may be restrained from oppression, by feeling and participating the burdens of the people, they should, at fixed periods, be reduced to a private station, return into that body from which they were originally taken, and the vacancies be supplied by frequent, certain, and regular elections, in which all, or any part of the former members, to be again eligible, or ineligible, as the laws shall direct.

SEC. 6. That elections of members to serve as representatives of the people, in assembly, ought to be free; and that all men, having sufficient evidence of permanent common interest with, and attachment to, the community, have the right of suffrage, and cannot be taxed or deprived of their property for public uses, without their own consent, or that of their representatives so elected, nor bound by any law to which they have not, in like manner, assembled, for the public good.

SEC. 7. That all power of suspending laws, or the execution of laws, by any authority, without consent of the representatives of the people, is injurious to their rights, and ought not to be exercised.

SEC. 8. That in all capital or criminal prosecutions a man hath a right to demand the cause and nature of his accusation, to be confronted with the accusers and witnesses, to call for evidence in his favor, and to a speedy trial by an impartial jury of twelve men of his vicinage, without whose unanimous consent he cannot be found guilty; nor can he be compelled to give evidence against himself; that no man be deprived of his liberty, except by the law of the land or the judgment of his peers.

SEC. 9. That excessive bail ought not to be required, nor excessive fines imposed, nor cruel and unusual punishments inflicted.

SEC. 10. That general warrants, whereby an officer or messenger may be commanded to search suspected places without evidence of a fact committed, or to seize any person or persons not named, or whose offence is not particularly described and supported by evidence, are grievous and oppressive, and ought not to be granted.

SEC. 11. That in controversies respecting property, and in suits between man and man, the ancient trial by jury is preferable to any other, and ought to be held sacred.

SEC. 12. That the freedom of the press is one of the great bulwarks of liberty, and can never be restrained but by despotic governments.

SEC. 13. That a well-regulated militia, composed of the body of the people, trained to arms, is the proper, natural, and safe defence of a free State; that standing armies, in time of peace, should be avoided, as dangerous to liberty; and that in all cases the military should be under strict subordination to, and governed by, the civil power.

SEC. 14. That the people have a right to uniform government; and, therefore, that no government separate from, or independent of the government of Virginia, ought to be erected or established within the limits thereof.

SEC. 15. That no free government, or the blessings of liberty, can be preserved to any people, but by a firm adherence to justice, moderation, temperance, frugality, and virtue, and by frequent recurrence to fundamental principles.

SEC. 16. That religion, or the duty which we owe to our Creator, and the manner of discharging it, can be directed only by reason and conviction, not by force or violence; and therefore all men are equally entitled to the free exercise of religion, according to the dictates of conscience; and that it is the mutual duty of all to practice Christian forbearance, love, and charity towards each other.

Questions

1. According to the Virginia Declaration of Rights, where does legitimate power reside?
2. What responsibilities does government have?
3. How would the declaration affect people in the long term?

Abigail and John Adams Debate the Rights of Women (1776)

John Adams (1735–1826) was not the only member of the Adams family who thought about the nature of people and governments. His wife, Abigail Adams (1744–1818), was an active Patriot in her own right and kept the family functioning while John was serving in Congress. The couple exchanged letters regularly. The correspondence reveals their differences of opinion on the issue of expanding the rights of women.

ABIGAIL ADAMS TO JOHN ADAMS, MARCH 31, 1776

I long to hear that you have declared an independancy — and by the way in the new Code of Laws which I suppose it will be necessary for you to make I desire you would Remember the Ladies, and be more generous and favourable to them than your ancestors. Do not put such unlimited power into the hands of the Husbands. Remember all Men would be tyrants if they could. If perticuliar care and attention is not paid to the Ladies we are determined to foment a Rebelion, and will not hold ourselves bound by any Laws in which we have no voice, or Representation.

That your Sex are Naturally Tyrannical is a Truth so thoroughly established as to admit of no dispute, but such of you as wish to be happy willingly give up the harsh title of Master for the more tender and endearing one of Friend. Why then, not put it out of the power of the vicious and the Lawless to use us with cruelty and indignity with impunity. Men of Sense in all Ages abhor those customs which treat us only as the vassals of your Sex. Regard us then as Beings placed by providence under your protection and in immitation of the Supreem Being make use of that power only for our happiness. . . .

JOHN ADAMS TO ABIGAIL ADAMS, APRIL 14, 1776

As to your extraordinary Code of Laws, I cannot but laugh. We have been told that our Struggle has loosened the bands of Government every where. That Children and Apprentices were disobedient — that schools and Colledges were grown turbulent — that Indians slighted their Guardians and Negroes grew insolent to their Masters. But your Letter was the first Intimation that another Tribe more numerous and powerful than all the rest were grown discontented — This is rather too coarse a Compliment but you are so saucy, I wont blot it out.

Depend upon it, We know better than to repeal our Masculine systems. Altho they are in full Force, you know they are little more than Theory. We dare not exert our Power in its full Latitude. We are obliged to go fair, and softly, and in Practice you know We are the subjects. We have only the Name of Masters, and rather than give up this, which would compleatly subject Us to the Despotism of the Peticoat, I hope General Washington, and all our brave Heroes would fight. I am sure every good Politician would plot, as long as he would against Despotism, Empire, Monarchy, Aristocracy, Oligarchy, or Ochlocracy [mob rule]. A fine Story indeed. I begin to think the Ministry as deep as they are wicked. After stirring up Tories, Landjobbers, Trimmers, Bigots, Canadians, Indians, Negroes, Hanoverians, Hessians, Russians, Irish Roman Catholicks, Scotch Renegadoes, at last they have stimulated the . . . [Ladies?] to demand new Priviledges and threaten to rebell.

ABIGAIL ADAMS TO JOHN ADAMS, MAY 7, 1776

I can not say that I think you very generous to the Ladies, for whilst you are proclaiming peace and good will to Men, Emancipating all Nations, you insist upon retaining an absolute power over Wives. But you must remember that Arbitary power is like most other things which are very hard, very liable to be broken — and notwithstanding all your wise Laws and Maxims we have it in our power not only to free ourselves but to subdue our Masters, and without violence throw both your natural and legal authority at our feet—

"Charm by accepting, by submitting sway
Yet have our Humour most when we obey."

I thank you for several Letters which I have received since I wrote Last. They alleviate a tedious absence, and I long earnestly for a Saturday Evening, and experience a similar pleasure to that which I used to find in the return of my Friend upon that day after a weeks absence. The Idea of a year dissolves all my Phylosophy.

Our Little ones whom you so often recommend to my care and instruction shall not be deficient in virtue or probity if the precepts of a Mother have their desired Effect, but they would be doubly inforced could they be indulged with the example of a Father constantly before them; I often point them to their Sire

"engaged in a corrupted State
Wrestling with vice and faction."

ABIGAIL ADAMS TO JOHN ADAMS, AUGUST 14, 1776

If you complain of neglect of Education in sons, What shall I say with regard to daughters, who every day experience the want of it. With regard to the Education of my own children, I find myself soon out of my debth, and destitute and deficient in every part of Education.

I most sincerely wish that some more liberal plan might be laid and executed for the Benefit of the rising Generation, and that our new constitution may be distinguished for Learning and Virtue. If we mean to have Heroes, Statesmen and Philosophers, we should have learned women. The world perhaps would laugh at me, and accuse me of vanity, But you I know have a mind too enlarged and liberal to disregard the Sentiment. If much depends as is allowed upon the early Education of youth and the first principals which are instilled take the deepest root, great benifit must arise from litirary accomplishments in women.

Questions

1. Scholars disagree whether this material demonstrates that Abigail Adams was in favor of women's suffrage. What do you think?

2. What specific rights does Abigail Adams argue that women should have?
3. What pragmatic arguments does she advance to support the idea of greater rights for women? How convincing is she?
4. What does the correspondence suggest about the Adamses' marriage?

James Madison, *The Federalist,* No. 10 (1787)

The advocates of the new Constitution had to persuade the American people to adopt it; that proved difficult (see text pp. 187–90). James Madison, along with Alexander Hamilton and John Jay, wrote a series of essays to help win support for the Constitution in the crucial state of New York. Scholars now generally agree that the essays, known collectively as The Federalist, *probably did not play a significant role in persuading New Yorkers. Nevertheless, scholars also agree that* The Federalist *is essential in understanding the mindset of the men who wrote the Constitution. Madison (1751–1836), one of the most important of the framers (see text pp. 184–87), penned* The Federalist, *No. 10, the most widely cited essay in the series. It is reprinted here in its entirety.*

THE FEDERALIST. NO. X.
To the People of the State of New-York.

Among the numerous advantages promised by a well constructed Union, none deserves to be more accurately developed than its tendency to break and control the violence of faction. The friend of popular governments, never finds himself so much alarmed for their character and fate, as when he contemplates their propensity to this dangerous vice. He will not fail therefore to set a due value on any plan which, without violating the principles to which he is attached, provides a proper cure for it. The instability, injustice and confusion introduced into the public councils, have in truth been the mortal diseases under which popular governments have every where perished; as they continue to be the favorite and fruitful topics from which the adversaries to liberty derive their most specious declamations. The valuable improvements made by the American Constitutions on the popular models, both ancient and modern, cannot certainly be too much admired; but it would be an unwarrantable partiality, to contend that they have as effectually obviated the danger on this side as was wished and expected. Complaints are every where heard from our most considerate and virtuous citizens, equally the friends of public and private faith, and of public and personal liberty; that our governments are too unstable; that the public good is disregarded in the conflicts of rival parties; and that measures are too often decided, not according to the rules of justice, and the rights of the minor party; but by the superior force of an interested and overbearing majority. However anxiously we may wish that these complaints had no foundation, the evidence of known facts will not permit us to deny that they are in some degree true. It will be found indeed, on a candid review of our situation, that some of the distresses under which we labor, have been erroneously charged on the operation of our governments; but it will be found, at the same time, that other causes will not alone account for many of our heaviest misfortunes; and particularly, for that prevailing and increasing distrust of public engagements, and alarm for private rights, which are echoed from one end of the continent to the other. These must be chiefly, if not wholly, effects of the unsteadiness and injustice, with which a factious spirit has tainted our public administration.

By a faction I understand a number of citizens, whether amounting to a majority or minority of the whole, who are united and actuated by some common impulse of passion, or of interest, adverse to the rights of other citizens, or to the permanent and aggregate interests of the community.

There are two methods of curing the mischiefs of faction: the one, by removing its causes; the other, by controlling its effects.

There are again two methods of removing the causes of faction: the one, by destroying the liberty which is essential to its existence; the other, by giving to every citizen the same opinions, the same passions, and the same interests.

It could never be more truly said than of the first remedy, that it is worse than the disease. Liberty is to faction, what air is to fire, an aliment without which it instantly expires. But it could not be a less folly to abolish liberty, which is essential to political life, because it nourishes faction, than it would be to wish the annihilation of air, which is essential to animal life, because it imparts to fire its destructive agency.

The second expedient is as impracticable, as the first would be unwise. As long as the reason of man continues fallible, and he is at liberty to exercise it, different opinions will be formed. As long as the connection subsists between his reason and his self-love, his opinions and his passions will have a reciprocal influence on each other; and the former will be objects to which the latter will attach themselves. The diversity in the faculties of men from which the rights of property originate, is not less an insuperable obstacle to a uniformity of interests. The protection of these faculties is the first object of Government. From the protection of different and unequal faculties of acquiring property, the possession of different degrees and kinds of property immediately results: and from the influence of these on the sentiments and views of the respective proprietors, ensues a division of the society into different interests and parties.

The latent causes of faction are thus sown in the nature of man; and we see them every where brought into different degrees of activity, according to the different circumstances of civil society. A zeal for different opinions concerning religion, concerning Government, and many other points, as well of speculation as of practice; an attachment to different leaders ambitiously contending for pre-eminence and power; or to persons of other descriptions whose fortunes have been interesting to the human passions, have in turn divided mankind into parties, inflamed them with mutual animosity, and rendered them much more disposed to vex and oppress each other, than to co-operate for their common good. So strong is this propensity of mankind to fall into mutual animosities, that where no substantial occasion presents itself, the most frivolous and fanciful distinctions have been sufficient to kindle their unfriendly passions, and excite their most violent conflicts. But the most common and durable source of factions, has been the various and unequal distribution of property. Those who hold, and those who are without property, have ever formed distinct interests in society. Those who are creditors, and those who are debtors, fall under a like discrimination. A landed interest, a manufacturing interest, a mercantile interest, a monied interest, with many lesser interests, grow up of necessity in civilized nations, and divide them into different classes, actuated by different sentiments and views. The regulation of these various and interfering interests forms the principal task of modern Legislation, and involves the spirit of party and faction in the necessary and ordinary operations of Government.

No man is allowed to be a judge in his own cause; because his interest would certainly bias his judgment, and, not improbably, corrupt his integrity. With equal, nay with greater reason, a body of men, are unfit to be both judges and parties, at the same time; yet, what are many of the most important acts of legislation, but so many judicial determinations, not indeed concerning the rights of single persons, but concerning the rights of large bodies of citizens; and what are the different classes of legislators, but advocates and parties to the causes which they determine? Is a law proposed concerning private debts? It is a question to which the creditors are parties on one side, and the debtors on the other. Justice ought to hold the balance between them. Yet the parties are and must be themselves the judges; and the most numerous party, or, in other words, the most powerful faction must be expected to prevail. Shall domestic manufactures be encouraged, and in what degree, by restrictions on foreign manufactures? are questions which would be differently decided by the landed and the manufacturing classes; and probably by neither, with a sole regard to justice and the public good. The apportionment of taxes on the various descriptions of property, is an act which seems to require the most exact impartiality; yet there is perhaps no legislative act in which greater opportunity and temptation are given to a predominant party, to trample on the rules of justice. Every shilling with which they over-burden the inferior number, is a shilling saved to their own pockets.

It is in vain to say, that enlightened statesmen will be able to adjust these clashing interests, and render them all subservient to the public good. Enlightened statesmen will not always be at the helm: Nor, in many cases, can such an adjustment be made at all, without taking into view indirect and remote considerations, which will rarely prevail over the immediate interest which one party may find in disregarding the rights of another, or the good of the whole.

The inference to which we are brought, is, that the *causes* of faction cannot be removed; and that relief is only to be sought in the means of controling its *effects*.

If a faction consists of less than a majority, relief is supplied by the republican principle, which enables the majority to defeat its sinister views by regular vote: It may clog the administration, it may convulse the society; but it will be unable to execute and mask its violence under the forms of the Constitution. When a majority is included in a faction, the form of popular government on the other hand enables it to sacrifice to its ruling passion or interest, both the public good and the rights of other citizens. To secure the public good, and private rights, against the danger of such a faction, and at the same time to preserve the spirit and the form of popular government, is then the great object to which our enquiries are directed: Let me add that it is the great desideratum, by which alone this form of government can be rescued from the opprobrium under which it has so long labored, and be recommended to the esteem and adoption of mankind.

By what means is this object attainable? Evidently by one of two only. Either the existence of the same passion or interest in a majority at the same time, must be prevented; or the majority, having such co-existent passion or interest, must be rendered, by their number and local situation, unable to concert and carry into effect schemes of oppression. If the impulse and the opportunity be suffered to coincide, we well know that neither moral nor religious motives can be relied on as an adequate control. They are not found to be such on the injustice and violence of individuals, and lose their efficacy in proportion to the number combined together; that is, in proportion as their efficacy becomes needful.

From this view of the subject, it may be concluded, that a pure Democracy, by which I mean, a Society, consisting of a small number of citizens, who assemble and administer the Government in person, can admit of no cure for the mischiefs of faction. A common passion or interest will, in almost every case, be felt by a majority of the whole; a communication and concert results from the form of Government itself; and there is nothing to check the inducements to sacrifice the weaker party, or an obnoxious individual. Hence it is, that such Democracies have ever been spectacles of turbulence and contention; have ever been found incompatible with personal security, or the rights of property; and have in general been as short in their lives, as they have been violent in their deaths. Theoretic politicians, who have patronized this species of Government, have erroneously supposed, that by reducing mankind to a perfect equality in their political rights, they would, at the same time, be perfectly equalized and assimilated in their possessions, their opinions, and their passions.

A Republic, by which I mean a Government in which the scheme of representation takes place, opens a different prospect, and promises the cure for which we are seeking. Let us examine the points in which it varies from pure Democracy, and we shall comprehend both the nature of the cure, and the efficacy which it must derive from the Union.

The two great points of difference between a Democracy and a Republic are, first, the delegation of the Government, in the latter, to a small number of citizens elected by the rest: secondly, the greater number of citizens, and greater sphere of country, over which the latter may be extended.

The effect of the first difference is, on the one hand to refine and enlarge the public views, by passing them through the medium of a chosen body of citizens, whose wisdom may best discern the true interest of their country, and whose patriotism and love of justice, will be least likely to sacrifice it to temporary or partial considerations. Under such a regulation, it may well happen that the public voice pronounced by the representatives of the people, will be more consonant to the public good, than if pronounced by the people themselves convened for the purpose. On the other hand, the effect may be inverted. Men of factious tempers, of local prejudices, or of sinister designs, may by intrigue, by corruption or by other means, first obtain the suffrages, and then betray the interests of the people. The question resulting is, whether small or extensive Republics are most favorable to the election of proper guardians of the public weal; and it is clearly decided in favor of the latter by two obvious considerations.

In the first place it is to be remarked that however small the Republic may be, the Representatives must be raised to a certain number, in order to guard against the cabals of a few; and that however large it may be, they must be limited to a certain number, in order to guard against the confusion of a multitude. Hence the number of Representatives in the two cases, not being in proportion to that of the Constituents, and being proportionally greatest in the small Republic, it follows, that if the proportion of fit characters, be not less, in the large than in the small Republic, the former will present a greater option, and consequently a greater probability of a fit choice.

In the next place, as each Representative will be chosen by a greater number of citizens in the large than in the small Republic, it will be more difficult for unworthy candidates to practise with success the vicious arts, by which elections are too often carried; and the suffrages of the people being more free, will be more likely to centre on men who possess the most attractive merit, and the most diffusive and established characters.

It must be confessed, that in this, as in most other cases, there is a mean, on both sides of which inconveniencies will be found to lie. By enlarging too much the number of electors, you render the representative too little acquainted with all their local circumstances and lesser interests; as by reducing it too much, you render him unduly attached to these, and too little fit to comprehend and pursue great and national objects. The Federal Constitution forms a happy combination in this respect; the great and aggregate interests being referred to the national, the local and particular, to the state legislatures.

The other point of difference is, the greater number of citizens and extent of territory which may be brought within the compass of Republican, than of Democratic Government; and it is this circumstance principally which renders factious combinations less to be dreaded in the former, than in the latter. The smaller the society, the fewer probably will be the distinct parties and interests composing it; the fewer the distinct parties and interests, the more frequently will a majority be found of the same party; and the smaller the number of individuals composing a majority, and the smaller the compass within which they are placed, the more easily will they concert and execute their plans of oppression. Extend the sphere, and you take in a greater variety of parties and interests; you make it less probable that a majority of the whole will have a common motive to invade the rights of other citizens; or if such a common motive exists, it will be more difficult for all who feel it to discover their own strength, and to act in unison with each other. Besides other impediments, it may be remarked, that where there is a consciousness of unjust or dishonorable purposes, communication is always checked by distrust, in proportion to the number whose concurrence is necessary.

Hence it clearly appears, that the same advantage, which a Republic has over a Democracy, in controlling the effects of faction, is enjoyed by a large over a small Republic — is enjoyed by the Union over the States composing it. Does this advantage consist in the substitution of Representatives, whose enlightened views and virtuous sentiments render them superior to local prejudices, and to schemes of injustice? It will not be denied, that the Representation of the Union will be most likely to possess these requisite endowments. Does it consist in the greater security afforded by a greater variety of parties, against the event of any one party being able to outnumber and oppress the rest? In an equal degree does the encreased variety of parties, comprised within the Union, encrease this security. Does it, in fine, consist in the greater obstacles opposed to the concert and accomplishment of the secret wishes of an unjust and interested majority? Here, again, the extent of the Union gives it the most palpable advantage.

The influence of factious leaders may kindle a flame within their particular States, but will be unable to spread a general conflagration through the other States: a religious sect, may degenerate into a political faction in a part of the Confederacy; but the variety of sects dispersed over the entire face of it, must secure the national Councils against any danger from that source: a rage for paper money, for an abolition of debts, for an equal division of property, or for any other improper or wicked project, will be less apt to pervade the whole body of the Union, than a particular member of it; in the same proportion as such a malady is more likely to taint a particular county or district, than an entire State.

In the extent and proper structure of the Union, therefore, we behold a Republican remedy for the diseases most incident to Republican Government. And according to the degree of pleasure and pride, we feel in being Republicans, ought to be our zeal in cherishing the spirit, and supporting the character of Federalists.

Questions

1. According to James Madison, what causes "factions" to develop?
2. Why does Madison believe factions are dangerous?
3. Given that assessment, can he be called an economic determinist? Why or why not?
4. Are there any similarities between what Madison hails as a neutralizing of interests and what critics today condemn as governmental gridlock? Why or why not?

Alexander Hamilton, *Report on Public Credit* (1790)

Demonstrating his admiration of British institutions and economic policies, Alexander Hamilton said in 1781 that "a national debt if it is not excessive will be to us a national blessing, it will be [a] powerful cement of our union." When he became the first secretary of the Treasury in 1789, Hamilton (1755–1804) tried to implement his ideas by devising innovative financial policies to overcome the fiscal problems that worked against the government under the Articles of Confederation. Below is Hamilton's view on public credit, including his position concerning a national debt.

Treasury Department, January 9, 1790.
[Communicated on January 14, 1790]

[To the Speaker of the House of Representatives]

The Secretary of the Treasury, in obedience to the resolution of the House of Representatives . . . has . . . applied himself to the consideration of a proper plan for the support of the Public Credit, with all the attention which was due to the authority of the House, and to the magnitude of the object.

In the discharge of this duty, he has felt . . . a deep and solemn conviction of the momentous nature of the truth contained in the resolution under which his investigations have been conducted, "That an *adequate* provision for the support of the Public Credit, is a matter of high importance to the honor and prosperity of the United States."

With an ardent desire that his well-meant endeavors may be conducive to the real advantage of the nation, and with the utmost deference to the superior judgment of the House, he now respectfully submits the result of his enquiries and reflections, to their indulgent construction.

In the opinion of the Secretary, the wisdom of the House, in giving their explicit sanction to the proposition which has been stated, cannot but be applauded by all, who will seriously consider, and trace through their obvious consequences, these plain and undeniable truths.

That exigencies are to be expected to occur, in the affairs of nations, in which there will be a necessity for borrowing.

That loans in times of public danger, especially from foreign war, are found an indispensable resource, even to the wealthiest of them.

And that in a country, which, like this, is possessed of little active wealth, or in other words, little monied capital, the necessity for that resource, must, in such emergencies, be proportionably urgent.

And as on the one hand, the necessity for borrowing in particular emergencies cannot be doubted, so on the other, it is equally evident, that to be able to borrow upon *good terms*, it is essential that the credit of a nation should be well established.

For when the credit of a country is in any degree questionable, it never fails to give an extravagant premium, in one shape or another, upon all the loans it has occasion to make. Nor does the evil end here; the same disadvantage must be sustained upon whatever is to be bought on terms of future payment.

From this constant necessity of *borrowing* and *buying dear,* it is easy to conceive how immensely the expences of a nation, in a course of time, will be augmented by an unsound state of the public credit.

To attempt to enumerate the complicated variety of mischiefs in the whole system of the social œconomy, which proceed from a neglect of the maxims that uphold public credit, and justify the solicitude manifested by the House on this point, would be an improper intrusion on their time and patience.

In so strong a light nevertheless do they appear to the Secretary, that on their due observance at the present critical juncture, materially depends, in his judgment, the individual and aggregate prosperity of the citizens of the United States; their relief from the embarrassments they now experience; their character as a People; the cause of good government.

If the maintenance of public credit, then, be truly so important, the next enquiry which suggests itself is, by what means is it to be effected? The ready answer to which question is, by good faith, by a punctual performance of contracts. States, like individuals, who observe their engagements, are respected and trusted: while the reverse is the fate of those, who pursue an opposite conduct. . . .

While the observance of that good faith, which is the basis of public credit, is recommended by the strongest inducements of political expediency, it is enforced by considerations of still greater authority. There are arguments for it, which rest on the immutable principles of moral obligation. And in proportion as the mind is disposed to contemplate, in the order of Providence, an intimate connection between public virtue and public happiness, will be its repugnancy to a violation of those principles.

This reflection derives additional strength from the nature of the debt of the United States. It was the price of liberty. The faith of America has been repeatedly pledged for it, and with solemnities, that give peculiar force to the obligation. There is indeed reason to regret that it has not hitherto been kept; that the necessities of the war, conspiring with inexperience in the subjects of finance, produced direct infractions; and that the subsequent period has been a continued scene of negative violation, or non-compliance. But a diminution of this regret arises from the reflection, that the last seven years have exhibited an earnest and uniform effort, on the part of the government of the union, to retrieve the national credit, by doing justice to the creditors of the nation; and that the embarrassments of a defective constitution, which defeated this laudable effort, have ceased.

From this evidence of a favorable disposition, given by the former government, the institution of a new one, cloathed with powers competent to calling forth the resources of the community, has excited correspondent expectations. A general belief, accordingly, prevails, that the credit of the United States will quickly be established on the firm foundation of an effectual provision for the existing debt. . . .

It cannot but merit particular attention, that among ourselves the most enlightened friends of good government are those, whose expectations are the highest.

To justify and preserve their confidence; to promote the encreasing respectability of the American name; to answer the calls of justice; to restore landed property to its due value; to furnish new resources both to agriculture and commerce; to cement more closely the union of the states; to add to their security against foreign attack; to establish public order on the basis of an upright and liberal policy. These are the great and invaluable ends to be secured, by a proper and adequate provision, at the present period, for the support of public credit.

To this provision we are invited, not only by the general considerations, which have been noticed, but by others of a more particular nature. It will procure to every class of the community some important advantages, and remove some no less important disadvantages. . . .

But these good effects of a public debt are only to be looked for, when, by being well funded, it has acquired an *adequate* and *stable* value. Till then, it has rather a contrary tendency. The fluctuation and insecurity incident to it in an unfunded state, render it a mere commodity, and a precarious one. As such, being only an object of occasional and particular speculation, all the money applied to it is so much diverted from the more useful channels of circulation, for which the thing itself affords no substitute: So that, in fact, one serious inconvenience of an unfunded debt is, that it contributes to the scarcity of money.

This distinction which has been little if at all attended to, is of the greatest moment. It involves a question immediately interesting to every part of the community; which is no other than this — Whether the public debt, by a provision for it on true principles, shall be rendered a *substitute* for money; or whether, by being left as it is, or by being provided for in such a manner as will wound those principles, and destroy confidence, it shall be suffered to continue, as it is, a pernicious drain of our cash from the channels of productive industry. . . .

Persuaded as the Secretary is, that the proper funding of the present debt, will render it a national blessing: Yet he is so far from acceding to the position, in the latitude in which it is sometimes laid down, that "public debts are public benefits," a position inviting to prodigality, and liable to dangerous abuse — that he ardently wishes to see it incorporated, as a fundamental maxim, in the system of public credit of the United States, that the creation of debt should always be accompanied with the means of extinguishment. This he regards as the true secret for rendering public credit immortal. And he presumes, that it is difficult to conceive a situation, in which there may not be an adherence to the maxim. At least he feels an unfeigned solicitude, that this may be attempted by the United States, and that they may commence their measures for the establishment of credit, with the observance of it.

Questions

1. Why does Alexander Hamilton believe it essential for a nation to have good public credit?
2. What does Hamilton think is required for the United States to have sound public credit?
3. How is the report at once economic and political in scope?

George Washington, Farewell Address (1796)

Foreign aid, especially the direct military aid that resulted from the French Alliance, proved essential to winning American independence. However, the alliance was made with the monarchy *of France. When revolution transformed France into a republic and then plunged it into war, the U.S. government faced a dilemma. Should the United States honor an alliance with a government (or political system, for that matter) that no longer existed?*

The country split over the issue as President Washington and the Federalist-dominated Congress embraced neutrality. In making that decision, Washington revealed his Federalist leaning. Yet his emphasis on keeping America out of harm's way also reflected his own views on foreign policy for the young, still militarily weak nation. In his Farewell Address of 1796, which also included extensive comments on "the baneful effects of the spirit of [political] parties," Washington clearly spelled out his views on foreign policy.

Observe good faith and justice toward all nations. Cultivate peace and harmony with all. Religion and morality enjoin this conduct. And can it be that good policy does not equally enjoin it? It will be worthy of a free, enlightened, and at no distant period a great nation to give to mankind the magnanimous and too novel example of a people always guided by an exalted justice and benevolence. Who can doubt that in the course of time and things the fruits of such a plan would richly repay any temporary advantages which might be lost by a steady adherence to it? . . .

In the execution of such a plan nothing is more essential than that permanent, inveterate antipathies against particular nations and passionate attachments for others should be excluded, and that in place of them just and amicable feelings toward all should be cultivated. The nation which indulges toward another an habitual hatred or an habitual fondness is in some degree a slave. It is a slave to its animosity or to its affection, either of which is sufficient to lead it astray from its duty and its interest. . . .

As avenues to foreign influence in innumerable ways, such attachments are particularly alarming to the truly enlightened and independent patriot. How many opportunities do they afford to tamper with domestic factions, to practice the arts of seduction, to mislead public opinion, to influence or awe the public councils! Such an attachment of a small or weak toward a great and powerful nation dooms the former to be the satellite of the latter. Against the insidious wiles of foreign influence (I conjure you to believe me, fellow-citizens) the jealousy of a free people ought to be *constantly* awake, since history and experience prove that foreign influence is one of the most baneful foes of republican government. But that jealousy, to be useful, must be impartial, else it becomes the instrument of the very influence to be avoided, instead of a defense against it. Excessive partiality for one foreign nation and excessive dislike of another cause those whom they actuate to see danger only on one side, and serve to veil and even second the arts of influence on the other. Real patriots who may resist the intrigues of the favorite are liable to become suspected and odious, while its tools and dupes usurp the applause and confidence of the people to surrender their interests.

The great rule of conduct for us in regard to foreign nations is, in extending our commercial relations to have with them as little *political* connection as possible. So far as we have already formed engagements let them be fulfilled with perfect good faith. Here let us stop.

Europe has a set of primary interests which to us have none or a very remote relation. Hence she must be engaged in frequent controversies, the causes of which are essentially foreign to our concerns. Hence, therefore, it must be unwise in us to implicate ourselves by artificial ties in the ordinary vicissitudes of her politics or the ordinary combinations and collisions of her friendships or enmities.

Our detached and distant situation invites and enables us to pursue a different course. If we remain one people, under an efficient government, the period is not far off when we may defy material injury from external annoyance; when we may take such an attitude as will cause the neutrality we may at any time resolve upon to be scrupulously respected; when belligerent nations, under the impossibility of making acquisitions upon us, will not lightly hazard the giving us provocation; when we may choose peace or war, as our interest, guided by justice, shall counsel.

Why forego the advantages of so peculiar a situation? Why quit our own to stand upon foreign ground? Why, by interweaving our destiny with that of any part of Europe, entangle our peace and prosperity in the toils of European ambition, rivalship, interest, humor, or caprice?

It is our true policy to steer clear of permanent alliances with any portion of the foreign world, so far, I mean, as we are now at liberty to do it; for let me not be understood as capable of patronizing infidelity to existing engagements. I hold the maxim no less applicable to public than to private affairs that honesty is always the best policy. I repeat, therefore, let those engagements be observed in their genuine sense. But in my opinion it is unnecessary and would be unwise to extend them.

Taking care always to keep ourselves by suitable establishments on a respectable defensive posture, we may safely trust to temporary alliances for extraordinary emergencies.

Harmony, liberal intercourse with all nations are recommended by policy, humanity, and interest. But even our commercial policy should hold an equal and impartial hand, neither seeking nor granting exclusive favors or preferences; consulting the natural course of things; diffusing and diversifying by gentle means the streams of commerce, but forcing nothing; establishing with powers so disposed, in order to give trade a stable course, to define the rights of our merchants, and to enable the Government to support them, conventional rules of intercourse, the best that present circumstances and mutual opinion will permit, but temporary and liable to be from time to time abandoned or varied as experience and circumstances shall dictate; constantly keeping in view that it is folly in one nation to look for disinterested favors from another; that it must pay with a portion of its independence for whatever it may accept under that character; that by such acceptance it may place itself in the condition of having given equivalents for nominal favors, and yet of being reproached with ingratitude for not giving more. There can be no greater error than to expect or calculate upon real favors from nation to nation. It is an illusion which experience must cure, which a just pride ought to discard.

In offering to you, my countrymen, these counsels of an old and affectionate friend I dare not hope they will make the strong and lasting impression I could wish — that they will control the usual current of the passions or prevent our nation from running the course which has hitherto marked the destiny of nations. But if I may even flatter myself that they may be productive of some partial benefit, some occasional good — that they may now and then recur to moderate the fury of party spirit, to warn against the mischiefs of foreign intrigue, to guard against the impostures of pretended patriotism — this hope will be a full recompense for the solicitude for your welfare by which they have been dictated.

How far in the discharge of my official duties I have been guided by the principles which have been delineated the public records and other evidences of my conduct must witness to you and to the world. To myself, the assurance of my own conscience is that I have at least believed myself to be guided by them.

In relation to the still subsisting war in Europe my proclamation of the 22d of April, 1793, is the index to my plan. Sanctioned by your approving voice and by that of your representatives in both Houses of Congress, the spirit of that measure has continually governed me, uninfluenced by any attempts to deter or divert me from it.

After deliberate examination, with the aid of the best lights I could obtain, I was well satisfied that our country, under all the circumstances of the case, had a right to take, and was bound in duty and interest to take, a neutral position. Having taken it, I determined as far as should depend upon me to maintain it with moderation, perseverance, and firmness. . . .

The inducements of interest for observing that conduct will best be referred to your own reflections and experience. With me a predominant motive has been to endeavor to gain time to our country to settle and mature its yet recent institutions, and to progress without interruption to that degree of strength and consistency which is necessary to give it, humanly speaking, the command of its own fortunes. . . .

Questions

1. What foreign policy guidelines does President Washington recommend for the United States?
2. Are Washington's reasons for following those guidelines convincing? Why or why not?
3. In what way has Washington's Farewell Address become part of a foreign policy debate that continues to the present?

The Sedition Act (1798)

As the textbook shows (see text p. 197), President Washington was in some measure correct when he warned of "the baneful effects of the spirit of [political] parties." Not least of all was the way that the Federalists responded to their declining popularity in the late 1790s.

In an effort to retain power, leading Federalists trampled on the rights of their political opponents and precipitated a major political crisis. It was evidenced and symbolized by the passage of the Alien and Sedition Acts of 1798. The Sedition Act, reprinted here, provoked a sharp response as a perceived assault on the Bill of Rights.

An Act in addition to the act, entitled "An act for the punishment of certain crimes against the United States."

SEC. 1. *Be it enacted . . . ,* That if any persons shall unlawfully combine or conspire together, with intent to oppose any measure or measures of the government of the United States, which are or shall be directed by proper authority, or to impede the operation of any law of the United States, or to intimidate or prevent any person holding a place or office in or under the government of the United States, from undertaking, performing or executing his trust or duty; and if any person or persons, with intent as aforesaid, shall counsel, advise or attempt to procure any insurrection, riot, unlawful assembly, or combination, whether such conspiracy, threatening, counsel, advice, or attempt shall have the proposed effect or not, he or they shall be deemed guilty of a high misdemeanor, and on conviction, before any court of the United States having jurisdiction thereof, shall be punished by a fine not exceeding five thousand dollars, and by imprisonment during a term not less than six months nor exceeding five years; and further, at the discretion of the court may be holden to find sureties for his good behaviour in such sum, and for such time, as the said court may direct.

Sec. 2. That if any person shall write, print, utter, or publish, or shall cause or procure to be written, printed, uttered or published, or shall knowingly and willingly assist or aid in writing, printing, uttering or publishing any false, scandalous and malicious writing or writings against the government of the United States, or either house of the Congress of the United States, or the President of the United States, with intent to defame the said government, or either house of the said Congress, or the said President or to bring them, or either of them, into contempt or disrepute; or to excite against them, or either or any of them, the hatred of the good people of the United States, or to stir up sedition within the United States, or to excite any unlawful combinations therein, for opposing or resisting any law of the United States, or any act of the President of the United States, done in pursuance of any such law, or of the powers in him vested by the constitution of the United States, or to resist, oppose, or defeat any such law or act, or to aid, encourage or abet any hostile designs of any foreign nation against the United States, their people or government, then such person, being thereof convicted before any court of the United States having jurisdiction thereof, shall be punished by a fine not exceeding two thousand dollars, and by imprisonment not exceeding two years.

Sec. 3. That if any person shall be prosecuted under this act, for the writing or publishing any libel aforesaid, it shall be lawful for the defendant, upon the trial of the cause, to give in evidence in his defence, the truth of the matter contained in the publication charged as a libel. And the jury who shall try the cause, shall have a right to determine the law and the fact, under the direction of the court, as in other cases.

Sec. 4. That this act shall continue to be in force until March 3, 1801, and no longer. . . .

Questions

1. What is the purported legal foundation of the Sedition Act?
2. At what point does it violate the First Amendment?
3. Should a sedition act ever be enacted? Why or why not?

Thomas Jefferson, First Inaugural Address (1801)

The 1800 presidential election was the first one to be marked by especially vicious mudslinging. Despite the political rancor, it was clear that Americans preferred the ideas of Thomas Jefferson and the Republicans to those of the Federalists, who were going into political decline. Ironically, a mix-up by Republicans unexpectedly threw the election into the House of Representatives, where Alexander Hamilton championed his longtime rival, Jefferson (1743–1826), over Aaron Burr.

Hamilton acted in part because he considered Burr to be a scoundrel. However, Hamilton also supported Jefferson in the belief that Jefferson as president would follow a more moderate course than Jefferson as Republican party leader. The first proof of Hamilton's insight came on March 4, 1801, when Jefferson delivered his stunning First Inaugural Address, reprinted here in full.

Friends and Fellow-Citizens.

Called upon to undertake the duties of the first executive office of our country, I avail myself of the presence of that portion of my fellow-citizens which is here assembled to express my grateful thanks for the favor with which they have been pleased to look toward me, to declare a sincere consciousness that the task is above my talents, and that I approach it with those anxious and awful presentiments which the greatness of the charge and the weakness of my powers so justly inspire. A rising nation, spread over a wide and fruitful land, traversing all the seas with the rich productions of their industry, engaged in commerce with nations who feel power and forget right, advancing rapidly to destinies beyond the reach of mortal eye — when I contemplate these transcendent objects, and see the honor, the happiness, and the hopes of this beloved country committed to the issue and the auspices of this day, I shrink from the contemplation, and humble myself before the magnitude of the undertaking. Utterly, indeed, should I despair did not the presence of many whom I here see remind me that in the other high authorities provided by our Constitution I shall find resources of wisdom, of virtue, and of zeal on which to rely under all difficulties. To you, then, gentlemen, who are charged with the sovereign functions of legislation, and to those associated with you, I look with encouragement for that guidance and support which may enable us to steer with safety the vessel in which we are all embarked amidst the conflicting elements of a troubled world.

During the contest of opinion through which we have passed the animation of discussions and of exertions has sometimes worn an aspect which might impose on strangers unused to think freely and to speak and to write what they think; but this being now decided by the voice of the nation, announced according to the rules of the Constitution, all will, of course, arrange themselves under the will of the law, and unite in common efforts for the common good. All, too, will bear in mind this sacred principle, that though the will of the majority is in all cases to prevail, that will to be rightful must be reasonable; that the minority possess their equal rights, which equal law must protect, and to violate would be oppression. Let us, then, fellow-citizens, unite with one heart and one mind. Let us restore to social intercourse that harmony and affection without which liberty and even life itself are but dreary things. And let us reflect that, having banished from our land that religious intolerance under which mankind so long bled and suffered, we have yet gained little if we countenance a political intolerance as despotic, as wicked, and capable of as bitter and bloody persecutions. During the throes and convulsions of the ancient world, during the agonizing spasms of infuriated man, seeking through blood and slaughter his long-lost liberty, it was not wonderful that the agitation of the billows should reach even this distant and peaceful shore; that this should be more felt and feared by some and less by others, and should divide opinions as to measures of safety. But every difference of opinion is not a difference of principle. We have called by different names brethren of the same principle. We are all Republicans, we are all Federalists. If there be any among us who would wish to dissolve this Union or to change its republican form, let them stand undisturbed as monuments of the safety with which error of opinion may be tolerated where reason is left free to combat it. I know, indeed, that some honest men fear that a republican government can not be strong, that this Government is not strong enough; but would the honest patriot, in the full tide of successful experiment, abandon a government which has so far kept us free and firm on the theoretic and visionary fear that this Government, the world's best hope, may by possibility want energy to preserve itself? I trust not. I believe this, on the contrary, the strongest Government on earth. I believe it the only one where every man, at the call of the law, would fly to the standard of the law, and would meet invasions of the public order as his own personal concern. Sometimes it is said that man can not be trusted with the government of himself. Can he, then, be trusted with the government of others? Or have we found angels in the forms of kings to govern him? Let history answer this question.

Let us, then, with courage and confidence pursue our own Federal and Republican principles, our attachment to union and representative government. Kindly separated by nature and a wide ocean from the exterminating havoc of one quarter of the globe; too high-minded to endure the degradations of the others; possessing a chosen country, with room enough for our descendants to the thousandth and thousandth generation; entertaining a due sense of our equal right to the use of our own faculties, to the acquisitions of our own industry, to honor and confidence from our fellow-citizens, resulting not from birth, but from our actions and their sense of them; enlightened by a benign religion, professed, indeed, and practiced in various forms, yet all of them inculcating honesty, truth, temperance, gratitude, and the love of man; acknowledging and adoring an overruling Providence, which by all its dispensations proves that it delights in the happiness of man here and his greater happiness hereafter — with all these blessings, what more is necessary to make us a happy and a prosperous people? Still one thing more, fellow-citizens — a wise and frugal Government, which shall restrain men from injuring one another, shall leave them otherwise free to regulate their own pursuits of industry and improvement, and shall not take from the mouth of labor the bread it has earned. This is the sum of good government, and this is necessary to close the circle of our felicities.

About to enter, fellow-citizens, on the exercise of duties which comprehend everything dear and valuable to you, it is proper you should understand what I deem the essential principles of our Government, and consequently those which ought to shape its Administration. I will compress them within the narrowest compass they will bear, stating the general principle, but not all its limitations. Equal and exact justice to all men, of whatever state or persuasion, religious or political; peace, commerce, and honest friendship with all nations, entangling alliances with none; the support of the State governments in all their rights, as the most competent administrations for our domestic concerns and the surest bulwarks against antirepublican tendencies; the preservation of the General Government in its whole constitutional vigor, as the sheet anchor of our peace at home and safety abroad; a jealous care of the right of election by the people — a mild and safe corrective of abuses which are lopped by the sword of revolution where peaceable remedies are unprovided; absolute acquiescence in the decisions of the majority, the vital principle of republics, from which is no appeal but to force, the vital principle and immediate parent of despotism; a well-disciplined militia, our best reliance in peace and for the first moments of war, till regulars may relieve them; the supremacy of the civil over the military authority; economy in the public expense, that labor may be lightly burthened; the honest payment of our debts and sacred preservation of the public faith; encouragement of agriculture, and of commerce as its handmaid; the diffusion of information and arraignment of all abuses at the bar of the public reason; freedom of religion; freedom of the press, and freedom of person under the protection of the habeas corpus, and trial by juries impartially selected. These principles form the bright constellation which has gone before us and guided our steps through an age of revolution and reformation. The wisdom of our sages and blood of our heroes have been devoted to their attainment. They should be the creed of our political faith, the text of civic instruction, the touchstone by which to try the services of those we trust; and should we wander from them in moments of error or of alarm, let us hasten to retrace our steps and to regain the road which alone leads to peace, liberty, and safety.

I repair, then, fellow-citizens, to the post you have assigned me. With experience enough in subordinate offices to have seen the difficulties of this the greatest of all, I have learnt to expect that it will rarely fall to the lot of imperfect man to retire from this station with the reputation and the favor which bring him into it. Without pretensions to that high confidence you reposed in our first and greatest revolutionary character, whose preeminent services had entitled him to the first place in his country's love and destined for him the fairest page in the volume of faithful history, I ask so much confidence only as may give firmness and effect to the legal administration of your affairs. I shall often go wrong through defect of judgment. When right, I shall often be thought wrong by those whose positions will not command a view of the whole ground. I ask your indulgence for my own errors, which will never be intentional, and your support against the errors of others, who may condemn what they would not if seen in all its parts. The approbation implied by your suffrage is a great consolation to me for the past, and my future solicitude will be to retain the good opinion of those who have bestowed it in advance, to conciliate that of others by doing them all the good in my power, and to be instrumental to the happiness and freedom of all.

Relying, then, on the patronage of your good will, I advance with obedience to the work, ready to retire from it whenever you become sensible how much better choice it is in your power to make. And may that Infinite Power which rules the destinies of the universe lead our councils to what is best, and give them a favorable issue for your peace and prosperity.

Questions

1. What is the significance of Jefferson saying "We are all Republicans, we are all Federalists"?
2. How does Jefferson make known his own political beliefs?
3. Would you consider the ideas expressed as current or outdated? Explain.

Connections Questions

1. How would the supporters of the Virginia Declaration of Rights be expected to react to Alexander Hamilton's *Report on Public Credit*? Why?
2. Is James Madison correct in warning against "faction," as he does in *The Federalist*, No. 10? Why or why not? What other ways might there be to prevent the growth of divisive politics?
3. What earlier documents could Abigail Adams cite in the debate with her husband? What would they show?

CHAPTER 8

Toward a Continental Nation 1790–1820

Thomas Jefferson,
Message to Congress (1803)

Thomas Jefferson, third president of the United States, was one of the lead-ing intellectual figures in the early republic. Jefferson's belief in the United States as a nation of independent yeomen farmers called for a surplus of new lands available for settlement. The president shared the prevailing view that the native Americans constituted a barrier to be removed. In the following message to Congress, Jefferson described the peaceful means by which he hoped to induce the Indians to sell their lands to the United States.

The Indian tribes residing within the limits of the United States have for a considerable time been growing more and more uneasy at the constant diminution of the territory they occupy. . . . and the policy has long been gaining strength with them of refusing absolutely all further sale on any con-dition. . . . In order peaceably to counteract this policy of theirs and to pro-vide an extension of territory which the rapid increase of our numbers will call for, two measures are deemed expedient. First. To encourage them to aban-don hunting, to apply [themselves] to the raising [of] stock, to agriculture, and domestic manufacture, and thereby prove to themselves that less land and labor will maintain them . . . better than in their former mode of living. The extensive forests necessary in the hunting life will then become useless, and they will see advantage in exchanging them for the means of improving their farms and of increasing their domestic comforts. Secondly. To multiply trad-ing houses among them, and place within their reach those things which will contribute more to their domestic comfort than the possession of extensive but uncultivated wilds. . . . In leading them thus to agriculture, to manufac-tures, and civilization; in bringing together their and our sentiments, and in preparing them ultimately to participate in the benefits of our Government, I trust and believe we are acting for their greatest good. . . . In one quarter this is particularly interesting . . . on the Mississippi . . . it is [desirable] to pos-sess a respectable breadth of country . . . so that we may present as firm a front on that as on our eastern border. We possess what is below the Yazoo, and can probably acquire a certain breadth from the Illinois and Wabash to the Ohio; but between the Ohio and Yazoo the country all belongs to the Chickasaws, the most friendly tribe within our limits, but the most decided against the alienation of lands. The portion of their country most important for us is ex-actly that which they do not inhabit. Their settlements are not on the Missis-sippi, but in the interior country. They have lately shown a desire to become agricultural, and this leads to the desire of buying implements and comforts.

In the strengthening and gratifying of these wants I see the only prospect of planting on the Mississippi itself the means of its own safety. Duty has required me to submit these views to the judgment of the Legislature, but as their disclosure might embarrass and defeat their effect, they are committed to the special confidence of the two Houses.

Questions

1. The United States claimed sovereignty over the native American nations but recognized the Indians' ownership of the lands they traditionally occupied. How does Jefferson propose to overcome this problematic situation?
2. Why does Jefferson believe that native Americans would be better off with less land?
3. Was there an alternative policy that Jefferson failed to explore? If so, what was it, and why did it go unutilized?

Noah M. Ludlow, From New York to Kentucky in 1815

Noah M. Ludlow (1795–1886) was born in New York City and took an early interest in the theater. Ludlow made his first stage appearance in Albany in 1813 with a theatrical troupe, and two years later he joined a touring company formed by Samuel Drake, a pioneering theatrical manager in the West. The troupe had ample opportunity to experience the transportation bottlenecks of the era. Ludlow describes his first trip to the West in his memoirs, excerpted here.

With the commencement of the year 1815, Mr. [Samuel] Drake was looking around for some actors and actresses bold and adventurous enough to risk their lives and fortunes in a Western wilderness, as Kentucky was then popularly supposed to be. . . . His course was to travel north-west in the State of New York, until he should reach Canandaigua; then to deflect to the southwest, strike the head waters of the Allegheny river, descend by boat to Pittsburgh, and perform there until the assembling of the State Legislature of Kentucky, early in December. . . .

Sometime about the latter part of July, 1815, our party started from Canandaigua for the head waters of the Allegheny River. Our means of transportation were a road-wagon, drawn by two horses, owned by Mr. Drake, and a light spring-wagon . . . drawn by one horse, and used for the convenience and comfort of his wife . . . the other portions of the company . . . were expected to walk the greater part of the way . . . and in this way we started for Olean, a settlement on the Allegheny . . . about one hundred and fifty miles south-west . . . through what was then almost a wilderness. . . .

Olean, in the summer of 1815, was a wild-looking place . . . Mr. Drake immediately made a trade, disposing of his wagons and horses, and purchasing a flat-bottomed boat, known in those days as an "Ark," or "Broad-horn." It was about twenty-five feet long by fifteen wide, boarded up at the sides, and covered with an elliptical roof about high enough to allow a man of medium stature to stand erect beneath the centre. It was quadrangular, and intended to be a kind of floating house. . . . In one end of this boat were two rooms, partitioned off as bed-rooms, one for Mr. Lewis and wife; the other for the three single young ladies. . . . The men . . . were expected to "rough it," and rough it we did. . . . For awhile . . . the good "Broad-horns" [sic] wended her slow but steady way wherever it pleased the current of old Allegheny to carry her. But the repose . . . was suddenly disturbed by . . . an alarming cry that the boat was going over a waterfall. . . . Looking . . . ahead . . . I saw a "mill-dam" made across the portion of the river we were on . . . five . . . plunged into the river . . . and . . . succeeded in getting the boat safely to shore. . . .

After resting a little, we set to work to retrace the course we had come, until we should reach that point at which . . . the boat had taken the wrong "chute," or fork of the river. This we effected with much labor, by passing a rope to the shore . . . those on shore pulled it along, while the manager, Mr. Drake, kept it from the shore with a large steering-oar; and thus, by . . . this way of "cordelling," practiced on the rivers of the West in those days . . . we . . . got out of our unpleasant situation. . . .

[At Pittsburgh] another "broad-horn" boat had been purchased, larger and more conveniently arranged than our former one . . . and . . . near the middle of November . . . we commenced our voyage down the Ohio. . . .

There was a great sameness in this water journey of about four hundred miles. . . . The point at which Mr. Drake proposed to disembark was known as Limestone and afterwards as Maysville, on the Kentucky side of the river. . . . This point we reached . . . about a week from the time we left Pittsburgh. After landing . . . I was requested by Mr. Drake to go up into the village . . . to procure a large wagon, that might be engaged to transport our trunks . . . to Frankfort . . . less than a hundred miles. . . .

I do not recollect how many days we were journeying to Frankfort, but it was not a disagreeable trip, except from being a very slow method of travelling. We did not make more than from twenty to twenty-five miles each day. . . . We found no "inns," except in one or two villages we passed through; yet we never had any difficulty in finding "houses of entertainment," as they were called, which simply were . . . farmers' houses, who would take you in, and feed you and your horse with such as they had, and only make a trifling charge.

Questions

1. Ludlow's account illustrates the relative ease of river travel downstream and the very opposite for travel upstream. What implications does this have for commerce west of the Appalachian Mountains?
2. Where did the bottlenecks occur in Ludlow's trip? How might they have been alleviated?
3. What dangers and inconveniences does water transportation entail? Why would that be an important political issue?

Journals of the Lewis and Clark Expedition (1805)

Shortly after completing the Louisiana Purchase, President Jefferson commissioned two army captains, William Clark (the younger brother of Revolutionary War hero George Rogers Clark) and Meriwether Lewis (Jefferson's personal secretary), to explore the new American territory. In the spring of 1804 Lewis (1774–1809) and Clark (1770–1838) led an expedition of twenty-five men up the Missouri River to what is today central North Dakota.

In the spring of 1805, they followed the Missouri and Columbia Rivers west to the Pacific. The following spring they returned to their point of departure at St. Louis. Their journals tell of a journey of discoveries as the men encountered new flora, fauna, and a rich variety of native American cultures. In the passages below, Clark and Lewis observe their surroundings as they travel west on the Missouri from the Yellowstone to the Musselshell River.

William Clark, May 1, Wednesday 1805
We set out at sun rise under a stiff Breeze from the East, the morning cool & cloudy. . . . One of the men . . . shot a gull or pleaver [plover], which is about

the size of an Indian hen, with a sharp pointed bill turned up & four inches
long, the head and neck of a light brown, the breast, the under feathers of the
2nd and 3rd joint of the wings, the short feathers of the upper part of the 3rd
joint of the wings, down the back, the back, the rump & tail white. The large
feathers of the 1st joints of the wing, the upper feathers of the 2nd joints of the
wings, on the body on the joints of the wing and the bill is black. The legs long
and of a sky blue. The feet webbed &c. This fowl may be properly styled the
Missouri Pleaver [probably a Hudsonian or marbled godwit in migration and
between its winter and summer plumage]. The wind became very hard and we
put to on the l.[eeward] side, as the wind continued with some degree of violence and the waves too high for the canoes; we were obliged to stay all day.

Meriwether Lewis, Thursday May 2, 1805
The wind continued violent all night nor did it abate much of its violence this
morning, when at daylight it was attended with snow which continued to fall
until about 10 A.M. Being about one inch deep, it formed a singular contrast
with the vegetation which was considerably advanced. Some flowers had put
forth in the plains, and the leaves of the cottonwood were as large as a dollar.
Sent out some hunters who killed two deer, three elk, and several buffalo; on
our way this evening we also shot three beaver along the shore. These animals
in consequence of not being hunted are extremely gentle; where they are
hunted they never leave their lodges in the day. The flesh of the beaver is esteemed a delicacy among us; I think the tail a most delicious morsal; when
boiled it resembles in flavor . . . fresh . . . codfish, and is usually sufficiently
large to afford a plentiful meal for two men. . . . One of the hunters who was
out today found several yards of scarlet cloth which had been suspended on
the bough of a tree near an old indian hunting camp, where it had been left
as a sacrifice to the deity by the indians . . . it being a custom with . . . all the
nations inhabiting the waters of the Missouri so far as they are known to us,
to offer or sacrifice in this manner to the deity whatever they may be possessed of which they think most acceptable to him, and very honestly making
their own feelings the test of those of the deity, [they] offer him the article
which they most prize themselves. This being the most usual method of wor-
shipping the great spirit as they term the deity, is practiced on interesting occasions, or to produce the happy eventuation of the important occurances incident to human nature, such as relief from hunger or malady, protection
from their enemies, or the delivering [to] them into their hands, and with such
as cultivate, to prevent the river's overflowing and destroying their crops &c.
Sacrifices of a similar kind are also made to the deceased by their friends and
relatives. The air was vary piercing this evening. The [water] friezed [sic] on
the oars as they rowed. The wind dying at 5 P.M. we set out.

Questions

1. Are Lewis and Clark describing a "wilderness"? Why or why not?
2. Why do Lewis and Clark describe these particular experiences in such detail?
3. Is Lewis a sympathetic observer of native American life? Why or why not?

William Henry Harrison, Speech to Tecumseh and the Prophet (1811) and Report to the Secretary of War (1814)

William Henry Harrison was elected president of the United States in 1840 largely because of his reputation as an Indian fighter. The nickname "Tippecanoe" celebrated Harrison's victory over the followers of the Shawnee chief Tecumseh (b.1768?) and his brother Tenskwatawa (the Prophet) at the Battle of Tippecanoe on November 7, 1811.

As governor of the Indiana Territory, Harrison (1773–1841) carried out the government policy of divesting native Americans of their land. Tecumseh and Tenskwatawa formed a coalition to resist this policy of piecemeal dispossession. In response, Harrison moved an army of seasoned Indian fighters to Tippecanoe Creek; this was near the hostile Indian encampment called Prophetstown. Convinced by the Prophet that they were invincible, the Indians swept into the American camp in the predawn darkness. But Harrison's men held their ground, formed a defensive line, and soon turned back the Indians with heavy losses.

Tecumseh's forces abandoned Prophetstown and, fighting in small bands, made war on settlers across the Northwest. Tecumseh joined forces with the British during the War of 1812 only to die at the Battle of the Thames on October 5, 1813. In his letter to the secretary of war, Harrison summarizes his success in implementing the government's Indian policy.

Harrison to Tecumseh and the Prophet, June 24, 1811:

Brothers, — Listen to me. I speak to you about matters of importance, both to the white people and yourselves; open your ears, therefore, and attend to what I shall say.

Brothers, this is the third year that all the white people in this country have been alarmed at your proceedings; you threaten us with war, you invite all the tribes in the north and west of you to join against us. . . .

Brothers, our citizens are alarmed, and my warriors are preparing themselves; not to strike you, but to defend themselves and their women and children. You shall not surprise us as you expect to do; you are about to undertake a vary rash act; as a friend, I advise you to consider well of it. . . . Do you really think that the handful of men that you have about you, are able to contend with the Seventeen Fires [the seventeen states then composing the United States], or even that the whole of the tribes united, could contend against the Kentucky Fire alone?

Brothers, I am myself of the long knife fire; as soon as they hear my voice, you will see them pouring forth their swarms of hunting shirt men, as numerous as the musquetoes [sic] on the shores of the Wabash; brothers, take care of their stings.

Harrison to the Secretary of War, March 22, 1814:
I received instruction from President Jefferson, shortly after his first election, to make efforts for extinguishing the Indian claims upon the Ohio, below the mouth of the Kentucky river, and to such other tracts as were necessary to connect and consolidate our settlements. It was at once determined, that the community of interests in the lands among the Indian tribes, which seemed to be recognized by the treaty of Greenville, should be objected to. . . . Care was taken . . . to place the title to such tracts as might be desireable to purchase . . . upon a footing that would facilitate the procuring of them, by getting the tribes who had no claim themselves, and who might probably interfere, to recognize the titles of those who were ascertained to posses [sic] them.

This was particularly the case with regard to the lands watered by the Wabash, which were declared to be the property of the Miamis, with the exception of the tract occupied by the Delawares on White river, which was to be considered the joint property of them and the Miamis. This arrangement was very much disliked by Tecumseh, and the banditti that he had assembled at Tippecanoe. He complained loudly, as well of the sales that had been made, as of the principle of considering a particular tribe as the exclusive proprietors of any part of the country, which he said the Great Spirit had given to all his red children. . . .

The question of the title to the lands south of the Wabash, has been thoroughly examined; every opportunity was afforded to Tecumseh and his party to exhibit their pretensions [land claims], and they were found to rest upon no other basis than that of their being the common property of all the Indians.

Questions

1. Would you consider Harrison's speech to Tecumseh a fair warning? Why or why not?

2. What was at the root of Indian–settler conflict? Could it have been re-solved in any other way? Why or why not?

3. How does Harrison's report demonstrate a clash between cultures? Explain.

Richard Mentor Johnson,
The Benefits of Slavery in Missouri

Richard Mentor Johnson (1780–1850) was born in a frontier settlement on the Ohio River. He studied law at Transylvania College, was admitted to the bar in 1802, and won election to the Kentucky state legislature in 1804. He served in the U.S. House of Representatives as an ardent Jeffersonian from 1807 to 1819.

In 1819 the Kentucky legislature elected Johnson to the U.S. Senate, where he served for the next decade. He warmly supported Andrew Jackson in the presidential election of 1828. Largely as a result of Jackson's support, Johnson was chosen to run as vice-president on the Democratic ticket with Martin Van Buren. Although he never married, Johnson was the father of two daughters born to a slave mistress whom he had inherited from his father.

The question of admitting Missouri as a slave state touched off heated debates leading to the Missouri Compromise of 1820 (see text pp. 220–21). The focal point of the Missouri debates was a proposal for the gradual abolition of slavery in Missouri. In Senator Johnson's opinion, slavery was not an evil but a blessing to the American republic. He puts forth that position in this speech.

. . . Can gentlemen sincerely believe that the cause of humanity will be promoted by still confining this population [i.e., slaves] within such limits, as that their relative numbers will oppose everlasting obstacles to their emancipation? Upon the most extensive principles of philanthropy, I say, let them spread forth with the growing extent of our nation. I am sure I plead the cause of humanity. I advocate the best interests of the sons of bondage, when I entreat you to give them room to be happy; and so disperse them as that, under the auspices of Providence, they may one day enjoy the rights of man, without convulsing the empire or endangering society. . . .

There is no just cause for irritation on this subject. We should suppress our feelings, when they threaten to transport us beyond the bounds of reason. Early habits beget strong prejudices, and under a heavy burden of them we all labor. But it becomes us to bring them to one common altar, and consume them together. Before we compel our brother to pluck the mote from his eye, it will be wise to take the beam from our own. On this occasion I cannot omit to mention my own feelings on a former occurrence. When I first came to Congress, it was with mingled emotions of horror and surprise that I saw citizens from the non-slaveholding States, as they are called — yes, and both branches of our National Legislature — riding in a coach and four, with a white servant seated before, managing the reins, another standing behind the coach, and both of these white servants in livery. Is this, said I to myself, the degraded condition of the citizen, on whose voice the liberties of a nation may depend? I could not reconcile it with my ideas of freedom; because, in the State where I received my first impressions, slaves alone were servile. All white men there are on an equality, and every citizen feels his independence. We have no classes — no patrician or plebeian rank. Honesty and honor form all the distinctions that are felt or known. Whatever may be the condition of a citizen with us, you must treat him as an equal. This I find is not so in every part of the non-slaveholding States, especially in your populous cities, where ranks and distinctions, the precursors of aristocracy, already begin to exist. They whose business it is to perform menial offices in other States, are as servile as our slaves in the West. Where is the great difference betwixt the conditions of him who keeps your stable, who blacks your boots, who holds your stirrups, or mounts behind your coach when you ride, and the slave who obeys the command of his master? There may be a nominal difference; but it would be difficult to describe its reality. In the one case it is called voluntary, because it is imposed by its own necessity, and in the other involuntary, because imposed by the will of another. Whatever difference there may be in the principle, the effects upon society are the same. The condition, in some respects, is in favor of the slave. He is supplied with food and clothing; and in the hour of sickness he finds relief. No anxious cares, in relation to age and infirmity, invade his breast. He fears no duns [demands for payment]: careless of the pressure of the times, he dreads not the coercion of payment, nor feels the cruelty of that code which confines the white servant in prison, because the iron hand of poverty has wrested from him the means of support for his family. Though slavery still must be confessed a bitter draught, yet where the stamp of nature marks the distinction, and when the mind, from early habit, is moulded to the condition, the slave often finds less bitterness in the cup of life than most white servants. What is the condition of many, who are continually saluting our ears with cries of want, even in this city? Men, women, boys, girls, from infancy to old age, craving relief from every passenger. Are they slaves? No. Among the slaves are no beggars; no vagrants; none idle for want of employ, or crying for want of bread. Every condition of life has its evils; and most evils have some palliative; though perhaps none less than those of white menials. Yet, sir, none are more lavish of their censures against slaveholders than those lordlings with livery servants of their own complexion. . . .

I never could stand having white servants dressed in livery. No, sir, when the honest laborer, the mechanic, however poor, or whatever his employment, visits my house, it matters not what company is there, he must sit with me at my board, and receive the same treatment as the most distinguished guest; because in him I recognise a fellow citizen and an equal.

The condition of the slave is but little understood by those who are not the eye-witnesses of his treatment. His sufferings are greatly aggravated in their apprehension. The general character of the slaveholding community can no more be determined, nor should they be any more stigmatized, by a particular instance of cruelty to a slave, than the character of the non-slaveholding community by a particular instance of cruelty in a parent towards his child, a guardian to his ward, or a master to his apprentice. No man among us can be cruel to his slave without incurring the execration of the whole community.

Questions

1. What does Johnson mean when he suggests that the westward extension of slavery might encourage its demise?
2. How is the enslavement of blacks supposed to encourage equality among whites?
3. What kind of rationalization is Johnson making? What issue or argument must he ignore to believe it?

Charles Ball, Life on a South Carolina Cotton and Rice Plantation

Charles Ball (1780–?) was born a slave in eastern Maryland. He worked there as a farmhand and for two years was hired out as a shipyard worker in Washington, D.C. Shortly after marrying and starting a family, Ball was sold to a South Carolina cotton planter. He was then sold to a planter in the Georgia upcountry. Eventually he managed to escape, and he settled near Philadelphia. There he told his story to Isaac Fisher, who later wrote Ball's slave narrative. In this passage, Ball describes aspects of life among a community of slaves in the South Carolina lowlands.

At the time I first went to Carolina, there were a great many African slaves in the country, and they continued to come in for several years afterwards. I became intimately acquainted with some of these men. Many of them believed there were several gods; some of whom were good, and others evil, and they prayed as much to the latter as to the former. I knew several who must have been, from what I have since learned, Mohamedans [Muslims]; though at that time, I had never heard of the religion of Mohamed.

There was one man on this plantation, who prayed five times every day, always turning his face to the east, when in the performance of his devotion.

There is, in general, very little sense of religious obligation, or duty, amongst the slaves on the cotton plantations; and Christianity cannot be, with propriety, called the religion of these people. They are universally subject to the grossest and most abject superstition; and uniformly believe in witchcraft, conjuration [conjuring — summoning the devil or spirits by incantation], and the agency of evil spirits in the affairs of human life. . . .

They have not the slightest religious regard for the Sabbath-day, and their masters make no efforts to impress them with the least respect for this sacred institution. My first Sunday on this plantation was but a prelude to all that followed; and I shall here give an account of it.

At the time I rose . . . a large number of the men, as well as some of the women, had already quitted the quarter, and gone about the business of the day. That is, they had gone to work for wages for themselves — in this manner: our overseer had, about two miles off, a field of near twenty acres, planted in cotton, on his own account. He was the owner of this land; but as he had no slaves, he was obliged to hire people to work it for him, or let it lie waste. . . . About twenty of our people went to work for him today, for which he gave them fifty cents each. . . .

On every plantation, with which I ever had any acquaintance, the people are allowed to make patches, as they are called — that is, gardens, in some remote and unprofitable part of the estate, generally in the woods, in which they plant corn, potatoes, pumpkins, melons, &c. for themselves.

These patches they must cultivate on Sunday, or let them go uncultivated. I think, that on this estate, there were about thirty of these patches. . . .

The vegetables that grew in these patches, were always consumed in the families of the owners [of the patches]; and the money that was earned by hiring out, was spent . . . sometimes for clothes, sometimes for better food . . . and sometimes for rum; but those who drank rum, had to do it by stealth. . . .

As I had nothing to do for myself, I went with Lydia, whose husband was still sick, to help her to work in her patch. . . . She had onions, cabbages, cucumbers, melons, and many other things in her garden.

In the evening, as we returned home, we were joined by the man who prayed five times a day; and at the going down of the sun, he stopped and prayed aloud in our hearing, in a language I did not understand. . . .

I must here observe, that when the slaves go out to work for wages on Sunday, their employers never flog them; and so far as I know never give them abusive language. . . . I worked faithfully, because I knew that if I did not, I could not expect payment; and those who hired me, knew that if I did not work well, they need not employ me.

Questions

1. Why does Ball emphasize the religious state of the slaves?
2. What is the significance of the vegetable patches?
3. Ball implies that men worked better for wages than they did as slaves. Why then didn't slaveholders replace slaves with wage labor?

Connections Questions

1. Noah Ludlow ("From New York to Kentucky") describes the American frontier just as Lewis and Clark ("Journals") do. Why do their viewpoints seem to differ?
2. Are Thomas Jefferson ("Message to Congress") and Richard Mentor Johnson ("The Benefits of Slavery") offering variations on the same argument? Why or why not?
3. How do Richard Mentor Johnson's remarks compare to the sentiments expressed in the South Carolina legislation of 1712 (Chapter 3, "An Act for the Better Order and Government of Negroes and Slaves") and the Mennonite statement of 1688 (Chapter 3, "Early Protests against Slavery")? Explain the differences.

CHAPTER 9

Toward a Capitalist Protestant Republic 1790–1820

Tench Coxe, "A Statement of the Arts and Manufactures of the United States of America, for the Year 1810"

Tench Coxe was a native of Philadelphia who held a number of minor government offices during the presidencies of George Washington and Thomas Jefferson. But Coxe's greatest influence was as a writer on economics.

Coxe (1755–1824) emphasized what he saw as a harmony of interests between a small but growing manufacturing sector and the dominant agricultural sector. He advocated a modest tariff on imported manufactures. Coxe also was one of the first observers to see the full economic implications of the cotton gin and increased cultivation of cotton in the South. In a report drafted for Albert Gallatin, Jefferson's secretary of the Treasury, Coxe noted the emergence of a cotton textile industry in the Northeast and tied its growth to the cultivation of cotton on southern plantations.

It is a fact of great importance . . . on the subject of the relation of manufactures to the landed interest, that none of the productions of the earth, whether of *natural growth* or *the fruits of cultivation,* in the middle, northern and eastern states, which can be considered as "raw materials," are now exported in an *unmanufactured* condition to foreign markets. . . .

Until the late revolution in the cultivation of cotton, by which it was converted, through the strenuous excitements of the friends of manufactures, from a petty object in little fields and gardens, into an article of extensive cultivation among the planters and farmers, there was no redundant [surplus] raw materials for the manufacture of cloths and stuffs, for apparel and furniture, in the United States. There is at this time no other redundant raw material.

The green seed cotton was the best adapted to the general quality and situation, and to the climate of the southern states. But its cultivation, though perfectly pleasant and easy, was very much restrained by the extraordinary difficulty of separating it from the seeds. This operation required so much manual industry, as greatly to impede the manufacture, and of course, for the time, to prevent an extensive cultivation. In the year 1793 *the invaluable . . . gin* was invented by a citizen of the United States [in a note Coxe identified "Mr. Eli Whitney, of Connecticut"], and was so improved and perfected, as to render it easy, it is said to separate the seeds from one hundred million of pounds weight of cotton wool by the employment of three or four hundred persons, although it is alleged that it would require three hundred thousand persons to effect the same by hand. . . . By employing this machinery, every vicinity can easily and expeditiously prepare its cotton for the manufacturing cards . . . to any extent, that the world could require, were it to clothe itself entirely in cotton manufactures. Thus has been added, by our own invention, to the machinery *to facilitate the manufacture of a staple production of our soil,* a single improvement movable by water, steam, cattle or hand, which has set loose these immense powers of agriculture, *to produce cotton wool.* . . .

The water spinners of cotton, in one of the states, have represented . . . that they can make eighty-two pounds and one half of yarn by each spindle in every year. But the owners of other spinning mills deem it unsafe to calculate upon more than fifty-two pounds of yarn per annum for each spindle. . . . At the lowest of the rates, the United States, had they 1,160,000 spindles, could work up into yarn the sixty-four millions of pounds weight of cotton, which are the maximum of our exportation, in a single year. . . . Sixty-four millions of pounds weight of cotton . . . would produce about 50,000,000 pounds of cotton yarn, and with the labor . . . of about 58,000 persons . . . one eighth part ought to be adult males. The remaining seven eighths, might be women and children. This employment of less than *an hundredth part of* our white population of 1810 would be no inconvenience to agriculture or commerce. . . . If the weaving of this be executed, as may be done with perfect ease, by the employment of 100,000 women (less than one sixth of our adult females) with *the fly shuttle,* during *one half* of each working day in the year, the quantity of cloth by the Rhode Island rule of four yards for every pound, would amount to about 200,000,000 of yards. This quantity of cotton cloth, at one third of a dollar per yard, would be worth about 67,000,000 dollars.

There is yet another operation, which can be effected by labor-saving means, and by a process superceding the labor of many hands. Machinery is now in actual operation in the United States, for printing cotton and linen cloths, by engraving rollers of copper, moved by water. Ten thousand yards have been printed, with ease in a single day, by one man and two boys, with these rollers. . . . Similar means are in constant use for staining and dying cotton and linen cloths of one colour, in the same expeditious manner, so as to make them fit for a greater variety of apparel and furniture. Were these operations to be performed, upon the whole quantity of cotton goods estimated in this statement, they would add seven or eight millions to their value, and would require but 50 or 60,000 men and children. . . . The total addition to the original value of our cotton crop alone would be at a rate, far exceeding the value of our exports of American growth. . . . A quantity of cotton wool equal to all that is now produced by the civilized and uncivilized nations of the world, could be raised on a very small portion of our southern soil.

Such are the benefits, which agriculture and the country at large may derive from the manufacture of *our only redundant raw material.* The states of Rhode Island and Massachusetts have expelled all doubts about the practicability of the cotton operations. With the smallest territory in the United

States, Rhode Island has already attained and introduced into her vicinity a cotton branch of our manufactures as valuable, as the cotton branch of any country in Europe was, at the time of the formation of our present constitution.

Questions

1. Coxe wanted workers in the United States to spin, weave, and print the cotton they cultivated rather than export it raw. Why?
2. What social and economic factors does Coxe ignore in his report?
3. What does this report suggest about the effect of inventions on a society? Can those effects be controlled? Why or why not?

Martin Van Buren, Against Unrestricted Male Suffrage (1821)

Martin Van Buren (1782–1862) was born to a family of Dutch descent in upstate New York. Van Buren became the leader of a powerful Jeffersonian organization known as the Albany Regency. Van Buren played a leading role in the convention that redrafted the New York constitution in 1821. The convention embraced the principle of universal suffrage for white men while increasing the property qualifications for black men. Van Buren initially favored maintaining a minimal property qualification. He suggested in the following remarks that unrestricted manhood suffrage threatened to sweep aside distinctions of race as well as class.

Mr. Van Buren . . . observed, that it was evident, and indeed some gentlemen did not seem disposed to disguise it, that the amendment proposed . . . contemplated nothing short of universal suffrage. Mr. V. B. did not believe that there were twenty members . . . who, were the bare naked question of universal suffrage put to them, would vote in its favor; and he was very sure that its adoption was not expected, and would not meet the views of their constituents. . . .

One word on the main question. . . . We had already reached the verge of universal suffrage. There was but one step beyond. And are gentlemen prepared to take that step? We were cheapening this invaluable right. He was disposed to go as far as any man in the extension of rational liberty; but he could not consent to undervalue this precious privilege, so far as to confer it with an undiscriminating hand upon every one, black or white, who would be kind enough to condescend to accept it. . . .

Mr. Van Buren said . . . he felt it a duty to make a brief explanation of the motives which governed him. The qualifications reported [for consideration] . . . were of three kinds, viz: the payment of a money tax — the performance of military duty, and working on the highway. The two former had met with his decided approbation; to the latter, he wished to add the additional qualification, that the elector [voter] should, if he paid no tax, performed no military duty, but offered his vote on the sole ground that he had labored on the highways, also be a *house-holder*. . . . The question then recurred [of] . . . abandoning all qualifications, and throwing open the ballot-boxes to every body — demolishing at one blow, the distinctive character of an elector, the proudest and most invaluable attribute of freemen[.]

Mr. Van Buren said, he had, . . . this day hinted at the numerous objections which he had . . . in regard to the right of suffrage: objections which he intended to make . . . to convince every member . . . of the dangerous and alarming tendency of that precipitate and unexpected prostration of all qualifications. At this moment, he would only say, that among the evils which would flow from a wholly unrestricted suffrage, the following would be the most injurious, viz. . . . That the character of the increased number of votes would be such as would render . . . elections rather a curse than a blessing; which would drive from the polls all sober minded people. . . .

Questions

1. Is Van Buren arguing for meritocracy over democracy? Why or why not?
2. Why does he fear expanding the electorate?
3. What does this document indicate about the way rights are extended in American society? Should the process be different? Why or why not? If so, how?

Lydia Maria Child,
The Mother's Book (1831)

Lydia Maria Child (1802–1880) was born in Medford, Massachusetts, and married a prominent Boston lawyer. Child was best known as a leading abolitionist, but she also enjoyed a successful career as a writer of fiction, juvenile literature, and works on domestic economy. Her most widely read work was The Mother's Book, *which explained to women in middle-class households how the mother's role in child rearing had assumed vast new meaning and significance.*

In Child's view, an internalized sense of self-restraint represented the central object of good parenting — children were not to be whipped into obedience but instructed in a manner that encouraged them to want to obey. In this passage, Child explores the means by which such a moral education could be accomplished.

I once saw a mother laugh very heartily at the distressed face of a kitten, which a child of two years old was pulling backward by the tail. At last, the kitten, in self-defense, turned and scratched the boy. He screamed, and his mother ran to him, kissed the wound, and beat the poor kitten, saying all the time, "Naughty kitten, to scratch John!" . . .

This little incident, trifling as it seems, no doubt had important effects on the character of the child. . . .

In the first place, the child was encouraged in cruelty, by seeing that it gave his mother amusement. . . .

In the next place, the kitten was struck for defending herself; this was injustice to the injured animal, and a lesson of tyranny to the boy. In the third place, striking the kitten because she had scratched him, was teaching him retaliation . . . the influence upon him is, that it is right to injure when we are injured. . . .

The mind of a child is not like that of a grown person . . . it is a vessel empty and pure — always ready to receive, and always receiving.

Every look, every movement, every expression, does something toward forming the character of the little heir to immortal life. . . .

The rule, then, for developing good affections in a child is, that he never be allowed to see or feel the influence of bad passions, even in the most trifling things; and in order to effect this, you must drive evil passions from your own heart. Nothing can be real that has not its home *within* us. The only sure way, as well as the easiest, to *appear* good, is to *be* good.

It is not possible to indulge anger, or any other wrong feeling, and conceal it entirely. If not expressed in words, a child *feels* the baneful influence. Evil enters into his soul, as the imperceptible atmosphere he breathes enters into his lungs: and the beautiful little image of God is removed farther and farther from his home in heaven.

Questions

1. What is Child's purpose in telling the story about the kitten?
2. Why would readers reject traditional notions of parenting in favor of Child's?
3. How does Child mix traditional and modern ideas in her argument?

Mercy Otis Warren, On the Writing of American History (1805)

Mercy Otis Warren (1728–1814) lived most of her life in Plymouth, Mass-achusetts. Through her brother (James Otis) and husband (James Warren), she knew many leaders of the American Revolution. Warren assumed the role of poet and historian of the Patriot cause. Her History of the Rise, Progress, and Termination of the American Revolution *appeared in three volumes in 1805.*

John Adams did not like it. He thought Warren downplayed his role in events, and the two engaged in a lengthy correspondence about the work. After five years of private arguing they reestablished a public cordiality, al-though Adams confided to a friend, "History is not the Province of the Ladies." Warren publicly confronts this male sense of propriety in the introduction to her History.

At a period when every manly arm was occupied, and every trait of talent or activity engaged, either in the cabinet or the field, apprehensive, that amidst the sudden convulsions, crowded scenes, and rapid changes, that flowed in quick succession, many circumstances might escape the more busy and active members of society [i.e., men], I have been induced to improve the leisure Providence had lent, to record as they passed, in the following pages, the new and unexperienced events exhibited in a land previously blessed with peace, liberty, simplicity, and virtue. . . .

Connected by nature, friendship, and every social tie, with many of the first patriots, and most influential characters on the continent; in the habits of confidential and epistolary intercourse with several gentlemen employed abroad in the most distinguished stations, and with others since elevated to the highest grades of rank and distinction, I had the best means of information, through a long period that the colonies were in suspense, waiting the operation of foreign courts, and the success of their own enterprising spirit.

The solemnity that covered every countenance, when contemplating the sword uplifted, and the horrors of civil war rushing to habitations not inured to scenes of rapine and misery; even to the quiet cottage, where only concord and affection had reigned; stimulated to observation a mind that had not yielded to the assertion, that all political attentions lay out of the road of female life.

It is true there are certain appropriate duties assigned to each sex; and doubtless it is the more peculiar province of masculine strength, not only to repel the bold invader of the rights of his country and of mankind, but in the nervous style of manly eloquence, to describe the blood-stained field, and relate the story of slaughtered armies.

Sensible of this, the trembling heart has recoiled at the magnitude of the undertaking, and the hand often shrunk back from the task; yet, recollecting that every domestic enjoyment depends on the unimpaired possession of civil and religious liberty, that a concern for the welfare of society ought equally to flow in every human breast, the work was not relinquished. The most interesting circumstances were collected, active characters portrayed, the principles of the times developed, and the changes marked; nor need it cause a blush to acknowledge, a detail was preserved with a view of transmitting it to the rising youth of my country, some of them in infancy, others in the European world, while the most interesting events lowered over their native land. . . .

The state of the public mind, appears at present to be prepared to weigh these reflections with solemnity, and to receive with pleasure an effort to trace the origin of the American revolution, to review the characters that effected it, and to justify the principles of the defection and final separation from the parent state. With an expanded heart, beating with high hopes of the continued freedom and prosperity of America, the writer indulges a modest expectation, that the following pages will be perused with kindness and candor: this she claims, both in consideration of her sex, the uprightness of her intentions, and the fervency of her wishes for the happiness of all the human race.

Questions

1. What different perspectives might Mercy Otis Warren bring to her project as a historian? Why would they matter in ways John Adams might not recognize?

2. Is the introduction excerpted here more a discussion about history or a manifesto? Explain.

3. What does the publication of Warren's work imply about American society in 1805?

Ezra Stiles Ely, *The Duty of Christian Freemen to Elect Christian Rulers* (1828)

As a Presbyterian clergyman in Philadelphia, Ezra Stiles Ely (1786–1861) strongly supported the Sabbatarian reforms of the Second Great Awakening, which urged Americans to oppose all secular activities on Sunday. When the Pennsylvania state senate refused to grant an act of incorporation to the Sabbatarian movement, Ely published extracts from a sermon he had delivered on the previous Fourth of July calling on Christians to unite and elect devout Christians to public office.

God, my hearers, requires a Christian faith, a Christian profession, and a Christian practice of all our public men; and we as Christian citizens ought, by the publication of our opinions, to require the same.

. . . Since it is the duty of all our rulers to serve the Lord and kiss the Son of God, it must be most manifestly the duty of all our Christian fellow-citizens to honour the Lord Jesus Christ and promote christianity by electing and supporting as public officers the friends of our blessed Saviour. Let it only be granted, that Christians have the same rights and privileges in exercising the elective franchise, which are here accorded to Jews and Infidels, and we ask no other evidence to show, that those who prefer a Christian ruler, may unite in supporting him, in preference to any one of a different character. It shall cheerfully be granted, that every citizen is eligible to every office, whatever may be his religious opinions and moral character; and that every one may constitutionally support any person whom he may *choose;* but it will not hence follow, that he is without accountability to his Divine Master for his choice; or that he may lay aside all his Christian principles and feelings when he selects his ticket and presents it at the polls. "In *all* thy ways acknowledge him," is a maxim which should dwell in a Christian's mind on the day of a public election as much as on the Sabbath; and which should govern him when conspiring with others to honour Christ, either at the Lord's table, or in the election of a Chief Magistrate. In elucidating the duty of private Christians in relation to the choice of their civil rulers, it seems to me necessary to remark,

That every Christian who has the right and the opportunity of exercising the elective franchise ought to do it. Many pious people feel so much disgust at the manner in which elections are conducted, from the first nomination to the closing of the polls, that they relinquish their right of voting for years together. But if all *pious* people were to conduct thus, then our rulers would be wholly elected by the *impious.* If all *good men* are to absent themselves from elections, then the *bad* will have the entire transaction of our public business. . . .

I propose, fellow-citizens, a new sort of union, or, if you please, a *Christian party in politics,* which I am exceedingly desirous all good men in our country should join: not by *subscribing a constitution* and the formation of a new society, to be added to the scores which now exist; but by adopting, avowing, and determining to act upon, truly religious principles in all civil matters. I am aware that the true Christians of our country are divided into many different denominations; who have, alas! too many points of jealousy and collision; still, a union to a very great extent, and for the most valuable purposes is not impracticable. For,

All Christians, of all denominations, may, and ought to, agree in determining, that they will never wittingly support for any public office, any person whom they know or believe to sustain, at the time of his proposed election, a bad moral character. In this, thousands of moralists, who profess no experimental acquaintance with Christianity, might unite and co-operate with *our Christian party.* And surely, it is not impossible, nor unreasonable for all classes of Christians to say within themselves, no man that we have reason to think is a liar, thief, gambler, murderer, debauchee, spendthrift, or openly immoral person in any way, shall have our support at any election. REFORMATION should not only be allowed, but encouraged; for it would be requiring too much to insist upon it, that a candidate for office *shall always have sustained an unblemished moral character,* and it would be unchristian not to forgive and support one who has proved his repentance by recantation and a considerable course of new obedience.

Some of the best men were once vile; but they have been washed from their sins. Present good moral character should be considered as essential to every candidate for the post of honour. In this affair I know we are very much dependent on testimony, and that we may be deceived; especially in those controverted elections in which all manner of falsehoods are invented and vended, wholesale and retail, against some of the most distinguished men of our country: but after all, we must exercise our candour and best discretion, as we do in other matters of belief. We must weigh evidence, and depend most on those who appear the most competent and credible witnesses. It will be natural for us to believe a man's neighbours and acquaintances in preference to strangers. When we have employed the lights afforded us for the illumination of our minds, we shall feel peace of conscience, if we withhold our vote from every one whom we believe to be an immoral man.

Come then, fellow Christians, and friends of good morals in society, let us determine thus far to unite; for thus far we may, and ought to, and shall unite, if we duly weigh the importance of a good moral character in a ruler. Let no love of *the integrity of a party* prevent you from striking out the name of every dishonest and base man from your ticket. You have a right to choose, and you glory in your freedom: make then your own election: and when all good *men* act on this principle it will not be a vain thing. Candidates then, must be moral men, or seem to be, or they will not secure an election. . . .

All who profess to be Christians of any denomination ought to agree that they will support no man as a candidate for any office, who is not professedly friendly to Christianity, and a believer in divine Revelation. We do not say that true or even pretended Christianity shall be made a constitutional test of admission to office; but we do affirm that Christians may in their elections lawfully prefer the avowed friends of the Christian religion to Turks, Jews, and Infidels. . . . While every religious system is tolerated in our country, and no one is established by law, it is still possible for me to think, that the friend of Christianity will make a much better governor of this commonwealth or President of the United States, than the advocate of Theism or Polytheism. . . . If three or four of the most numerous denominations of Christians in the United States, the Presbyterians, the Baptists, the Methodists and Congregationalists for instance, should act upon this principle, our country would never be dishonoured with an *avowed infidel* in her national cabinet or capitol. . . . Let a man be of good moral character, and let him profess to believe in and advocate the Christian religion, and we can all support him. At one time he will be a Baptist, at another an Episcopalian, at another a Methodist, at another a Presbyterian of the American, Scotch, Irish, Dutch, or German stamp, and always a friend to our common Christianity. . . .

Let us elect men who dare to acknowledge the Lord Jesus Christ for their Lord in their public documents. Which of our Presidents has ever done this? It would pick no infidel's pocket, and break no Jew's neck, if our President should be so singular as to let it be known, that he is a *Christian* by his Messages, and an advocate for the Deity of Christ by his personal preference. . . .

We are a Christian nation: we have a right to demand that all our rulers in their conduct shall conform to Christian morality; and if they do not, it is the duty and privilege of Christian freemen to make a new and a better election.

May the Lord Jesus Christ for ever reign in and over these United States, and call them peculiarly his own. *Amen.*

Questions

1. How does Ely define Christianity?
2. What are the dangers inherent in this kind of proposal?

3. Are Ely's ideas based on the American experience as it occurred from colonization through the 1820s? Why or why not?

Benjamin Rush, *Essays Literary, Moral, and Philosophical* (1798)

Benjamin Rush (1745–1813) studied medicine in Philadelphia and at the University of Edinburgh. He returned to Philadelphia in 1769 to practice medicine and promote American republican values. For Rush, republicanism implied a host of social and moral reforms as Americans distinguished their society from that of monarchical Great Britain. Here he advocates improved education for young women to prepare them to function in the role of republican mothers (see text pp. 248–49). Rush addressed his remarks on women's education to "The Visitors of the Young Ladies' Academy in Philadelphia, 28th July 1787."

The first remark that I shall make upon this subject, is, that female education should be accommodated to the state of society, manners, and government of the country, in which it is conducted.

This remark leads me at once to add, that the education of young ladies, in this country, should be conducted upon principles very different from what it is in Great Britain, and in some respects, different from what it was when we were part of a monarchical empire.

There are several circumstances in the situation, employments, and duties of women in America, which require a peculiar mode of education. . . .

The equal share that every citizen has in the liberty, and the possible share he may have in the government of our country, make it necessary that our ladies should be qualified to a certain degree by a peculiar and suitable education, to concur in instructing their sons in the principles of liberty and government. . . .

Vocal music should never be neglected, in the education of a young lady, in this country. Besides preparing her to join in that part of public worship which consists in psalmody, it will enable her to soothe the cares of domestic life. The distress and vexation of a husband — the noise of a nursery, and, even, the sorrows that will sometimes intrude into her own bosom, may all be relieved by a song, where sound and sentiment unite to act upon the mind. . . .

The attention of our young ladies should be directed, as soon as they are prepared for it, to the reading of history — travels — poetry — and moral essays. These studies are accommodated, in a peculiar manner, to the present state of society in America, and when a relish is excited for them, in early life, they subdue that passion for reading novels, which so generally prevails among the fair sex. . . . As yet the intrigues of a British novel, are . . . foreign to our manners. . . . Let it not be said, that the tales of distress, which fill modern novels, have a tendency to soften the female heart into acts of humanity. The fact is the reverse of this. The abortive sympathy which is excited by the recital of imaginary distress, blunts the heart to that which is real; and, hence, we sometimes see instances of young ladies, who weep away a whole forenoon over the criminal sorrows of a fictitious Charlotte . . . turning with disdain at three o'clock from the sight of a beggar, who solicits in feeble accents or signs, a small portion only of the crumbs which fall from their fathers' tables. . . .

It should not surprize [*sic*] us that British customs, with respect to female education have been transplanted into our American schools and families. . . . It is high time to awake from this servility — to study our own character — to examine the age of our country — and to adopt manners in every thing, that shall be accommodated to our state of society, and to the forms of our government. In particular it is incumbent upon us to make ornamental accomplishments yield to principles and knowledge, in the education of our women. . . . The influence of female education would be still more extensive and useful in domestic life. The obligations of gentlemen to qualify themselves by knowledge and industry to discharge the duties of benevolence, would be encreased [*sic*] by marriage; and the patriot — the hero — and the legislator, would find the sweetest regard of their toils, in the approbation and applause of their wives. Children would discover the marks of maternal prudence and wisdom in every station of life; for it has been remarked that there have been few great or good men who have not been blessed with wise and prudent mothers. . . . I know that the elevation of the female mind, by means of moral, physical and religious truth, is considered by some men as unfriendly to the domestic character of a woman. But this is a prejudice of little minds, and springs from the same spirit which opposes the general diffusion of knowledge among the citizens of our republic. If men believe that ignorance is favourable to the government of the female sex, they are certainly deceived; for a weak and ignorant woman will always be governed with the greatest difficulty. . . . It will be in our power, LADIES, to correct the mistakes and practice of our sex upon these subjects, by demonstrating, that the female temper can only be governed by reason, and that the cultivation of reason in women, is alike friendly to the order of nature, and to private as well as public happiness.

Questions

1. What areas does Rush urge American women to study? Why?
2. Where in these remarks does Rush show his antagonism toward the British?
3. What benefits does he believe will come from educating American women?

Connections Questions

1. How do Martin Van Buren's views of the electorate ("Against Unrestricted Male Suffrage") compare to those of James Madison (Chapter 7, *The Federalist*, No. 10")?

2. How might Benjamin Rush (*"Essays Literary, Moral, and Philosophical"*) critique Van Buren?

3. Who seems to have a more truly republican view of women — Benjamin Rush or Mercy Otis Warren ("On the Writing of American History")? Why?

CHAPTER 10

The Economic Revolution 1820–1840

Jacob Pusey, A Textile Manufacturer
Discusses His Enterprise (1832)

In 1832 Secretary of the Treasury Louis McLane responded to a congressional resolution by asking manufacturers a series of questions about their business. The purpose of the inquiry was to determine their attitudes toward the protective tariff (see text p. 261). Jacob Pusey owned and operated a cotton textile mill in Delaware. His answers give an indication of the precariousness of the American textile industry. The new law enacted in July 1832 responded to Pusey's concerns and those of other manufacturers by retaining a 50 percent tariff on imported cotton cloth.

QUESTIONS.

ANSWERS.

1. State and county in which the manufactory is situated?

2. Kind or description of the manufactory; and whether water, steam, or other power?

3. When established; and whether a joint stock concern?

4. Capital invested in ground and buildings, and water power, and in machinery?

5. Average amount in materials, and in cash for the purchase of materials and payment of wages?

6. Annual rate of profit on the capital invested since the establishment of the manufactory; distinguishing between the rate of profit upon that portion of the capital which is borrowed, after providing for the interest upon it, and the rate of profit upon that portion which is not borrowed?

7. Cause of the increase, (or decrease, as the case may be,) of profit?

1. Delaware State, Newcastle county.

2. Cotton spinning, by water power.

3. In the year 1814; private property.

4. $30,000 [$423,000 in 1990 dollars].

5. Variable. When in full operation about $10,000 must be afloat in materials and manufactures on hand, with provision for payment of wages.

6. The first seven years sunk all the capital invested, and the last ten years have recovered about two-thirds of it; though some of the last ten were years of loss: my books will not distinguish between the two kinds of capital.

7. Frequently by competition in the home market the profits are reduced to cost and charges;

QUESTIONS.

ANSWERS.

sometimes (when the business would not have been affected by home competition,) the profits are reduced to nothing, by overimportation of other descriptions of goods causing such a press for money in seaports as to put down the price of yarn when the stock in market was not greater than ordinary; and vice versa for increased profits.

8. Rates of profit on capital otherwise employed in the same State and county?

8. Not known to the writer.

9. Amount of articles annually manufactured since the establishment of the manufactory? Description, quality, and value of each kind?

9. From 70,000 to 100,000 lbs. cotton yarn per annum; the quantity varying in the year according to the demand in some measure. It is difficult to ascertain the value, as the price has varied since the commencement from sixty-four cents in 1814, to eighteen cents per lb. in 1830.

10. Quantity and value of different kinds of raw materials used, distinguishing between foreign products and domestic products?

10. 350 bales of cotton, valued for 1831, at $10,500; all the produce of the United States.

11. Cost in the United States of similar articles of manufacture imported from abroad, and from what countries?

11. Very little, if any; cotton yarn is imported of the degree of coarseness which is manufactured at this mill.

12. Number of men, women, and children employed, and average wages of each class?

12. 6 men, average $6 each per week; 12 women, average $2 each per week; 25 children, average $1.25 per week.

13. How many hours a day employed; and what portion of the year?

13. 11 hours per day, exclusive of meals, and about 50 weeks in the year.

14. Rate of wages of similar classes otherwise employed in the same State and county, in other States, and in foreign countries?

14. Not known to the writer.

QUESTIONS.	ANSWERS.

QUESTIONS.

15. Number of horses or other animals employed?
16. Whether the manufactures find a market at the manufactory? If not, how far they are sent to a market?
17. Whether foreign articles of the like kinds enter into competition with them at such place of sale; and to what extent?
18. Where are the manufactures consumed?
19. Whether any of the manufactures are exported to foreign countries? and if so, where?
20. Whether the manufacture is sold by the manufacturer for cash? and if on credit, at what credit? if bartered, for what?
21. Whether the cost of the manufactured article (to the manufacturer) has increased or decreased; and how much in each year, from the establishment of the manufactory; and whether the increase has been in the materials or the labor, and at what rate?
22. The prices at which the manufactures have been sold by the manufacturer since the establishment?

23. What rate of duty [i.e., tariff] is necessary to enable the manufacturer to enter into competition in the home market with similar articles imported?
24. What has been the rate of your profits, annually, for the last three years? . . .

ANSWERS.

15. Seven.
16. A small portion sold at the factory; the remainder sent 40 miles by land and water conveyance.
17. No foreign article of like kind is imported that I know of in latter years; domestic competition had settled that in the reduced price.
18. In Pennsylvania and the southern and western States.
19. None of this kind exported, known to the writer, until woven.

20. Much the largest part is sold on a credit, generally 6 months, after having lain in store sometimes three or four months.
21. The cost has decreased both in the material and labor; rather more in the material; have not sufficient data to answer more particularly; the labor has been rather higher since 1824; material has fluctuated, having been sold some years at 10 to 15 cents, and others at 25 to 30 cents.
22. In 1814 sixty-four cents per lb.; gradually declining till 1820, it was twenty-eight cents; then advancing till 1822, it was 34 or 35 cents; then gradually declining till 1831, it was 18 cents, (except excited prices in 1825, a few months.)
23. Not known.

24. Less than four per cent, after providing for necessary proportion of repairs.

QUESTIONS.

25. What portion of the cost of your manufactures consists of the price of the raw material, what portion of the wages of labor, and what portion of the profits of capital?

26. What amount of the agricultural productions of the country is consumed in your establishment, and what amount of other domestic productions?

27. What quantity or amount of manufactures, such as you make, are produced in the United States; and what amount in your own State?

28. If the duty upon the foreign manufacture of the kind of goods which you make were reduced to 12½ per cent, with a corresponding reduction on all the imports, would it cause you to abandon your business, or would you manufacture at reduced prices?

29. If it would cause you to abandon your business, in what way would you employ your capital?

30. Is there any pursuit in which you could engage, from which you

ANSWERS.

25. About ½ for raw material; ¼ for labor in the factory; 1–20, or sometimes 1–15, might be profit; the balance is made up by contingent expenses, wastage, etc., etc.

26. About $2,000 in value of agricultural and vegetable productions; $1,000 in domestic dry goods and groceries.

27. No data to answer from as respects the United States; upwards of 20,000 lbs. of cotton yarn are produced in this county in one week; (no other county in this State manufactures cotton).

28. There can be no question but a *present* abandonment of business would be the consequence, as manufacturing at reduced prices would soon destroy the capital. All who could hold their property a few years would do an excellent business under such prices, both for raw material and manufactured goods, *as British monopoly would then dictate,* taken in connexion with the then low prices for bread, and meat, and labor.

29. Under such circumstances, I should have no capital, as purchasers for such property could not be found at any price; but, admitting a very small amount could be realized, agriculture or merchandizing would be the next business, in order to get bread, though both branches are well filled.

30. Certain loss would result, and total ruin would follow such an

QUESTIONS.	ANSWERS.
could derive greater profits, even after a reduction of the import duties to 12½ per cent?	import duty; and twenty-five cents per day for my manual labor would be better than that; the effect (of such a change in the duties) on agriculture or other business might be to deter a man from engaging in them without the necessary experience, which he could not have if his time had been spent in manufacturing.

Newcastle, March 10th, 1832.
JACOB PUSEY, Cotton Spinner

Questions

1. Why are the questions and answers so precise?
2. What is Jacob Pusey's view of the protective tariff?
3. According to Pusey, what would be the ripple effects of a low tariff?

A Mill Worker Describes
Her Work and Life (1844)

The majority of workers in the early years of the textile industry were young women from New England farm families (see text pp. 262–63). Their experience differed greatly from that of workers in the post–Civil War era; antebellum employers offered housing and education as well as jobs. In Lowell, Massachusetts, the women mill hands even published their own poetry and other compositions in The Lowell Offering. *The following letters, written by a worker identified only as "Susan," were published in 1844.*

Dear Mary:

In my last I told you I would write again, and say more of my life here; and this I will now attempt to do.

I went into the mill to work a few days after I wrote to you. It looked very pleasant at first, the rooms were so light, spacious, and clean, the girls so pretty and neatly dressed, and the machinery so brightly polished or nicely painted. The plants in the windows, or on the overseer's bench or desk, gave a pleasant aspect to things. You will wish to know what work I am doing. I will tell you of the different kinds of work.

There is, first, the carding-room, where the cotton flies most, and the girls get the dirtiest. But this is easy, and the females are allowed time to go out at night before the bell rings — on Saturday night at least, if not on all other nights. Then there is the spinning-room, which is very neat and pretty. In this room are the spinners and doffers. The spinners watch the frames; keep them clean, and the threads mended if they break. The doffers take off the full bobbins, and put on the empty ones. They have nothing to do in the long intervals when the frames are in motion, and can go out to their boarding-houses, or do any thing else that they like. In some of the factories the spinners do their own doffing, and when this is the case they work no harder than the weavers. These last have the hardest time of all — or can have, if they choose to take charge of three or four looms, instead of the one pair which is the allotment. And they are the most constantly confined. The spinners and dressers have but the weavers to keep supplied, and then their work can stop. The dressers never work before breakfast, and they stay out a great deal in the afternoons. The drawers-in, or girls who draw the threads through the harnesses, also work in the dressing-room, and they all have very good wages — better than the weavers who have but the usual work. The dressing-rooms are very neat, and the frames move with a gentle undulating motion which is really graceful. But these rooms are kept very warm, and are disagreeably scented with the "sizing," or starch, which stiffens the "beams," or unwoven webs. There are many plants in these rooms, and it is really a good greenhouse for them. The dressers are generally quite tall girls, and must have pretty tall minds too, as their work requires much care and attention.

I could have had work in the dressing-room, but chose to be a weaver; and I will tell you why. I disliked the closer air of the dressing-room, though I might have become accustomed to that. I could not learn to dress so quickly as I could to weave, nor have work of my own so soon, and should have had to stay with Mrs. C. two or three weeks before I could go in at all, and I did not like to be "lying upon my oars" so long. And, more than this, when I get well learned I can have extra work, and make double wages, which you know is quite an inducement with some.

Well, I went into the mill, and was put to learn with a very patient girl — a clever old maid. I should be willing to be one myself if I could be as good as she is. You cannot think how odd every thing seemed to me. I wanted to laugh at every thing, but did not know what to make sport of first. They set me to threading shuttles, and tying weaver's knots, and such things, and now

I have improved so that I can take care of one loom. I could take care of two if I only had eyes in the back part of my head, but I have not got used to "looking two ways of a Sunday" yet.

At first the hours seemed very long, but I was so interested in learning that I endured it very well; and when I went out at night, the sound of the mill was in my ears, as of crickets, frogs, and jewsharps [small musical instrument; it twangs], all mingled together in strange discord. After that it seemed as though cotton-wool was in my ears, but now I do not mind it at all. You know that people learn to sleep with the thunder of Niagara in their ears, and a cotton mill is no worse, though you wonder that we do not have to hold our breath in such a noise.

It makes my feet ache and swell to stand so much, but I suppose I shall get accustomed to that too. The girls generally wear old shoes about their work, and you know nothing is easier; but they almost all say that when they have worked here a year or two they have to procure shoes a size or two larger than before they came. The right hand, which is the one used in stopping and starting the loom, becomes larger than the left; but in other respects the factory is not detrimental to a young girl's appearance. Here they look delicate, but not sickly; they laugh at those who are much exposed, and get pretty brown; but I, for one, had rather be brown than pure white. I never saw so many pretty looking girls as there are here. Though the number of men is small in proportion there are many marriages here, and a great deal of courting. I will tell you of this last sometime.

You wish to know minutely of our hours of labor. We go in at five o'clock; at seven we come out to breakfast; at half-past seven we return to our work, and stay until half-past twelve. At one, or quarter-past one four months in the year, we return to our work, and stay until seven at night. Then the evening is all our own, which is more than some laboring girls can say, who think nothing is more tedious than a factory life.

When I first came here, which was the last of February, the girls ate their breakfast before they went to their work. The first of March they came out at the present breakfast hour, and the twentieth of March they ceased to "light up" the rooms, and come out between six and seven o'clock.

You ask if the girls are contented here: I ask you, if you know of *any one* who is perfectly contented. Do you remember the old story of the philosopher, who offered a field to the person who was contented with his lot; and when one claimed it, he asked him why, if he was so perfectly satisfied, he wanted his field. The girls here are not contented; and there is no disadvantage in their situation which they do not perceive as quickly, and lament as loudly, as the sternest opponents of the factory system do. They would scorn to say they were contented, if asked the question; for it would compromise their Yankee spirit — their pride, penetration, independence, and love of "freedom and equality" to say that they were *contented* with such a life as this.

Yet, withal, they are cheerful. I never saw a happier set of beings. They appear blithe in the mill, and out of it. If you see one of them, with a very long face, you may be sure that it is because she has heard bad news from home, or because her beau has vexed her. But, if it is a Lowell trouble, it is because she has failed in getting off as many "sets" or "pieces" as she intended to have done; or because she had a sad "break-out," or "break-down," in her work, or something of that sort.

You ask if the work is not disagreeable. Not when one is accustomed to it. It tried my patience sadly at first, and does now when it does not run well; but, in general, I like it very much. It is easy to do, and does not require very violent exertion, as much of our farm work does.

You also ask how I get along with the girls here. Very well indeed. . . .

Dear Mary: . . .

The mill girls are the prettiest in the city. You wonder how they can keep neat. Why not? There are no restrictions as to the number of pieces to be washed in the boarding-house. And, as there is plenty of water in the mill, the girls can wash their laces and muslins and other nice things themselves, and no boarding woman ever refuses the conveniences for starching and ironing. You say too that you do not see how we can have so many conveniences and comforts at the price we pay for board. You must remember that the boarding-houses belong to the companies, and are let to the tenants far below the usual city rent — sometimes the rent is remitted. Then there are large families, so that there are the profits of many individuals. The country farmers are quite in the habit of bringing their produce to the boarding-houses for sale, thus reducing the price by the omission of the market-man's profit. So you see there are many ways by which we get along so well.

You ask me how the girls behave in the mill, and what are the punishments. They behave very well while about their work, and I have never heard of punishments, or scoldings, or anything of that sort. Sometimes an overseer finds fault, and sometimes offends a girl by refusing to let her stay out of the mill, or some deprivation like that; and then, perhaps, there are tears and pouts on her part, but, in general, the tone of intercourse between the girls and overseers is very good — pleasant, yet respectful. When the latter are fatherly sort of men the girls frequently resort to them for advice and assistance about other affairs than their work. Very seldom is this confidence abused; but, among the thousands of overseers who have lived in Lowell, and the tens of thousands of girls who have in time been here, there are legends still told of wrong suffered and committed. "To err is human," and when the frailties of humanity are exhibited by a factory girl it is thought of for worse than are the errors of any other persons.

The only punishment among the girls is dismission from their places. They do not, as many think, withhold their wages; and as for corporal punishment — mercy on me! To strike a female would cost any overseer his place. If the superintendents did not take the affair into consideration the girls would turn out [go on strike], as they did at the Temperance celebration, "Independent day;" and if they didn't look as pretty, I am sure they would produce as deep an impression. . . .

Do you wish to hear anything more about the overseers? Once for all, then, there are many very likely intelligent public-spirited men among them. They are interested in the good movements of the day; teachers in the Sabbath schools; and some have represented the city in the State Legislature. They usually marry among the factory girls, and do not connect themselves with their inferiors either. Indeed, in almost all the matches here the female is superior in education and manner, if not in intellect, to her partner.

The overseers have good salaries, and their families live very prettily. I observe that in almost all cases the mill girls make excellent wives. They are good managers, orderly in their households, and "neat as waxwork." It seems as though they were so delighted to have houses of their own to take care of, that they would never weary of the labor and the care. . . .

Questions

1. How enthusiastic is the author about factory work? To what extent is she critical?
2. Does she believe her co-workers are contented? Why or why not?
3. What is her overall view of factory work?

Harriet Martineau, *Society in America* (1837)

Harriet Martineau (1802–1876) joined a steady stream of European visitors to the United States in the early nineteenth century. She published her observations after a two-year stay from 1834 to 1836. Martineau enthusiastically embraced the radical social implications of the Industrial Revolution and regarded the United States as a brave social experiment in human equality.

An ardent feminist and abolitionist, Martineau noted that the subordination of women and slaves in the United States contradicted the egalitarian principles enunciated in the Declaration of Independence. But she also saw signs of progress in New England's new industrial order. The Waltham plan offered young American women of modest means an alternative to domestic service; to Martineau, this system suggested the manner by which the United States could protect itself from the ills of poverty that infected the industrial society in Britain.

The morals of the female factory population may be expected to be good when it is considered of what class it is composed. Many of the girls are in the factories because they have too much pride for domestic service. Girls who are too proud for domestic service as it is in America, can hardly be low enough for any gross immorality; or to need watching; or not to be trusted to avoid the contagion of evil example. To a stranger, their pride seems to take a mistaken direction, and they appear to deprive themselves of a respectable home and station, and many benefits, by their dislike of service: but this is altogether their own affair. They must choose for themselves their way of life. But the reasons of their choice indicate a state of mind superior to the grossest dangers of their position.

I saw a bill fixed up in the Waltham mill which bore a warning that no young lady who attended dancing-school that winter should be employed: and that the corporation had given directions to the overseer to dismiss any one who should be found to dance at the school. I asked the meaning of this; and the overseer's answer was, "Why, we had some trouble last winter about the dancing-school. It must, of course, be held in the evening, as the young folks are in the mill all day. They are very young, many of them; and they forget the time, and everything but the amusement, and dance away till two or three in the morning. They are unfit for their work the next day; or, if they get properly through their work, it is at the expense of their health. So we have forbidden the dancing-school; but, to make up for it, I have promised them that, as soon as the great new room at the hotel is finished, we will have a dance once a-fortnight. We shall meet and break up early; and my wife and I will dance; and we will all dance together."

I was sorry to see one bad and very unnecessary arrangement, in all the manufacturing establishments. In England, the best friends of the poor are accustomed to think it the crowning hardship of their condition that solitude is wholly forbidden to them. It is impossible that any human being should pass his life as well as he might do who is never alone. . . . The silence, freedom and collectedness of solitude are absolutely essential to the health of the mind. . . . In the dwellings of the English poor, parents and children are crowded into one room. . . . All wise parents above the rank of poor, make it a primary consideration so to arrange their families as that each member may, at some hour have some place where he may enter in, and shut his door, and feel himself alone. If possible, the sleeping places are so ordered. In America, where space is of far less consequence . . . these same girls have no private apartments, and sometimes sleep six or eight in a room, and even three in a bed. This is very bad. . . .

Now are the days when these gregarious habits should be broken through. . . . If the change be not soon made, the American factory population, with all its advantages of education and of pecuniary sufficiency, will be found, as its numbers increase, to have been irreparably injured by its subjection to a grievance . . . to which poverty exposes artisans in old countries.

Questions

1. Why do the young women at Waltham prefer factory work to domestic service?
2. What is the problem associated with the dancing school?
3. What dangers does Martineau see in crowded dormitory living?

Frances Anne Kemble,
A Railroad Journey South (1838)

Frances Anne (Fanny) Kemble (1809–1893) was born into a family of famous English actors. When Kemble was twenty years old, she made her reluctant debut as Juliet in Shakespeare's Romeo and Juliet *and was an instant success. Accompanied by her father, she came to the United States in 1832 for an American tour; Kemble delighted both theater audiences and New England intellectuals.*

Kemble abandoned her stage career rather suddenly in 1834 when she married Pierce Butler, a well-to-do American. In December 1838 Fanny, along with her husband, a small daughter, a baby, and an Irish servant, left Philadelphia by train on a trip that would take them to a family-owned slave plantation on the Georgia coast. In these excerpts from a letter to her friend Harriet St. Leger, Kemble describes the trip as far as North Carolina.

Dearest Harriet,

On Friday morning [December 21, 1838] we started from Philadelphia, by railroad, for Baltimore. It is a curious fact enough, that half the routes that are traveled in America are either temporary or unfinished — one reason, among several, for the multitudinous accidents which befall wayfarers. At the very outset of our journey, and within scarce a mile of Philadelphia, we crossed the Schuylkill, over a bridge, one of the principal piers of which is yet incomplete, and the whole building (a covered wooden one, of handsome dimensions) filled with workmen, yet occupied about its construction. But the Americans are impetuous in the way of improvement, and have all the impatience of children about the trying of a new thing, often greatly retarding their own progress by hurrying unduly the completion of their works, or using them in a perilous state of incompleteness. Our road lay for a considerable length of time through flat low meadows that skirt the Delaware, which at this season of the year, covered with snow and bare of vegetation, presented a most dreary aspect. We passed through Wilmington . . . , and crossed a small stream called the Brandywine, the scenery along the banks of which is very beautiful. For its historical associations I refer you to the life of Washington. I cannot say that the aspect of the town of Wilmington, as viewed from the railroad cars, presented any very exquisite points of beauty; I shall therefore indulge in a few observations upon these same railroad cars just here.

And first, I cannot but think that it would be infinitely more consonant with comfort, convenience, and common sense, if persons obliged to travel during the intense cold of an American winter (in the Northern states), were to clothe themselves according to the exigency of the weather, and so do away with the present deleterious custom of warming close and crowded carriages with sheet iron stoves, heated with anthracite coal. No words can describe the foulness of the atmosphere, thus robbed of all vitality by the vicious properties of that dreadful combustible, and tainted besides with the poison emitted at every respiration from so many pairs of human lungs. These are facts which the merest tyro [beginner] in physiological science knows, and the utter disregard of which on the part of the Americans renders them the amazement of every traveler from countries where the preservation of health is considered worth the care of a rational creature. I once traveled to Harrisburg in a railroad car, fitted up to carry sixty-four persons, in the midst of which glowed a large stove. The trip was certainly a delectable one. Nor is there any remedy for this: an attempt to open a window is met by a universal scowl and shudder; and indeed it is but incurring the risk of one's death of cold, instead of one's death of heat. The windows, in fact, form the walls on each side of the carriage, which looks like a long greenhouse upon wheels; the seats, which each contain two persons (a pretty tight fit too), are placed down the whole length of the vehicle, one behind the other, leaving a species of aisle in the middle for the uneasy (a large portion of the traveling community here) to fidget up and down, for the tobacco chewers to spit in, and for a whole tribe of little itinerant fruit and cake sellers to rush through, distributing their wares at every place where the train stops. Of course nobody can well sit immediately in the opening of a window when the thermometer is twelve degrees below zero; yet this, or suffocation in foul air, is the only alternative. I generally prefer being half frozen to death to the latter mode of martyrdom.

Attached to the Baltimore cars was a separate apartment for women. It was of comfortable dimensions, and without a stove; and here I betook myself with my children, escaping from the pestilential atmosphere of the other compartment, and performing our journey with ease enough. My only trial here was one which I have to encounter in whatever direction I travel in America, and which, though apparently a trivial matter in itself, has caused me infinite trouble, and no little compassion for the rising generation of the United States — I allude to the ignorant and fatal practice of the women of stuffing their children from morning till night with every species of trash [food] which comes to hand. . . .

We pursued our way from Wilmington to Havre de Grace on the railroad, and crossed one or two inlets from the Chesapeake, of considerable width, upon bridges of a most perilous construction, and which, indeed, have given way once or twice in various parts already. They consist merely of wooden piles driven into the river, across which the iron rails are laid, only just raising the train above the level of the water. To traverse with an immense train, at full steam-speed, one of these creeks, nearly a mile in width, is far from agreeable, let one be never so little nervous; and it was with infinite cordiality each time that I greeted the first bush that hung over the water, indicating our approach to *terra firma*. At Havre de Grace we crossed the Susquehanna in a steamboat, which cut its way through the ice an inch in thickness with marvelous ease and swiftness, and landed us on the other side, where we again entered the railroad carriages to pursue our road. . . .

Toward four o'clock, as we approached the Roanoke, the appearance of the land improved; there was a good deal of fine soil well farmed, and the river, where we crossed it, although in all the naked unadornment of wintry banks, looked very picturesque and refreshing as it gushed along, broken by rocks and small islands into rapid reaches and currents. Immediately after crossing it, we stopped at a small knot of houses, which, although christened Weldon, and therefore pretending to be a place, was rather the place where a place was intended to be. Two or three rough pine warerooms, or station houses, belonging to the railroad; a few miserable dwellings, which might be either not half built up, or not quite fallen down, on the banks of a large millpond; one exceedingly dirty-looking old wooden house, whither we directed our steps as to the inn; but we did not take our ease in it, though we tried as much as we could. . . .

My poor little children, overcome with fatigue and sleep, were carried, and we walked from the *hotel* at Weldon to the railroad, and by good fortune obtained a compartment to ourselves.

It was now between eight and nine o'clock, and perfectly dark. The carriages were furnished with lamps, however, and, by the rapid glance they cast upon the objects which we passed, I endeavored in vain to guess at the nature of the country through which we were traveling; but, except the tall shafts of the ever-lasting pine trees which still pursued us, I could descry nothing, and resigned myself to the amusing contemplation of the attitudes of my companions, who were all fast asleep.

Between twelve and one o'clock [in the early morning of Sunday, December 23, 1838], the engine stopped, and it was announced to us that we had traveled as far upon the railroad as it was yet completed, and that we must transfer ourselves to stagecoaches; so in the dead middle of the night we crept out of the train, and taking our children in our arms, walked a few yards into an open space in the woods, where three four-horse coaches stood waiting to receive us. . . .

The horrors of that night's journey I shall not easily forget. The road lay almost the whole way through swamps, and was frequently itself under water. It was made of logs of wood (a corduroy road), and so dreadfully rough and unequal, that the drawing a coach over it at all seemed perfectly miraculous. I expected every moment that we must be overturned into the marsh, through which we splashed, with hardly any intermission, the whole night long. Their drivers in this part of the country deserve infinite praise both for skill and care; but the roadmakers, I think, are beyond all praise for their noble confidence in what skill and care can accomplish.

You will readily imagine how thankfully I saw the first whitening of daylight in the sky. I do not know that any morning was ever more welcome to me than that which found us still surrounded by the pine swamps of North Carolina, which, brightened by the morning sun, and breathed through by the morning air, lost something of their dreary desolateness to my senses. . . .

Questions

1. What is the state of the Transportation Revolution when Kemble encounters it?

2. What "American" characteristics does the transportation system suggest to Kemble?

3. What cultural and personal factors might influence Kemble's observations?

The Autobiography of
Benjamin Franklin (1818)

A native of Boston, Benjamin Franklin (1706–1790) established himself as a printer in Philadelphia and soon rose to prominence in colonial politics. He also became famous in both America and Europe as a natural philosopher keenly interested in the scientific concerns of the day, such as electricity.

As an American who was proud of the practicality of his countrymen, Franklin focused his scientific inquiry on practical applications: after demonstrating the electrical nature of lightning, for example, he invented the lightning rod. Bifocal eyeglasses and the Franklin stove also originated in Franklin's inventive workshop. During the nineteenth century, Franklin was remembered as a mechanical genius whose wit and wisdom expressed the practical idealism of the American democrat. In the following passage, he describes his efforts to achieve moral perfection.

. . . I conceived the bold and arduous project of arriving at *moral perfection.* I wished to live without committing any fault at any time, and to conquer all that either natural inclination, custom, or company might lead me into. As I knew, or thought I knew, what was right and wrong, I did not see why I might not *always* do the one and avoid the other. But I soon found I had undertaken a task of more difficulty than I had imagined. While my attention was taken up, and employed in guarding against one fault, I was often surprised by another. . . . I concluded, at length, that the mere speculative conviction that it was our interest to be completely virtuous, was not sufficient to prevent our slipping; and that the contrary habits must be broken, and good ones acquired and established, before we can have any dependence on a steady, uniform rectitude of conduct. For this purpose I therefore tried the following method. . . .

I made a little book, in which I allotted a page for each of the virtues. I ruled each page with red ink, so as it have seven columns, one for each day of the week, marking each column with a letter for the day. I crossed these columns with thirteen red lines, marking the beginning of each line with the first letter of one of the virtues [T for Temperance, S for Silence, etc.], on which line, and in its proper column, I might mark, by a little black spot, every fault I found upon examination to have been committed respecting that virtue upon that day.

I determined to give a week's strict attention to each of the virtues successively. Thus, in the first week, my great guard was to avoid every least offense against *Temperance,* leaving the other virtues to their ordinary chance, only marking every evening the faults of the day. Thus, if in the first week I could keep my first line, marked T, clear of spots, I supposed the habit of that virtue so much strengthened, and its opposite weakened, that I might venture extending my attention to include the next, and for the following week both lines clear of spots. . . .

I entered upon the execution of this plan for self-examination, and continued it with occasional intermissions for some time. I was surprised to find myself so much fuller of faults than I had imagined; but I had the satisfaction of seeing them diminish. . . . I always carried my little book with me.

. . . [The virtue] *Order* gave me the most trouble . . . and my faults in it vexed me so much, and I made so little progress in amendment, and had such frequent relapses, that I was almost ready to give up the attempt, and content myself with a faulty character in that respect, like the man who, in buying an ax of a smith . . . desired to have the whole of its surface as bright as the edge. The smith consented to grind it bright for him if he would turn the wheel; he turned, while the smith pressed the broad face of the ax hard and heavily on the stone, which made the turning of it very fatiguing. The man came every now and then from the wheel to see how the work went on, and at length would take his ax as it was, without further grinding. "No," said the smith, "turn on, turn on, we shall have it bright by-and-by; as yet, it is only speckled." "Yes," said the man, "but *I think I liked a speckled ax best.*" . . . for something, that pretended to be reason, was every now and then suggesting to me that such extreme nicety as I exacted of myself might be a kind of foppery in morals, which, if it were known, would make me ridiculous; that a perfect character might be attended with the inconvenience of being envied and hated; and that a benevolent man should allow a few faults in himself, to keep his friends in countenance. . . .

In reality, there is, perhaps, no one of our natural passions so hard to subdue as *pride*. Disguise it, struggle with it, stifle it, mortify it as much as one pleases, it is still alive, and will every now and then peep out and show itself; you will see it, perhaps, often in this history; for, even if I could conceive that I had completely overcome it, I should probably be proud of my humility. —

Questions

1. How successful is Franklin in transforming himself?
2. What proved to be the greatest obstacle? Why?
3. How does this passage suggest Franklin's strengths as a political leader?

Charles Grandison Finney, On Conversion (1821)

Charles Grandison Finney (1792–1875) was the leading revivalist of the early nineteenth century. He was born in Connecticut, but his family moved westward to Oneida County, New York, where Finney grew up. The religious experience he describes in this account ended his career as a lawyer and inspired his work as a revivalist. Finney's dramatic preaching stressed the importance of the immediate acceptance of God's grace through Jesus Christ. Finney emphasized people's need to assume moral responsibility for themselves. Those who flocked to his revivals hoped to experience God's regenerating grace in essentially the same way Finney had.

On a Sunday evening in the autumn of 1821 I made up my mind that I would settle the question of my soul's salvation at once, that if it were possible I would make my peace with God. . . .

During Monday and Tuesday my convictions increased, but still it seemed as if my heart grew harder. I could not shed a tear. I could not pray. . . .

Tuesday night I had become very nervous, and in the night a strange feeling came over me as if I were about to die. I knew that if I did I would sink down to hell, but I quieted myself as best I could until morning.

At an early hour I started for the office. But just before I arrived at the office, it seemed as if an inward voice confronted me with questions like these: "What are you waiting for? Did you not promise to give your heart to God? And what are you trying to do? Are you endeavoring to work out a righteousness of your own?"

Just at this point the whole question of Gospel salvation opened to my mind in a manner most marvelous. I think I then saw, as clearly as I ever have in my life, the reality and fullness of the atonement of Christ. I saw that his work was a finished work, and that instead of having, or needing, any righteousness of my own to recommend me to God, I had to submit to the righteousness of God through Christ. Gospel salvation seemed to be an offer to be accepted, and that it was full and complete. All that was necessary on my part was my own consent to give up my sins and accept Christ. Salvation was not achieved by my own works, but was to be found entirely in the Lord Jesus Christ, who presented himself before me as my God and my Savior.

Without being distinctly aware of it, I had stopped in the street right where the inward voice seemed to arrest me. How long I remained in that position I cannot say. But after this distinct revelation had stood for some little time before my mind, the question seemed to be, "Will you accept it now, today?"

I replied, "Yes, I will accept it today, or I will die in the attempt." . . .

The thought was pressing me of the rashness of my promise that I would give my heart to God that day or die in the attempt. It seemed to me as if that was binding upon my soul, and yet I was going to break my vow. A great sinking and discouragement came over me, and I felt almost too weak to stand upon my knees.

Just at this moment I again thought I heard someone approach me, and I opened my eyes to see whether it were so. But right there the revelation of my pride was distinctly shown to me as the great difficulty that stood in the way. An overwhelming sense of my wickedness in being ashamed to have a human being see me on my knees before God took such powerful possession of me that I cried at the top of my voice and exclaimed that I would not leave that place if all the men on earth and all the devils in hell surrounded me. "What!" I said, "such a degraded sinner as I am, on my knees confessing my sins to the great and holy God, ashamed to have any human being find me on my knees endeavoring to make my peace with my offended God!" The sin appeared awful, infinite. It broke me down before the Lord.

Just at that point this passage of scripture seemed to drop into my mind with a flood of light: "Then shall you go and pray unto me, and I will hearken to you. Then shall you seek me and find me, when you shall search for me with all your heart."

I instantly seized hold of this with my heart. I had intellectually believed the Bible before, but never had the truth been in my mind that faith was a voluntary trust instead of an intellectual state. I was as conscious of trusting at that moment in God's truthfulness as I was of my own existence. Somehow I knew that that was a passage of scripture, though I do not think I had ever read it. I knew that it was God's word, and God's voice, as it were, that spoke to me.

I cried to him, "Lord, I take Thee at Thy word. Now Thou knowest that I do search for Thee with all my heart, and that I have come here to pray to Thee; and Thou hast promised to hear me." . . .

But how was I to account for the quiet of my mind? I tried to recall my convictions, to get back again the load of sin under which I had been laboring. But all sense of sin, all consciousness of present sin or guilt, had departed from me. I said to myself, "What is this, that I cannot arouse any sense of guilt in my soul, as great a sinner as I am?" I tried in vain to make myself anxious about my present state. I was so quiet and peaceful that I tried to feel concerned about that, lest it should be a result of my having grieved the Spirit away. But take any view of it I would, I could not be anxious at all about my soul and about my spiritual state. The repose of my mind was unspeakably great. I cannot describe it in words. The thought of God was sweet to my mind, and the most profound spiritual tranquillity had taken full possession of me. This was a great mystery, but it did not distress or perplex me. . . .

[That evening] There was no fire and no light in this back room; nevertheless it appeared to me as if it were perfectly light. As I went in and shut the door after me, it seemed as if I met the Lord Jesus Christ face to face. It seemed to me that I saw him as I would see any other man. He said nothing, but looked at me in such a manner as to break me right down at his feet. It seemed to me a reality that he stood before me, and I fell down at his feet and poured out my soul to him. I wept aloud like a child and made such confessions as I could with my choked words. It seemed to me that I bathed his feet with my tears, and yet I had no distinct impression that I touched him.

I must have continued in this state for a good while, but my mind was too much absorbed with the interview to remember anything that I said. As soon as my mind became calm enough I returned to the front office and found that the fire I had made of large wood was nearly burned out. But as I turned and was about to take a seat by the fire, I received a mighty baptism of the Holy Spirit. Without any expectation of it, without ever having the thought in my mind that there was any such thing for me, without any memory of ever hearing the thing mentioned by any person in the world, the Holy Spirit descended upon me in a manner that seemed to go through me, body and soul. I could feel the impression, like a wave of electricity, going through and through me. Indeed it seemed to come in waves of liquid love, for I could not express it in any other way. It seemed like the very breath of God. I can remember distinctly that it seemed to fan me, like immense wings.

No words can express the wonderful love that was spread abroad in my heart. I wept aloud with joy and love. I literally bellowed out the unspeakable overflow of my heart. These waves came over me, and over me, and over me, one after the other, until I remember crying out, "I shall die if these waves continue to pass over me." I said, "Lord, I cannot bear any more," yet I had no fear of death. . . .

In this state I was taught the doctrine of justification by faith as a present experience. That doctrine had never taken possession of my mind. I had never viewed it distinctly as a fundamental doctrine of the Gospel. Indeed, I did not know at all what it meant in the proper sense. But I could now see and understand what was meant by the passage, "Being justified by faith, we have peace with God through our Lord Jesus Christ." I could see that the moment I believed, while up in the woods, all sense of condemnation had entirely dropped out of my mind, and that from that moment I could not feel a sense of guilt or condemnation by any effort I could make. My sense of guilt was gone, my sins were gone, and I do not think I felt any more sense of guilt than if I never had sinned.

This was just the revelation I needed. I felt myself justified by faith, and, so far as I could see, I was in a state in which I did not sin. Instead of feeling that I was sinning all the time, my heart was so full of love that it overflowed. My cup ran over with blessing and with love. I could not feel that I was sinning against God, nor could I recover the least sense of guilt for my past sins. Of this experience of justification I said nothing to anybody at the time.

Questions

1. How does Charles Grandison Finney's Christianity differ from that of the Puritans? of those who experienced the First Great Awakening?
2. What physical and psychological changes did Finney undergo?
3. When Finney's "cup ran over," what changes occurred in his life?

Lyman Beecher, On the Temperance Movement (1812)

Lyman Beecher (1775–1863) served as a pastor in both Congregational and Presbyterian churches and founded one of America's most remarkable families. Beecher was a complex man who wanted to spread the word of God — and check the growth of Roman Catholicism. A graduate of Yale College, he led parishes in New York, Connecticut, Massachusetts, and Ohio. Many of his eleven children, including daughters Catharine and Harriet Beecher Stowe as well as sons Henry Ward and Edward, achieved distinction. This selection from Beecher's autobiography describes his commitment to temperance reform soon after he became pastor of the Congregational Church in Litchfield, Connecticut.

Soon after my arrival at Litchfield I was called to attend the ordination at Plymouth of Mr. Heart, ever after that my very special friend. I loved him as he did me. He said to me one day, "Beecher, if you had made the least effort to govern us young men, you would have had a swarm of bees about you; but, as you have come and mixed among us, you can do with us what you will."

Well, at the ordination at Plymouth, the preparation for our creature comforts, in the sitting-room of Mr. Heart's house, besides food, was a broad sideboard covered with decanters and bottles, and sugar, and pitchers of water. There we found all the various kinds of liquors then in vogue. The drinking was apparently universal. This preparation was made by the society as a matter of course. When the Consociation [of ministers] arrived, they always took something to drink round; also before public services, and always on their return. As they could not all drink at once, they were obliged to stand and wait as people do when they go to mill.

There was a decanter of spirits also on the dinner-table, to help digestion, and gentlemen partook of it through the afternoon and evening as they felt the need, some more and some less; and the sideboard, with the spillings of water, and sugar, and liquor, looked and smelled like the bar of a very active grog-shop. None of the Consociation were drunk; but that there was not, at times, a considerable amount of exhilaration, I can not affirm.

When they had all done drinking, and had taken pipes and tobacco, in less than fifteen minutes there was such a smoke you couldn't see. And the noise I can not describe; it was the maximum of hilarity. They told their stories, and were at the height of jocose talk. They were not old-fashioned Puritans. They had been run down. Great deal of spirituality on Sabbath, and not much when they got where there was something good to drink.

I think I recollect some animadversions [criticisms] were made at that time by the people on the amount of liquor drank, for the tide was swelling in the drinking habits of society.

The next ordination was of Mr. Harvey, in Goshen, and there was the same preparation, and the same scenes acted over, and then afterward still louder murmurs from the society at the quantity and expense of liquor consumed.

These two meetings were near together, and in both my alarm, and shame, and indignation were intense. 'Twas that that woke me up for the war. And silently I took an oath before God that I would never attend another ordination of that kind. I was full. My heart kindles up at the thoughts of it now.

There had been already so much alarm on the subject, that at the General Association [of ministers] at Fairfield in 1811, a committee of three had been appointed to make inquiries and report measures to remedy the evil. A committee was also appointed by the General Association of Massachusetts for the same purpose that same month, and to confer with other bodies.

I was a member of [the] General Association which met in the year following at Sharon, June, 1812, when said committee reported. They said they had attended to the subject committed to their care; that intemperance had been for some time increasing in a most alarming manner; but that, after the most faithful and prayerful inquiry, they were obliged to confess they did not perceive that any thing could be done.

The blood started through my heart when I heard this, and I rose instanter, and moved that a committee of three be appointed immediately, to report at this meeting the ways and means of arresting the tide of intemperance.

The committee was named and appointed. I was chairman, and on the following day brought in a report, the most important paper that ever I wrote.

ABSTRACT OF REPORT.

The General Association of Connecticut, taking into consideration the undue consumption of ardent spirits, the enormous sacrifice of property resulting, the alarming increase of intemperance, the deadly effect on health, intellect, the family, society, civil and religious institutions, and especially in nullifying the means of grace and destroying souls, recommend,

1. Appropriate discourses on the subject by all ministers of Association.

2. That District Associations abstain from the use of ardent spirits at ecclesiastical meetings.

3. That members of Churches abstain from the unlawful vending, or purchase and use of ardent spirits where unlawfully sold; exercise vigilant discipline, and cease to consider the production of ardent spirits a part of hospitable entertainment in social visits.

4. That parents cease from the ordinary use of ardent spirits in the family, and warn their children of the evils and dangers of intemperance.

5. That farmers, mechanics, and manufacturers substitute palatable and nutritious drinks, and give additional compensation, if necessary, to those in their employ. . . .

Immense evils, we are persuaded, afflict communities, not because they are incurable, but because they are tolerated; and great good remains often unaccomplished merely because it is not attempted.

Questions

1. What is the evil that so offends Beecher? Why?
2. How does Beecher respond?
3. What does Beecher believe is at stake in this situation? Explain.

Connections Questions

1. Does the factory worker Susan ("A Mill Worker Describes Her Work and Her Life") have the same concerns as Harriet Martineau ("*Society in America*")? Why or why not?
2. How does Frances Kemble's journey ("A Railroad Journey South") show the United States as a work in progress?
3. Who seems to have a more forgiving sense of faith, Charles Finney ("On Conversion") or Lyman Beecher ("On the Temperance Movement")? Explain.

CHAPTER 11

A Democratic Revolution 1820–1844

Henry Clay, Speech on the Tariff (1824)

A Virginia native, Henry Clay (1777–1852) migrated to Kentucky, where he established himself as a substantial slaveholding planter and lawyer. A strong nationalist and War Hawk, Clay won election to the House of Representatives in 1810 and became Speaker of the House in the following year. A candidate for president in 1824, Clay advocated what he called the "American System" and later played a leading role in building the Whig opposition to Andrew Jackson.

Clay's American System envisioned an integrated national economy in which a protective tariff would encourage domestic manufacturing while it generated revenues to support federally financed harbors, canals, and other sizable internal improvements. Clay was largely successful in his immediate aim, and the Tariff of 1824 with its increased rates passed. But his larger goal of harnessing the federal government to the development of the national economy fell victim to sectional rivalry and charges of elitism.

In the following extracts from his two-day-long speech of March 1824 in the House of Representatives, Clay argues why it is in the nation's interest to impose a tariff on imports to protect domestic manufacturing.

. . . And what is this tariff? It seems to have been regarded as a sort of monster, huge and deformed; a wild beast, endowed with tremendous powers of destruction, about to be let loose among our people, if not to devour them, at least to consume their substance. But let us calm our passions, and deliberately survey this alarming, this terrific being. The sole object of the tariff is to tax the produce of foreign industry, with the view of promoting American industry. The tax is exclusively levelled at foreign industry. . . .

It has been treated as an imposition of burthens upon one part of the community by design for the benefit of another; as if, in fact, money were taken from the pockets of one portion of the people and put into the pockets of another. But, is that a fair representation of it? No man pays the duty assessed on the foreign article by compulsion, but voluntarily; and this voluntary duty, if paid, goes into the common exchequer, for the common benefit of all. . . . According to the opponents of the domestic policy, the proposed system will force capital and labor into new and reluctant employments; we are not prepared, in consequence of the high price of wages, for the successful establishment of manufactures, and we must fail in the experiment. We have seen that the existing occupations of our society, those of agriculture, commerce, navigation, and the learned professions, are overflowing with competitors, and that the want of employment is severely felt. Now what does this bill propose? To open a new and extensive field of business, in which all that choose may enter. There is no compulsion upon any one to engage in it. An option only is given to industry, to continue in the present unprofitable pursuits, or to embark in a new and promising one. The effect will be to lessen the competition in the old branches of business and to multiply our resources for increasing our comforts and augmenting the national wealth. The alleged fact of the high price of wages is not admitted. The truth is, that no class of society suffers more, in the present stagnation of business, than the laboring class. That is a necessary effect of the depression of agriculture, the principal business of the community. The wages of able-bodied men vary from five to eight dollars per month; and such has been the want of employment, in some parts of the Union, that instances have not been unfrequent, of men working merely for the means of present subsistence. . . . We are now, and ever will be, essentially, an agricultural people. Without a material change in the fixed habits of the country, the friends of this measure desire to draw to it, as a powerful auxiliary to its industry, the manufacturing arts. The difference between a nation with, and without the arts, may be conceived, by the difference between a keel-boat and a steam-boat, combatting the rapid torrent of the Mississippi. How slow does the former ascend, hugging the sinuosities of the shore, pushed on by her hardy and exposed crew, now throwing themselves in vigorous concert on their oars, and then seizing the pendant boughs of over-hanging trees: she seems hardly to move; and her scanty cargo is scarcely worth the transportation! With what ease is she not passed by the steam-boat, laden with the riches of all quarters of the world, with a crowd of gay, cheerful, and protected passengers, now dashing into the midst of the current, or gliding through the eddies near the shore. . . . The adoption of the restrictive system, on the part of the United States, by excluding the produce of foreign labor, would extend the consumption of American produce, unable, in the infancy and unprotected state of the arts, to sustain a competition with foreign fabrics. Let our arts breathe under the shade of protection; let them be perfected as they are in England, and we shall then be ready, as England now is said to be, to put aside protection, and to enter upon the freest exchanges. . . .

Other and animating considerations invite us to adopt the policy of this system. Its importance, in connexion with the general defence in time of war, cannot fail to be duly estimated. Need I recal [sic] to our painful recollection the sufferings, for the want of an adequate supply of absolute necessaries, to which the defenders of their country's rights and our entire population were subjected during the late war [the War of 1812]? Or to remind the committee of the great advantage of a steady and unfailing source of supply, unaffected alike in war and in peace? Its importance, in reference to the stability of our Union, that paramount and greatest of all our interests, cannot fail warmly to recommend it, or at least to conciliate the forbearance of every patriot bosom. Now our people present the spectacle of a vast assemblage of jealous rivals, all eagerly rushing to the sea-board, jostling each other in their way, to hurry off to glutted foreign markets the perishable produce of their labor. The tendency of that policy, in conformity to which this bill is prepared, is to transform these competitors into friends and mutual customers; and, by the reciprocal exchanges of their respective productions, to place the confederacy upon the most solid of all foundations, the basis of common interest. . . .

Even if the benefits of the policy were limited to certain sections of our country, would it not be satisfactory to behold American industry, wherever situated, active, animated, and thrifty, rather than persevere in a course which renders us subservient to foreign industry? But these benefits are twofold, direct, and collateral, and in the one shape or the other, they will diffuse themselves throughout the Union. All parts of the Union will participate, more or less, in both. As to the direct benefit, it is probable that the North and the East will enjoy the largest share. But the West and the South will also participate in them. . . . And where the direct benefit does not accrue, that will be enjoyed of supplying the raw material and provisions for the consumption of artisans. . . . I appeal to the South — to the high-minded, generous, and patriotic South — with which I have so often co-operated. . . . Of what does it complain? A possible temporary enhancement [i.e., price increase] in the objects of consumption. Of what do we complain? A total incapacity, produced by the foreign policy, to purchase, at any price, necessary foreign objects of consumption. In such an alternative, inconvenient only to it, ruinous to us, can we expect too much from Southern magnanimity? . . .

Questions

1. How does Clay go about mounting a defense of the proposed tariff?
2. Why does he make reference to the War of 1812?
3. Is this speech outdated or still relevant to debate on national economic policy? Explain.

Amos Kendall, The Beginnings of Grass-Roots Democracy (1830)

Amos Kendall (1789–1869) was born on an impoverished farm in western Massachusetts. With the meager support his family could offer and his own ambitious efforts, he graduated from Dartmouth College in 1811, studied law, and in 1814 sought brighter prospects in the West. Kendall settled in Kentucky, where he briefly tutored the sons of Henry Clay before establishing himself as a lawyer and newspaper editor. In 1816 he moved to the state capital of Frankfort to take charge of the influential Argus of Western America *and was soon joined by co-editor Francis P. Blair. Although Kendall and Blair supported Clay in the presidential election of 1824, they helped carry Kentucky for Jackson in 1828.*

After Jackson's victory, Kendall moved to Washington and became one of the most influential members of the new president's informal "Kitchen Cabinet"; in fact, Kendall was the principal author of Jackson's Bank Veto Message. In 1830, with Jackson's political support, Kendall founded the Washington, D.C., Globe, *with Blair as its editor. Kendall also became a powerful dispenser of Democratic patronage as postmaster general (1835–1840). In the following extracts from private letters written to Blair in Kentucky, Kendall examines the altered political landscape that produced Jackson's victory, and he assesses its significance for the future.*

AMOS KENDALL TO FRANCIS P. BLAIR, JANUARY 28, 1830:

The Democratic ascendancy in our state can only be maintained by diminishing the power of lawyers. I can think of no way so effectual to do that as to induce our farmers and mechanics to take a part in the *nomination* of candidates as well as their election. Now, our lawyers, big and little, thrust themselves out and forestall the field, and no modest farmer or mechanic dare come in competition with their pretentions. If the people could be made sensible of the wrong and injury done them by these upstarts, they would be ready to apply the remedy. . . . Let meetings of the democratic Jackson men be called in each militia company of the county on the same day. . . . By such means, the people would take the government into their own hands and send to the Legislature sounder men and better politicians. The Lawyers would not attend all these company meetings and an entire class of politicians would spring up opposed to them. . . .

By this plan the town aristocracies and the influence of rich men in the country would be measurably disarmed.

AMOS KENDALL TO FRANCIS P. BLAIR, AUGUST 27, 1830:

There is to be a new paper here entitled the "American Statesman and Work-ingmen's Advocate" devoted to Mr. [Henry] Clay. It will be a poor concern; but the factious object is seen by the title. . . . I am not sorry to see the efforts made to organize the workingmen. If Mr. Clay shall succeed in teaching them their strength, they will hurl him and all the factious lawyers out of power and almost out of sight. They are whetting a razor to cut their own throat. I would rejoice to see the *real* workingmen take a decisive stand in politics and place more of themselves in public office. Besides, their notions in relation to the U.S. Bank and many other matters are not very congenial to the objects of H. Clay. I know his only object is to *use* them; but he ought to remember the old proverb — "Do not meddle with edge-tools."

Questions

1. How does Kendall propose to attack "town aristocracies"?
2. What is his view of Henry Clay?
3. Is Kendall a political radical or conservative? Explain.

William Leggett, Opposition to Banks and Monopoly (c. 1832)

William Leggett (1801–1839) was possibly the most insightful political writer in the Jacksonian camp. Leggett was born in New York City and briefly lived a frontier life with his parents in Illinois. In 1829 Leggett became joint owner and editor (with William Cullen Bryant) of the New York Evening Post. *An enthusiastic and sophisticated supporter of Jackson's war against the Second Bank of the United States (see text pp. 294–95), Leggett developed the theoretical implications of Jacksonian antimonopoly and equal-rights rhetoric. In the following editorial, Leggett offers a practical description of the*

operation of unregulated banks as he explains how bank-sponsored specula-
tion entraps the unwary and makes honest producers the victims of financial
corruption.

Our primary ground of opposition to banks as they at present exist is that they are a species of monopoly. All corporations are liable to the objection that whatever powers or privileges are given to them, are so much taken from the government of the people. Though a state legislature may possess a constitutional right to create bank incorporations, yet it seems very clear to our apprehension that the doing so is an invasion of the grand republican principle of Equal Rights — a principle which lies at the bottom of our constitution, and which, in truth, is the corner-stone of our national government. . . .

Let us trace the progress of a new banking institution. Let us imagine a knot of speculators to have possessed themselves, by certain acts of collusion, bribery, and political management, of a bank charter; and let us suppose them commencing operations under their corporate privileges. They begin by lending their capital. After that, if commercial business is active, and the demand for money urgent, they take care to put as many of their notes in circulation as possible. For awhile this does very well and the Bank realizes large profits. Every thing seems to flourish; merchants extend their operations. . . . Others, in the meanwhile, stimulated by the same appearance of commercial prosperity, borrow money (that is notes) from the bank, and embark in enterprises of a different nature. They purchase lots, build houses, set railway and canal projects on foot, and every thing goes on swimmingly. The demand for labour is abundant, property of all kinds rises in price, and speculators meet each other in the streets, and exult in their anticipated fortunes.

But by and by things take a different turn. . . . The bank now perceives that it has extended itself too far. Its notes, which, until now, circulated currently enough, begin to return in upon it in demand for specie; while, at the same time, the merchants, whom it has been all along eager to serve, now call for increased accommodations. But the bank cannot accommodate them any longer. Instead of increasing its loans, it is obliged to require payment of those which it had previously made. . . . The merchants, unable to get the amount of accommodation necessary to sustain their operations, are forced to suspend payment. . . . Then follows wider derangement. One commercial house after another becomes bankrupt, and finally the bank itself, by these repeated losses forced to discontinue its business, closes its doors, and hands over its affairs for the benefit of its creditors. . . . On investigation it is discovered, most likely, that the whole capital of the institution has been absorbed by its losses. The enormous profits which it made during the first part of its career, had been regularly withdrawn by the stockholders, and the deluded creditor has nothing but a worthless bit of engraved paper to show for the valuable consideration which he parted with for what he foolishly imagined [to be] money.

Questions

1. What is Leggett's view of banking?
2. Why, according to Leggett, do banks fail?
3. What assumptions does Leggett make about the way banks and the national economy work?

Seth Luther, Address to the
Working Men of New England (1832)

Seth Luther (1817?–1846) is thought to have been born in Providence, Rhode Island. Luther became a strong voice for workingmen in Jacksonian America. A carpenter by trade, he had little formal education but was an avid reader of newspapers and books. Luther was a leading figure in the fight for the ten-hour work day. In the following speech, delivered to a gathering of workingmen, Luther described an "American System" dedicated not to expanding manufactures but to securing the equality of men.

I would ask if persons not possessing one hundred and thirty four dollars in soil, are permitted to address this meeting. If so, I wish to make a few remarks. This community seems to be divided into two parties. Not Jackson men and Clay men . . . but the Aristocracy and Democracy. The term Aristocracy denotes a privileged class. Although the Constitution of the United States acknowledges no hereditary right, yet there exists among us a class well deserving the name of Aristocrats. I will mention some of their privileges. . . . Sir, this aristocracy of wealth claims the right to shut up in the Cotton Mill the almost infant child for . . . 13 or 14 hours per diem, with only 20 or 30 minutes for each meal . . . thereby depriving them of the best of all earthly good, an education. . . . Sir, we are in favor of an American System that will benefit all interests. But we are not satisfied with *the* System, whatever it may be, which enables a favored few to accumulate mountains of wealth, at the expense of our dearest interests. . . . We hear the philanthropist moaning over the fate of the Southern slave, when there are thousands of children in this State as truly slaves as the blacks of the South. . . .

Sir, we find the aristocracy in all countries, using their efforts, either directly or indirectly, to hold the poorer classes in ignorance; that they may rivet the chains of oppression more effectually. Where, Sir, is the difference in the effect between Southern measures, and measures now practiced by the Manufacturer, to accomplish this dreadful object?

Much, Sir, have we heard respecting the happiness of a manufacturing population. The Hon. H.[enry] Clay . . . draws a most beautiful picture. He has seen *one* Cotton Mill in Cincinnati. . . . He exclaims, " 'Tis a paradise!" — But . . . one of my friends remarked, if a *Cotton Mill* is paradise, it is "Paradise Lost." . . . we would presume to advise the Hon. Senator from Kentucky to . . . see . . . instead of rosy cheeks, the *pale,* the *sickly,* the *haggard,* countenance of the ragged child from six to twelve years of age. Haggard from the worse than slavish confinement in the cotton mill.

Questions

1. According to Seth Luther, how are the workers oppressed?
2. What does Luther believe the factory system creates?
3. Do you agree with his comparison of northern workers to southern slaves? Why or why not?

People v. Cooper (1836)

Workers during the Age of Jackson fought to improve conditions; though their efforts were often thwarted, they did enjoy some victories. In 1836 leading members of the United Society of the Journeymen Cordwainers (shoemakers) of the City of Hudson were tried by the State of New York for engaging in a conspiracy against their employers for the purpose of demanding higher wages. The following account of the trial, People v. Cooper *(1836), was reported by the attorneys in the case.*

The defendants were indicted under the statute for a combination and conspiracy to raise their wages, etc., to "the great injury of trade and commerce." They were indicted at the instance of Eli Mosier, a boss shoemaker, of the city of Hudson. . . .

The first count charges, "that the defendants, not being content to work for the usual prices, but combining to increase their wages, and the wages of other journeymen . . . did on the 15th of September, 1835, combine together with other workmen, and agree that none of them, would after that day, work at any lower prices than those mentioned in the list, to the great damage of the boss shoemakers, and the injury of trade and commerce, and against the statute."

The second count charges, "that the defendants . . . did thereby agree . . . that any member who should work for less, should be expelled from the society and . . . that any boss who should refuse to pay their rates of wages should be fined, and no member of the society would work for him until he paid his fine. . . ."

SOLOMON SHATTOCK, sworn. I am a boss shoemaker. Several of the members of the society . . . left my employ because I would not give them the wages on their list. None but Defries left the first time — the rest did not leave until afterwards. Several members of the society . . . said that if I did not pay the fine they would leave me. . . . At the time Defries left me, I was paying the prices on their list to him — but in consequence of my not giving the full price to the other men Defries left me. . . .

His Hon. Judge Wilcoxon then charged the Jury in substance as follows: . . .

If the journeymen shoemakers of the city of Hudson had a right to combine, then the Journeymen [everywhere] . . . had a right to combine and to control the labor of every mechanical State in the Union. The question for consideration was whether the controlling the labor of the country in this manner had a tendency to injure trade. For instance, in a manufacturing establishment where there were a hundred hands, and where contracts had to be performed in a given time, would not a sudden combination and refusal to work, cause the ruin of the individual? . . .

The cause was then committed to the Jury. . . . The Jury were together about 209 minutes. . . . The next morning they delivered in Court the following verdict: The Jurors find the Prisoners Not Guilty.

Questions

1. Summarize the charges brought against the journeymen cordwainers.
2. Why does the judge fear journeymen's associations?
3. If the cordwainers had been found guilty, what kind of recourse would they have had for their grievances?

Francis P. Blair, Protecting "Domestic Industry" (1842)

Francis P. Blair (1791–1876) was born in Abington, Virginia, and settled in Frankfort, Kentucky, after graduating from Transylvania University. Both as a political advisor to Andrew Jackson and as a newspaper editor, Blair played a leading role in developing the Jacksonians' political appeal to southern and western planters, yeomen farmers, and workingmen in the urban North. In January 1842 his Washington, D.C., Globe attacked a Whig tariff proposal to protect "domestic industry" and commented on the changed meaning of the term.

In the good old days of the Republic, when every man minded his own business and left others to take care of their own; when dependence was placed on personal exertion alone, and people did not look up to HERCULES Congress to get them out of the slough into which they had plunged by their own folly and improvidence; in those times, domestic industry was a different thing from what it is now. If we are to believe the assertions of members of Congress advocating a protective tariff, there is no other domestic industry than that employed in our great manufactories. According to their definition, tending spinning jennies in a stupendous brick building, six or seven stories high, some ten or twenty miles from home, surrounded by hundreds of strapping "operatives," from all quarters of the world, with tremendous whiskers, is your only domestic industry for the young and blooming daughters of the land.

"DOMESTIC INDUSTRY" is no longer represented by the ruddy matron sitting at her own fireside in her own home, turning the spinning wheel with one foot and rocking a chubby bantling with the other, while singing it to sleep with lullabies. . . .

"DOMESTIC INDUSTRY," according to the tariff definition, is not that of the healthy mechanic or artisan, who works for himself at his own shop, or if he goes abroad, returns home to his meals every day, and sleeps under his own roof every night; whose earnings are regulated by the wants of the community at large, not by the discretion of a penurious master; whose hours of labor depend on universal custom; who, when the sun goes down, is a freeman until he rises again; who can eat his meals in comfort, and sleep as long as nature requires. . . . Domestic industry is nothing but bondage in its most oppressive form, labor in its utmost extremity of degradation.

"DOMESTIC INDUSTRY," according to the protective tariff cant, is that which separates wives, husbands, parents and children; annihilates every domestic tie and association, and renders all domestic duties subservient to the will, not of a husband or parent, but that of an unfeeling taskmaster, to whom the sacrifice of every moment of time, and every comfort of life, is wealth and prosperity.

Questions

1. What ironic meaning does Blair find in the term *domestic industry?*
2. How does Blair define the "healthy mechanic"? In Blair's view, why is the mechanic's "health" in jeopardy?
3. What is Blair's implied criticism of the factory system?

Connections Questions

1. Do the documents in this section suggest that Americans wanted the economy to remain as it was during the eighteenth century, or that they believed the new industrial system could be reformed to their benefit? Explain.
2. What are the limits of democracy as espoused by Amos Kendall ("The Beginnings"), Seth Luther ("Address"), and Francis Blair ("Protecting")? Why did their ideas stop where they did?
3. Can you make a defense of the "aristocracies" attacked by their various Democratic critics? Why or why not?

CHAPTER 12

The Ferment of Reform 1820–1860

Henry David Thoreau, *Walden* (1854)

Henry David Thoreau (1817–1862) was born and lived most of his life in Concord, Massachusetts. A graduate of Harvard, Thoreau taught for a time in Concord but soon devoted himself to the transcendentalist movement (see text pp. 312–13). His most famous works, an account of his residence at Walden Pond and the essay "On Civil Disobedience," although not widely read in his day, have become an enduring legacy of transcendentalism.

In contrast to Ralph Waldo Emerson, whose romantic individualism stayed aloof from material conditions, Thoreau offered a subversive twist to a principal tenet of liberal capitalism: the proposition that individuals exchange labor for leisure to promote future pleasure. If the highest sphere of individual pleasure is transcendental meditation, Thoreau reasoned, an individual should strive to exchange the least labor for the most leisure.

ECONOMY

When I wrote the following pages, or rather the bulk of them, I lived alone, in the woods, a mile from any neighbor, in a house which I had built myself, on the shore of Walden Pond, in Concord, Massachusetts, and earned my living by the labor of my hands only. I lived there two years and two months. At present I am a sojourner in civilized life again. . . . It would be some advantage to live a primitive and frontier life, though in the midst of an outward civilization, if only to learn what are the gross necessaries of life and what methods have been taken to obtain them. . . . By the words, *necessary of life,* I mean whatever, of all that man obtains by his own exertions, had been from the first, or from long use has become, so important to human life that few, if any whether from savageness, or poverty, or philosophy, ever attempt to do without it. . . .

Though we are not so degenerate but that we might possibly live in a cave or a wigwam or wear skins to-day, it certainly is better to accept the advantages, though so dearly bought, which the invention and industry of mankind offer. In such a neighborhood as this, boards and shingles, lime and bricks, are cheaper and more easily obtained than suitable caves. . . .

Near the end of March, 1845, I borrowed an axe and went down to the woods by Walden Pond. . . . It is difficult to begin without borrowing, but perhaps it is the most generous course thus to permit your fellow-men to have an interest in your enterprise. . . .

I hewed the main timbers six inches square, most of the studs on two sides only, and the rafters and floor timbers on one side, leaving the rest of the bark on, so that they were just as straight and much stronger than sawed ones. Each stick was carefully mortised or tenoned by its stump, for I had borrowed other tools by this time. . . .

By the middle of April, for I made no haste in my work, but rather made the most of it, my house was framed and ready for raising. . . . At length, in the beginning of May, with the help of some of my acquaintances, rather to improve so good an occasion for neighborliness than from any necessity, I set up the frame of my house. . . . Before winter I built a chimney, and shingled the sides of my house. . . . I have thus a tight shingled and plastered house, ten feet wide by fifteen long, and eight-feet posts, with a garret and a closet, a large window on each side. . . .

One says to me, "I wonder that you do not lay up money; you love to travel." . . . But I am wiser than that. . . . I say to my friend, Suppose we try who will get there first. The distance is thirty miles; the fare ninety cents. That is almost a day's wages. . . . Well, I start now on foot, and get there before night. . . . You will in the meanwhile have earned your fare, and arrive there some time to-morrow, or possibly this evening, if you are lucky enough to get a job in season. . . .

Such is the universal law, which no man can ever outwit, and with regard to the railroad even we may say it is as broad as it is long. To make a railroad round the world available to all mankind is equivalent to grading the whole sur-face of the planet. Men have an indistinct notion that if they keep up this ac-tivity of joint stocks and spades long enough all will at length ride somewhere, in next to no time, and for nothing; but though a crowd rushes to the depot, and the conductor shouts "All aboard!" when the smoke is blown away and the vapor condensed, it will be perceived that a few are riding, but the rest are run over, — and it will be called, and will be, "A melancholy accident." . . .

For more than five years I maintained myself thus solely by the labor of my hands, and I found that, by working about six weeks in a year, I could meet all the expenses of living. The whole of my winters, as well as most of my sum-mers, I had free and clear for study. . . .

As I preferred some things to others, and especially valued my free-dom. . . . I did not wish to spend my time in earning rich carpets or other fine furniture, or delicate cookery, or a house in the Grecian or the Gothic style just yet. . . . In short, I am convinced, both by faith and experience that to maintain one's self on this earth is not a hardship but a pastime, if we live simply and wisely. . . .

Questions

1. What is Thoreau's view of material progress?
2. What, if any, are the weaknesses of Thoreau's philosophy? Can his ideas be extended easily from an individual to a family? Why or why not?

3. By living alone at Walden, did Thoreau flee from the challenges of the outside world or lead by example? Explain.

Nathaniel Hawthorne,
The Blithedale Romance (1852)

Nathaniel Hawthorne (1804–1864) was a native of Salem, Massachusetts, and a graduate of Bowdoin College. Living for a year at Brook Farm, Hawthorne drew on that experience as well as the themes of moral reform and feminism in writing his novel The Blithedale Romance. *As did Herman Melville (the two writers admired each other's work), Hawthorne explored the human isolation of individualism and the destructive capacity of moral crusades.*

Whereas most reformers identified with the antislavery movement, Hawthorne and Melville distanced themselves from the certitude of moral reform (see text p. 316). In the following passage from The Blithedale Romance, *the narrator describes the romantic idealism of the Brook Farm community and the sense of moral isolation that followed its demise.*

If ever men might lawfully dream awake, and give utterance to their wildest visions, without dread of laughter or scorn on the part of the audience — yes, and speak of earthly happiness, for themselves and mankind, as an object to be hopefully striven for, and probably attained — we . . . were those very men. We had left the rusty iron framework of society behind us. We had broken through many hindrances that are powerful enough to keep most people on the weary tread-mill of the established system, even while they feel its irksomeness almost as intolerable as we did. . . . It was our purpose — a generous one, certainly, and absurd, no doubt, in full proportion with its generosity — to give up whatever we had theretofore attained, for the sake of showing mankind the example of a life governed by other than the false and cruel principles, on which human society has all along been based. . . . We meant to lessen the laboring man's great burthen of toil, by performing our due share of it. . . . We sought our profit by mutual aid, instead of wresting it by the strong hand from an enemy, or filching it craftily from those less shrewd than ourselves. . . .

The experiment, so far as its original projectors were concerned, proved long ago a failure, first leaping into Fourierism [see text pp. 363–364], and dying, as it well deserved, for this infidelity to its own higher spirit. . . .

My subsequent life has passed — I was going to say, happily — but, at all events, tolerably enough. I am now at middle-age — well, well, a step or two beyond the midmost point. . . . I live very much at my ease, and fare sumptuously every day. . . . As regards human progress . . . let them believe in it who can, and aid in it who choose! . . . I lack a purpose. . . . I by no means wish to die. Yet, were there any cause, in this whole chaos of human struggle, worth a sane man's dying for, and which my death would benefit, then — provided, however, the effort did not involve an unreasonable amount of trouble — methinks I might be bold to offer my life. . . . Farther than that, I should be loth to pledge myself.

Questions

1. What was the purpose of Brook Farm?
2. Why did it fail?
3. Do you think Hawthorne would have been inclined to repeat Thoreau's experience at Walden Pond? Why or why not?

Rebecca Cox Jackson, On the Shakers

Rebecca Cox Jackson (1795–1871) was a free African-American woman who renounced a relatively secure life with her husband in Philadelphia to become an itinerant Methodist preacher. During the 1830s she traveled throughout the countryside, accompanied by a younger disciple, Rebecca Perot. The two "Rebeccas" became committed Shakers in 1843 and eventually settled in the community of Watervliet near Albany, New York. But they remained ambivalent about the Shaker desire for isolation; in 1851 they resumed their ministry in the free black community. Jackson later founded her own Shaker family in Philadelphia.

In the 1840s Jackson began writing a memoir of her religious experiences; these included powerful dreams and visions. She expresses three key elements of the Shaker faith in the passages below: that believers received the direct guidance of the Holy Ghost; that Mother Ann Lee (the movement's founder) represented the female embodiment of a God with both male and female attributes; and that the millennium — the end of human time — was near.

Monday evening, February 18, 1850. I was instructed concerning the atmosphere and its bounds. I saw its form — it is like the sea, which has her bounds. . . . It covered land and sea, so far above all moving things, and yet so far beneath the starry heavens. Its face is like the face of the sea, smooth and gentle when undisturbed by the wind. So is the atmosphere, when undisturbed by the power of the sun and moon. When agitated by these, it rages like the sea and sends forth its storms upon the earth. Nothing can live above it. A bird could no more live or fly above its face, than a fish can live or swim out of the water. It is always calm and serene between its face and the starry heaven. The sight, to me, was beautiful.

March 1, 1850. . . . Prayer given to me by Mother Ann Lee: "Oh God, my Everlasting Father, to Thee do I lift up my soul in prayer and thanksgiving for the gift of Thy dear Son, our Blessed Savior, who has begotten to us a living hope. And to Thee, Holy Mother Wisdom, do I lift up my soul in prayer and thanksgiving, for the gift of Thy Holy Daughter, whose blessed Spirit has led me and instructed me in this, the holy way of God, lo! these many years, and has borne with my infirmities and many shortcomings. And lo! Thou hast comforted me in all my sorrows and Thy blessed Spirit comforts me today."

Then I saw our Heavenly Parents look on me and smile, and Mother Ann gave me sweet counsel. And I was greatly strengthened in the way of God.

March 15, 1850. After I came to Watervliet . . . and saw how the Believers seemed to be gathered to themselves, in praying for themselves and not for the world, which lay in midnight darkness, I wondered how the world was to be saved, if Shakers were the only people of God on earth, and they seemed to be busy in their own concerns, which were mostly temporal. . . .

Then seeing these at ease in Zion, I cried in the name of Christ and Mother that He in mercy would do something for the helpless world. At that time, it seemed as if the whole world rested upon me. I cried to the Lord both day and night, for many months, that God would make a way that the world might hear the Gospel — that God would send spirits and angels to administer to their understanding, that they might be saved in the present tense, for I knew by revelation, that it was God's will that they should be.

Questions

1. How does a sense of religious fervor shape the decisions made by Rebecca Cox Jackson?
2. What is her criticism of the Shakers at Watervliet?
3. How do Jackson's religious views differ from those predominating in the mid-nineteenth century?

Angelina E. Grimké, Breaking Out of Women's "Separate Sphere" (1838)

Angelina Grimké (1805–1879) was born in Charleston, South Carolina, and was raised in a wealthy, aristocratic, and conservative family. Deeply influenced by her older sister, Sarah, Angelina soon rejected Charleston society, converted from the Episcopal to the Quaker faith during a visit to Philadelphia, and soon thereafter embraced moral reform (see text p. 324). She wrote to William Lloyd Garrison in 1835 to express her support for abolitionism. When Garrison published her letter in his newspaper, The Liberator, *the public reform career of Angelina Grimké began.*

Grimké soon advocated women's rights in conjunction with abolitionism. One of her principal opponents was Catharine Beecher (see Chapter 20, "The Christian Family"). Although she was an early advocate of education for women, Beecher also was a leading figure in defining the domestic sphere of women. Defending this sphere from the public activity of abolitionist women, Beecher published An Essay on Slavery and Abolitionism, with Reference to the Duty of American Females *(1837). The following passage comes from Grimké's reply to Beecher.*

I come now to that part of thy book, which is, of all others, the most important to the women of this country; thy "general views in relation to the place woman is appointed to fill by the dispensations of heaven." . . .

Thou sayest, "Heaven has appointed to one sex the *superior,* and to the other the *subordinate* station. . . ." This is an assertion without proof. Thou further sayest, that "it was designed that the mode of gaining influence and exercising power should be *altogether different and peculiar.*" Does the Bible teach this? . . . Did Jesus . . . give a different rule of action to men and women? . . . I read in the Bible, that Miriam, and Deborah, and Huldah, were called to fill *public stations* in Church and State. I find Anna, the prophetess, speaking in the temple "unto all them that looked for redemption in Jerusalem." . . . I see them even standing on Mount Calvary, around his cross . . . but he never *rebuked* them; He never told them it was unbecoming *their sphere of life* to mingle in the crowds which followed his footsteps. . . .

Thou sayest . . . "make no claims, and maintain no rights, but what are the gifts of honor, rectitude and love." From whom does woman receive her *rights*? From God, or from man? . . . I understand . . . her *rights* are an integral part of her moral being; they cannot be withdrawn; they must live with her forever. Her rights lie at the foundation of all her duties; and, so long as the divine commands are binding upon her, so long must her rights continue. . . .

Thou sayest, "In this country, petitions to Congress, in reference to official duties of legislators, seem IN ALL CASES, to fall entirely without the sphere of female duty. Men are the proper persons to make appeals to the rulers whom they appoint," etc. Here I entirely dissent from thee. The fact that women are denied the right of voting for members of Congress, is but a poor reason why they should also be deprived of the right of petition. If their numbers are counted to swell the number of Representatives in our State and National Legislatures, the *very least* that can be done is to give them the right of petition in all cases whatsoever. . . . If not, they are mere slaves, known only through their masters.

Questions

1. How does Angelina Grimké go about attacking Beecher's position?
2. What does Grimké regard as the proper relationship between a woman's moral being and her rights? To what extent can the two be separated?
3. Why does Grimké believe women are entitled to the right of petition?

Elizabeth Cady Stanton, Seneca Falls Resolutions (1848)

Elizabeth Cady Stanton (1815–1902) and Lucretia Mott (1793–1880) met in 1840 at the World Anti-Slavery Convention held in London. Stanton attended with her husband, the abolitionist Henry B. Stanton. Mott, a Quaker minister, attended as a delegate for the American Anti-Slavery Society. The convention's decision to deny recognition to women consigned Stanton and Mott to the gallery as observers, and they resolved to link the struggle against slavery with one for women's rights. In 1848 they convened the first women's rights convention at Seneca Falls, New York, with Stanton drafting its famous "Declaration of Sentiments" and Resolutions. She used the Declaration of Independence as a model.

When, in the course of human events, it becomes necessary for one portion of the family of man to assume among the people of the earth a position different from that which they have hitherto occupied, but one to which the laws of nature and nature's God entitle them, a decent respect to the opinions of mankind requires that they should declare the causes that impel them to such a course.

We hold these truths to be self-evident: that all men and women are created equal; that they are endowed by their Creator with certain inalienable rights. . . . Whenever any form of government becomes destructive of these ends, it is the right of those who suffer from it to refuse allegiance to it, and to insist upon the institution of a new government. . . .

The history of mankind is a history of repeated injuries and usurpations on the part of man toward woman, having in direct object the establishment of an absolute tyranny over her. To prove this, let facts be submitted to a candid world.

He has never permitted her to exercise her inalienable right to the elective franchise. . . .

He has withheld from her rights which are given to the most ignorant and degraded men — both natives and foreigners. . . .

He has made her, if married, in the eye of the law, civilly dead.

He has taken from her all right in property, even to the wages she earns. . . .

After depriving her of all rights as a married woman, if single, and the owner of property, he has taxed her to support a government which recognizes her only when her property can be made profitable to it. . . .

He has denied her the facilities for obtaining a thorough education, all colleges being closed against her. . . .

He has created a false public sentiment by giving the world a different code of morals for men and women, by which moral delinquencies which exclude women from society, are not only tolerated, but deemed of little account in man. . . .

He has endeavored, in every way that he could, to destroy her confidence in her own powers, to lessen her self-respect and to make her willing to lead a dependent and abject life. . . .

Resolved, That all laws which prevent woman from occupying such a station in society as her conscience shall dictate, or which place her in a position inferior to that of man, are contrary to the great precept of nature, and therefore of no force or authority.

Resolved, That woman is man's equal — was intended to be so by the Creator, and the highest good of the race demands that she should be recognized as such. . . .

Resolved, That it is the duty of the women of this country to secure to themselves their sacred right to the elective franchise. . . .

Questions

1. Note the parallels to the Declaration of Independence. What is their intended effect?

2. What do the three resolutions reveal about the state of the women's movement in 1848?

3. Is this a radical document for the times? Why or why not?

William Lloyd Garrison,
"Commencement of *The Liberator*" (1831)

*In 1829 William Lloyd Garrison (1805–1879) broke with traditional abo-
litionist proposals for gradual emancipation to demand immediate abolition
of slavery in the United States. Later that year Garrison added his voice to
those of African-American freedmen in the North who denounced the American Colonization Society as a thinly disguised plot to remove free blacks, not
slaves, from America. Garrison also launched the Boston* Liberator *to express
his views; the paper's first number appeared on January 1, 1831.*

Publication of The Liberator *and the bloody slave rebellion led by Nat
Turner in Southampton County, Virginia, in August 1831 (see text p. 331) re-
inforced each other in ways that unsettled northern and southern whites; the
supporters of Andrew Jackson even attempted to silence the abolitionist "in-
cendiaries." The following excerpts are from Garrison's opening editorial,
"Commencement of* The Liberator," *in the inaugural issue.*

In Park Street Church, on the Fourth of July, 1829, in an address on slavery, I unreflectingly assented to the popular but pernicious doctrine of gradual abolition. I seize this opportunity to make a full and unequivocal recantation, and thus publicly to ask pardon of my God, of my country, and of my
brethren, the poor slaves, for having uttered a sentiment so full of timidity, injustice and absurdity. . . .

I am aware, that many object to the severity of my language; but is there
not cause for severity? I will be as harsh as truth, and as uncompromising as
justice. On this subject, I do not wish to think, or speak, or write, with moderation. No! no! Tell a man, whose house is on fire, to give a moderate alarm;
tell him to moderately rescue his wife from the hands of the ravisher; tell the
mother to gradually extricate her babe from the fire into which it has fallen;
but urge me not to use moderation in a cause like the present! I am in earnest.
I will not equivocate — I will not excuse — I will not retreat a single inch,
AND I WILL BE HEARD. . . .

It is pretended, that I am retarding the cause of emancipation by the
coarseness of my invective, and the precipitancy of my measures. The charge

is not true. On this question, my influence, humble as it is, is felt at this moment to a considerable extent, and shall be felt in coming years — not perniciously, but beneficially—not as a curse, but as a blessing; and POSTERITY WILL BEAR TESTIMONY THAT I WAS RIGHT.

Questions

1. What is the effect of Garrison's rhetoric? Is it excessive? Why or why not?
2. Why does Garrison refuse to compromise? Is he right to do so?
3. What role does an uncompromising critic like William Lloyd Garrison play in social change? Is his contribution crucial or not? Explain.

Theodore Dwight Weld, *American Slavery as It Is* (1839)

Theodore Dwight Weld (1803–1895) was converted to the evangelistic ministry by Charles Grandison Finney. Weld, however, moved beyond his mentor's interest in temperance and joined the newly invigorated abolitionist crusade. A founding member of the American Anti-Slavery Society, Weld organized a group of antislavery ministers who toured the country preaching against the sin of slavery. Weld married Angelina Grimké in 1838 at the height of his reform career, which ended shortly after the abolitionist schism of 1840.

Like others in the abolitionist cause during the 1830s, Weld aimed to convince all who would listen that slavery was morally wrong. Evangelical abolitionists, he believed, would launch a moral reformation across the land, and the slaves would be set free. Weld's best-known effort to produce such a moral reformation, written in collaboration with Sarah and Angelina Grimké, was American Slavery as It Is: Testimony of a Thousand Witnesses. *The book was a compilation of documentary information, especially from southern newspapers, to support the moral argument against slavery.*

PUNISHMENTS.
I. Floggings.

The slaves are terribly lacerated with whips, paddles, etc.; red pepper and salt are rubbed into their mangled flesh; hot brine and turpentine are poured into their gashes; and innumerable other tortures inflicted upon them.

We will in the first place, prove by a cloud of witnesses, that the slaves are whipped with such inhuman severity, as to lacerate and mangle their flesh in the most shocking manner, leaving permanent scars and ridges; after establishing this, we will present a mass of testimony, concerning a great variety of other tortures. The testimony, for the most part, will be that of the slaveholders themselves, and in their own chosen words. A large portion of it will be taken from the advertisements, which they have published in their own newspapers, describing by the scars on their bodies made by the whip, their own runaway slaves. To copy these advertisements *entire* would require a great amount of space, and flood the reader with a vast mass of matter irrelevant to the *point* before us; we shall therefore insert only so much of each, as will intelligibly set forth the precise point under consideration. In the column under the word "witnesses," will be found the name of the individual, who signs the advertisement, or for whom it is signed, with his or her place of residence, and the name and date of the paper, in which it appeared, and generally the name of the place where it is published. Opposite the name of each witness, will be an extract, from the advertisement, containing his or her testimony.

WITNESSES.	TESTIMONY.
Mr. D. Judd, jailor, Davidson Co., Tennessee, in the "Nashville Banner," Dec. 10th, 1838.	"Committed to jail as a runaway, a negro woman named Martha, 17 or 18 years of age, has *numerous scars of the whip* on her back."
Mr. Robert Nicoll, Dauphin st. between Emmanuel and Conception st's, Mobile, Alabama, in the "Mobile Commercial Advertiser."	"Ten dollars reward for my woman Siby, *very much scarred about the neck and ears by whipping.*"
Mr. Bryant Johnson, Fort Valley, Houston Co., Georgia, in the "Standard of Union," Milledgeville Ga., Oct. 2, 1838.	"Ranaway [*sic*], a negro woman, named Maria, *some scars on her back occasioned by the whip.*"
Mr. James T. De Jarnett, Vernon, Autauga Co., Alabama, in the "Pensacola Gazette," July 14, 1838.	"Stolen a negro woman, named Celia. On examining her back you will find *marks caused by the whip.*"
Maurice Y. Garcia, Sheriff of the County of Jefferson, La., in the "New Orleans Bee," August 14, 1838.	"Lodged in jail, a mulatto boy, *having large marks of the whip,* on his shoulders and other parts of his body."
R. J. Bland, Sheriff of Claiborne Co., Miss., in the "Charleston (S.C.) Courier," August 28, 1838.	"Was committed a negro boy, named Tom, is *much marked with the whip.*"
Mr. James Noe, Red River Landing, La., in the "Sentinel," Vicksburg, Miss., August 22, 1837.	"Ranaway, a negro fellow named Dick — has *many scars* on his back from being *whipped.*"

WITNESSES.	TESTIMONY.
William Craze, jailor, Alexandria, La. in the "Planter's Intelligencer," Sept. 26, 1838.	"Committed to jail, a negro slave — his back is *very badly scarred.*"
John A. Rowland, jailor, Lumberton, North Carolina, in the "Fayetteville (N. C.) Observer," June 20, 1838.	"Committed, a mulatto fellow — his back shows *lasting impressions of the whip,* and leaves no doubt of his being a SLAVE."
J. K. Roberts, sheriff, Blount county, Ala., in the "Huntsville Democrat," Dec. 9, 1838.	"Committed to jail, a negro man — his back *much marked* by the whip."
Mr. H. Varillat, No. 23 Girod street, New Orleans — in the "Commercial Bulletin," August 27, 1838.	"Ranaway, the negro slave named Jupiter — has a *fresh mark* of a cowskin on one of his cheeks."
Mr. Cornelius D. Tolin, Augusta, Ga., in the "Chronicle and Sentinel," Oct. 18, 1838.	"Ranaway, a negro man named Johnson — he has a *great many marks of the whip* on his back."
W. H. Brasseale, sheriff, Blount county, Ala., in the "Huntsville Democrat," June 9, 1838.	"Committed to jail, a negro slave named James —*much scarred* with a whip on his back."
Mr. Robert Beasley, Macon, Ga., in the "Georgia Messenger," July 27, 1837.	"Ranaway, my man Fountain — he is marked *on the back with the whip.*"
Mr. John Wotton, Rockville, Montgomery county, Maryland, in the "Baltimore Republican," Jan. 13, 1838.	"Ranaway, Bill — has *several* LARGE SCARS on his back from a *severe* whipping in *early* life."
D. S. Bennett, sheriff, Narchitoches, La., in the "Herald," July 21, 1838.	"Committed to jail, a negro boy who calls himself Joe — said negro bears *marks of the whip.*"
Messrs. C. C. Whitehead and R. A. Evans, Marion, Georgia, in the Milledgeville (Ga.) "Standard of Union," June 26, 1838.	"Ranaway, negro fellow John — from being whipped, has *scars on his back, arms, and thighs.*"
Mr. Samuel Stewart, Greensboro, Ala., in the "Southern Advocate," Huntsville, Jan. 6, 1838.	"Ranaway, a boy named Jim — with the marks of the *whip* on the small of the back, reaching round to the flank."
Mr. John Walker, No. 6, Banks' Arcade, New Orleans, in the "Bulletin," August 11, 1838.	"Ranaway, the mulatto boy Quash — *considerably marked* on the back and other places with the lash."

WITNESSES.	TESTIMONY.
Mr. Jesse Beene, Cahawba, Ala., in the "State Intelligencer," Tuskaloosa, Dec. 25, 1837.	"Ranaway, my negro man Billy — he has the *marks of the whip.*"
Mr. John Turner, Thomaston, Upson county, Georgia — in the "Standard of Union," Milledgeville, June 26, 1838.	"Left, my negro man named George — has *marks of the whip very plain* on his thighs."
James Derrah, deputy sheriff, Claiborne county, Mi., in the "Port Gibson Correspondent," April 15, 1837.	"Committed to jail, negro man Toy — he has been *badly whipped.*"
S. B. Murphy, sheriff, Wilinson county, Georgia — in the Milledge-ville "Journal," May 15, 1838.	"Brought to jail, a negro man named George — he has a *great many scars from the lash.*"
Mr. L. E. Cooner, Branchville Orangeburgh District, South Carolina—in the Macon "Messenger," May 25, 1837.	"One hundred dollars reward, for my negro Glasgow, and Kate, his wife. Glasgow is 24 years old — has *marks of the whip* on his back. Kate is 26 — has a *scar* on her cheek, *and several marks of a whip.*"
John H. Hand, jailor, Parish of West Feliciana, La., in the "St. Francisville Journal," July 6, 1837.	"Committed to jail, a negro boy named John, about 17 years old — his back *badly marked* with the *whip,* his upper lip and chin *severely bruised.*"

Questions

1. How does this information put slavery and its spokesmen on the defensive?
2. Does the selection have a weakness? If so, what is it?
3. Is this a religious, political, or emotional attack on slavery? Explain.

Connections Questions

1. Who is the more effective social critic — Henry David Thoreau ("*Walden*") or William Lloyd Garrison ("Commencement")? Explain.
2. Using the Stanton and Weld documents ("Seneca Falls Resolutions"; "*American Slavery*"), comment on the importance of framing an issue when calling for social change. In other words, why do the authors use their respective approaches?
3. Could slavery have been effectively attacked without recourse to religion? Why or why not?

CHAPTER 13

Sections and Sectionalism 1840–1860

Frederick Law Olmsted, Slave Management on a Mississippi Plantation (1852)

In the two decades preceding the Civil War, various writers traveled throughout the South to report their observations on the lives and labors of slaves and masters. The keenest of those observers may have been landscape architect Frederick Law Olmsted (1822–1903), who later won fame for his design (with Calvert Vaux) of Central Park. Olmsted first journeyed through the South in 1852 on a commission from the New York Times.

In the following selection Olmsted describes an extremely large plantation in Mississippi. Contemporary management philosophy held that plantations employing more than a hundred slaves were difficult if not impossible to govern. Thus owners often broke up very large estates into smaller, more manageable units. Each had its own overseer, and either the owner or a manager was in direct charge of the entire operation.

SLAVE MANAGEMENT ON THE LARGEST SCALE

The estate I am now about to describe, was situated upon a tributary of the Mississippi, and accessible only by occasional steamboats; even this mode of communication being frequently interrupted at low stages of the rivers. The slaves upon it formed about one twentieth of the whole population of the county, in which the blacks considerably out-number the whites. . . .

The property consisted of four adjoining plantations, each with its own negro-cabins, stables and overseer, and each worked to a great extent independently of the others, but all contributing their crop to one [cotton] gin-house and warehouse, and all under the general superintendence of a bailiff or manager, who constantly resided upon the estate, and in the absence of the owner, had vice-regal power over the overseers, controlling, so far as he thought fit, the economy of all the plantations. . . .

. . . The overseers were superior to most of their class, and, with one exception, frank, honest, temperate and industrious, but their feelings toward negroes were such as naturally result from their occupation. They were all married, and lived with their families, each in a cabin or cottage, in the hamlet of the slaves of which he had especial charge. Their wages varied from $500 to $1,000 a year each. . . .

. . . Of course, to secure their own personal safety and to efficiently direct the labor of such a large number of ignorant, indolent, and vicious negroes, rules, or rather habits and customs, of discipline, were necessary, which would in particular cases be liable to operate unjustly and cruelly. It is apparent, also, that, as the testimony of negroes against them would not be received as evidence in court, that there was very little probability that any excessive severity would be restrained by fear of the law. A provision of the law intended to secure a certain privilege to slaves, was indeed disregarded under my own observation, and such infraction of the law was confessedly customary with one of the overseers, and was permitted by the manager, for the reason that it seemed to him to be, in a certain degree, justifiable and expedient under the circumstances, and because he did not like to interfere unnecessarily in such matters.

In the main, the negroes appeared to be well taken care of and abundantly supplied with the necessaries of vigorous physical existence. A large part of them lived in commodious and well-built cottages, with broad galleries in front, so that each family of five had two rooms on the lower floor, and a loft. The remainder lived in log-huts, small and mean in appearance, but those of their overseers were little better, and preparations were being made to replace all of these by neat boarded cottages. Each family had a fowl-house and hog-sty (constructed by the negroes themselves), and kept fowls and swine, feeding the latter during the summer on weeds and fattening them in the autumn on corn *stolen* (this was mentioned to me by the overseers as if it were a matter of course) from their master's corn-fields. I several times saw gangs of them eating the dinner which they had brought, each for himself, to the field, and observed that they generally had plenty, often more than they could eat, of bacon, corn-bread, and molasses. The allowance of food is weighed and measured under the eye of the manager by the drivers, and distributed to the head of each family weekly: consisting of — for each person, 3 pounds of pork, 1 peck [8 quarts] of meal; and from January to July, 1 quart of molasses. Monthly, in addition, 1 pound tobacco, and 4 pints salt. No drink is ever served but water, except after unusual exposure, or to ditchers working in water, who get a glass of whisky at night. All hands cook for themselves after work at night, or whenever they please between nightfall and daybreak, each family in its own cabin. Each family had a garden, the products of which, together with eggs, fowls and bacon, they frequently sold, or used in addition to their regular allowance of food. Most of the families bought a barrel of flour every year. The manager endeavored to encourage this practice, and that they might spend their money for flour instead of liquor, he furnished it to them at rather less than what it cost him at wholesale. There were many poor whites within a few miles who would always sell liquor to the negroes, and encourage them to steal, to obtain the means to buy it of them. These poor whites were always spoken of with anger by the overseers, and they each had a standing offer of much more than the intrinsic value of their land, from the manager, to induce them to move away. . . .

Near the first quarters we visited there was a large blacksmith's and wheelwright's shop, in which a number of mechanics were at work. Most of them, as we rode up, were eating their breakfast, which they warmed at their fires. Within and around the shop there were some fifty plows which they were putting in order. The manager inspected the work, found some of it faulty, sharply reprimanded the workmen for not getting on faster, and threatened one of them with a whipping for not paying closer attention to the directions which had been given him. He told me that he once employed a white man from the North, who professed to be a first-class workman, but he soon found he could not do nearly as good work as the negro mechanics on the estate, and the latter despised him so much, and got such high opinions of themselves in consequence of his inferiority, that he had been obliged to discharge him in the midst of his engagement.

HOURS OF LABOR

Each overseer regulated the hours of work on his own plantation. I saw the negroes at work before sunrise and after sunset. At about eight o'clock they were allowed to stop for breakfast, and again about noon, to dine. The length of these rests was at the discretion of the overseer or drivers, usually, I should say, from half an hour to an hour. There was no rule.

OVERSEERS

The number of hands directed by each overseer was considerably over one hundred. The manager thought it would be better economy to have a white man over every fifty hands, but the difficulty of obtaining trustworthy overseers prevented it. Three of those he then had were the best he had ever known. He described the great majority as being passionate, careless, inefficient men, generally intemperate, and totally unfitted for the duties of the position. The best overseers, ordinarily, are young men, the sons of small planters, who take up the business temporarily, as a means of acquiring a little capital with which to purchase negroes for themselves.

PLOW-GIRLS

The plowing, both with single and double mule teams, was generally performed by women, and very well performed, too. I watched with some interest for any indication that their sex unfitted them for the occupation. Twenty of them were plowing together, with double teams and heavy plows. They were superintended by a male negro driver, who carried a whip, which he frequently cracked at them, permitting no dawdling or delay at the turning; and they twitched their plows around on the head-land, jerking their reins, and yelling to their mules, with apparent ease, energy, and rapidity. Throughout the Southwest the negroes, as a rule, appear to be worked much harder than in the eastern and northern slave States. I do not think they accomplish as much daily, as agricultural laborers at the North usually do, but they certainly labor much harder, and more unremittingly. They are constantly and steadily driven up to their work, and the stupid, plodding, machine-like manner in which they labor, is painful to witness. This was especially the case with the hoe-gangs. One of them numbered nearly two hundred hands (for the force of two plantations was working together), moving across the field in parallel lines, with a considerable degree of precision. I repeatedly rode through the lines at a canter, with other horsemen, often coming upon them suddenly, without producing the smallest change or interruption in the dogged action of the laborers, or causing one of them to lift an eye from the ground. A very tall and powerful negro walked to and fro in the rear of the line, frequently cracking his whip, and calling out, in the surliest manner, to one and another, "Shove your hoe, there! shove your hoe!" But I never saw him strike any one with the whip.

DISCIPLINE

The whip was evidently in constant use, however. There were no rules on the subject, that I learned; the overseers and drivers punished the negroes whenever they deemed it necessary, and in such manner, and with such severity, as they thought fit. "If you do n't work faster," or "If you do n't work better," or "If you do n't recollect what I tell you, I will have you flogged," are threats which I have often heard. I said to one of the overseers, "It must be very disagreeable to have to punish them as much as you do?" "Yes, it would be to those who are not used to it — but it's my business, and I think nothing of it. Why, sir, I would n't mind killing a nigger more than I would a dog." I asked if he had ever killed a negro? "Not quite," he said, but overseers were often obliged to. Some negroes are determined never to let a white man whip them, and will resist you, when you attempt it; of course you must kill them in that case. Once a negro, whom he was about to whip in the field, struck at his head with a hoe. He parried the blow with his whip, and drawing a pistol tried to shoot him, but the pistol missing fire he rushed in and knocked him down with the butt of it. At another time a negro whom he was punishing, insulted and threatened him. He went to the house for his gun, and as he was returning, the negro, thinking he would be afraid of spoiling so valuable a piece of property by firing, broke for the woods. He fired at once, and put six buck-shot into his hips. He always carried a bowie-knife, but not a pistol.

Questions

1. How does Olmsted's description of slavery differ from that of Theodore Weld (Chapter 12, *American Slavery*)?
2. What does Olmsted say about slave discipline?
3. Is Olmsted acting as a critic of slavery or as a reporter of its conditions? Cite examples in support of your answer.

Thomas R. Dew, "The Virtues of Slavery, The Impossibility of Emancipation" (1831)

Although one usually thinks of abolition as a northern enterprise, the early debates on it took place south of the Mason-Dixon Line. Many southerners believed that in the long run slavery would work against the moral and economic interests of the region. The dilemma centered on the disposition of slaves. Even the critics of slavery believed in the moral and intellectual inferiority of those enslaved. The continued presence of freed slaves in the South had little support on either side.

The argument stretched from the eighteenth century well into the nineteenth, and it ended only after the invention of the cotton gin made cotton king — and the slave economy very profitable. The last major debate in the South over emancipation occurred in the Virginia legislature in 1831; this commentary on it was written by Thomas R. Dew, president of the College of William and Mary as well as a staunch defender of the "peculiar institution."

We have now, we think, proved our position, that slave labor, in an economical point of view, is far superior to free negro labor; and have no doubt that if an immediate emancipation of negroes were to take place, the whole southern country would be visited with an immediate general famine, from which the productive resources of all the other States of the Union could not deliver them.

It is now easy for us to demonstrate the second point in our argument — that the slave is not only *economically* but *morally* unfit for freedom. And first, idleness and consequent want are, of themselves, sufficient to generate a catalogue of vices of the most mischievous and destructive character. . . .

The great evil, however, of these schemes of emancipation, remains yet to be told. They are admirably calculated to excite plots, murders and insurrections; whether gradual or rapid in their operation, this is the inevitable tendency. . . . Two totally different races, as we have before seen, cannot easily harmonize together, . . . and even when [the negro is] free, . . . idleness will produce want and worthlessness, and his very worthlessness and degradation will stimulate him to deeds of rapine and vengeance; he will oftener engage in plots and massacres, and thereby draw down on his devoted head, the vengeance of the provoked whites. . . . [L]iberate [our] slaves, and every year you would hear of insurrections and plots, and every day would perhaps record a murder. . . .

[Thomas Jefferson] has supposed the master in a continual passion — in the constant exercise of the most odious tyranny, and the child, a creature of imitation, looking on and learning. But is not this master sometimes kind and indulgent to his slaves? . . . We may rest assured, in this intercourse between a good master and his servant, more good than evil may be taught the child; the exalted principles of morality and religion may thereby be sometimes indelibly inculcated upon his mind. . . . Look to the slave-holding population of our country, and you everywhere find them characterized by noble and elevated sentiments, by humane and virtuous feelings. . . .

Let us now look a moment to the slave, and contemplate his position. Mr. Jefferson has described him as hating, rather than loving his master, and as losing, too, all that *amor patriae* [love of country] which characterizes the true patriot. We assert again, that Mr. Jefferson is not borne out by the fact. We are well convinced that there is nothing but the mere relations of husband and wife, parent and child, brother and sister, which produce a closer tie, than the relation of master and servant. We have no hesitation in affirming, that throughout the whole slaveholding country, the slaves of a good master are his warmest, most constant, and most devoted friends; they have been accustomed to look up to him as their supporter, director and defender. Everyone acquainted with southern states, knows that the slave rejoices in the elevation and prosperity of his master; and the heart of no one is more gladdened at the successful debut of young master or miss on the great theatre of the world, than that of either the young slave who has grown up with them, and shared in all their sports, and even partaken of all their delicacies — or the aged one who has looked on and watched them from birth to manhood, with the kindest and most affectionate solicitude, and has ever met from them all the kind treatment and generous sympathies of feeling, tender hearts. . . .

Questions

1. To what extent is this a "moral" argument? Explain.
2. Why is Dew's treatment of Thomas Jefferson significant and even surprising?
3. In Dew's mind, how do blacks act when they become free? As slaves? Does he explain the difference?

Memories of a Slave Childhood

Despite southerners' claims that slaves were happy and well treated, the evidence is overwhelming that those in bondage resented their condition and fought back whenever and however they could. Slaveowners recognized this, and to keep their slaves in line they resorted to harsh disciplinary measures or, when that failed, sold "problem" slaves to planters west of the Mississippi.

The following excerpt displays not only the anger felt by slaves over their treatment, but the subtle interplay that took place among slaves as well as between slave and master. The source is an interview from the 1930s with an elderly woman who had spent her youth as a slave.

[The] overseer . . . went to my father one morning and said, "Bob, I'm gonna whip you this morning." Daddy said, "I ain't done nothing," and he said, "I know it, I'm gonna whip you to keep you from doing nothing," and he hit him with that cowhide — you know it would cut the blood out of you with every lick if they hit you hard — and daddy was chopping cotton, so he just took up his hoe and chopped right down on that man's head and knocked his brains out. Yes'm, it killed him, but they didn't put colored folks in jail then, so when old Charlie Merrill, the nigger trader, come along they sold my daddy to him, and he carried him way down in Mississippi. Ole Merrill would buy all the time, buy and sell niggers just like hogs. They sold him Aunt Phoebe's little baby that was just toddling long, and Uncle Dick — that was my mammy's brother.

The way they would whip you was like they done my oldest sister. They tied her, and they had a place just like they're gonna barbecue a hog, and they would strip you and tie you and lay you down. . . . Old Aunt Fanny had told marster that my sister wouldn't keep her dress clean, and that's what they was whipping her 'bout. So they had her down in the cellar whipping her, and I was real little. I couldn't say "Big Sis," but I went and told Mammy. "Old Marster's got 'Big Jim' down there in the cellar beating her," and mammy got out of bed and went in there and throwed Aunt Fan out the kitchen door, and they had to stop whipping Big Sis and come and see about Aunt Fan. You see, she would tell things on the others, trying to keep from getting whipped herself. I seed mistress crack her many a time over the head with a broom, and I'd be so scared she was gonna crack me, but she never did hit me, 'cept slap me when I'd turn the babies over. I'd get tired and make like I was sleep, and would ease the cradle over and throw the baby out. I never would throw mammy's out, though. Old Miss would be setting there just knitting and watching the babies; they had a horn and every woman could tell when it was time to come and nurse her baby by the way they would blow the horn. The white folks was crazy 'bout their nigger babies, 'cause that's where they got their profit. . . . When I'd get tired, I would just ease that baby over and Mistress would slap me so hard; I didn't know a hand could hurt so bad, but I'd take the slap and get to go out to play. She would slap me hard and say, "Git on out of here and stay till you wake up," and that was just what I wanted, 'cause I'd play then. . . .

Questions

1. How and why does this document differ from the previous two (Frederick Law Olmsted, "Slave Management"; Thomas R. Dew, "The Virtues of Slavery")?
2. According to the speaker, where is the profit in slavery found?
3. What is the overriding sense of this woman's childhood?

Carl Schurz, A German Immigrant in Philadelphia (1855)

Carl Schurz (1829–1906) was part of the great tide of German immigrants who came to the United States in the two decades before the Civil War. A participant in the liberal German revolution of 1848, Schurz was forced to flee to Switzerland when the movement collapsed. He arrived in Philadelphia in 1852 and four years later moved to Watertown, Wisconsin, where he became the leader of the large community of German immigrants in the Old Northwest. In 1855 he returned to Europe for a visit.

Schurz later had a distinguished career as a Union general during the Civil War, newspaper editor, secretary of the interior, and United States senator. He also authored the report for Andrew Johnson on conditions in the postwar South (see Chapter 16, "Report on Conditions").

In this letter to a German-American acquaintance, Schurz reflects on his new and old homes.

Philadelphia, March 25, 1855.

To Gottfried Kinkel

You seem to surmise that my visit to Europe means that I am returning there for good, and I see that many of my friends have the same idea. It is my intention that this visit shall be a mere interlude in my American life. As long as there is no upheaval of affairs in Europe it is my firm resolve to regard this country not as a transient or accidental abode, but as the field for my usefulness. I love America and I am vitally interested in the things about me — they no longer seem strange. I find that the question of liberty is in its essence the same everywhere, however different its form. Although I do not regard the public affairs of this country with the same devotion as those of our old home, it is not mere ambition nor eagerness for distinction that impels me to activity. My interest in the political contests of this country is so strong, so spontaneous, that I am profoundly stirred. More self-control is required for me to keep aloof than to participate in them. These are the years of my best strength. Shall I devote myself wholly to the struggle for existence while I have hopes that I may soon be independent in that respect? I venture to say that I am neither avaricious nor self-indulgent.

If I now seek material prosperity, it is only that I may be free to follow my natural aspirations. Or shall I again subject myself to that dreary condition of waiting, which must undermine the strongest constitution when it is the only occupation? We have both tasted its bitterness; and I am burning with the desire to be employed with visible, tangible things and no longer to be bound to dreams and theories. I have a holy horror of the illusory fussiness which characterizes the life of the professional refugees. My devotion to the cause of the old Fatherland has not abated but my expectations have somewhat cooled; I have only faint hopes for the next few years. Even if the revolution should come sooner than I expect, I do not see why I should not utilize the intervening time. I feel that here I can accomplish something. I am convinced of it when I consider the qualities of the men who are now conspicuous. This inspires me, and even if the prospects of success did not correspond with my natural impulses, I should suddenly find that I had involuntarily entered into the thick of the fight. In these circumstances, why should I wish to return to Europe? I am happy that I have a firm foothold and good opportunities.

After my return from Europe I expect to go to Wisconsin. I transferred some of my business interests there when on my last trip to the West. The German element is powerful in that State, the immigrants being so numerous, and they are striving for political recognition. They only lack leaders that are not bound by the restraints of money-getting. There is the place where I can find a sure, gradually expanding field for my work without truckling to the nativistic elements, and there, I hope, in time, to gain influence that may also become useful to our cause. . . .

Questions
1. Why does Schurz love America?
2. What belief has he left behind, or at least modified substantially?

3. Does Schurz appear to be an exceptional or typical immigrant? Explain. How might he seem to immigrant-wary Americans in 1855?

The American ("Know-Nothing") Party Platform (1856)

America has existed as a nation of immigrants since 1607. But there has been a continuous pattern in which those whose ancestors came earlier display hostility and prejudice toward those who come later, especially from different parts of the world. Many of the detested newcomers to the United States in the mid-nineteenth century were Catholics from Germany and Ireland; Protestants feared that the papacy intended to take over the government of the United States.

A number of nativist societies arose to combat the "alien menace." In 1850 several of them combined to form the Order of the Star-Spangled Banner, which adopted a pledge of secrecy; if people asked about their program, they replied, "I know nothing." The Know-Nothings (as they came to be called) and other nativist groups created the American party, which in 1856 nominated former president Millard Fillmore as its presidential candidate. The party polled almost 900,000 votes in the election that year.

I. An humble acknowledgment to the Supreme Being who rules one universe, for His protecting care vouchsafed to our fathers in their revolutionary struggle, and hitherto manifested to us, their descendants, in the preservation of the liberties, the independence and the union of these states.

II. The perpetuation of the Federal Union, as the palladium of our civil and religious liberties, and the only sure bulwark of American independence.

III. *Americans must rule America;* and to this end, *native*-born citizens should be selected for all state, federal, or municipal offices of government employment, in preference to naturalized citizens — *nevertheless,*

IV. Persons born of American parents residing temporarily abroad, shall be entitled to all the rights of native-born citizens; but

V. No person should be selected for political station (whether of native or foreign birth), who recognizes any alliance or obligation of any description to any foreign prince, potentate or power, who refuses to recognize the federal and state constitutions (each within its own sphere), as paramount to all other laws, as rules of particular [political] action.

VI. The unequalled recognition and maintenance of the reserved rights of the several states, and the cultivation of harmony and fraternal good-will between the citizens of the several states, and to this end, non-interference by Congress with questions appertaining solely to the individual states, and non-intervention by each state with the affairs of any other state.

VII. The recognition of the right of the native-born and naturalized citizens of the United States, permanently residing in any territory thereof, to frame their constitutions and laws, and to regulate their domestic and social affairs in their own mode, subject only to the provisions of the Federal Constitution, with the right of admission into the Union whenever they have the requisite population for one representative in Congress. *Provided, always,* That none but those who are citizens of the United States, under the Constitution and laws thereof, and who have a fixed residence in any such territory, are to participate in the formation of the constitution, or in the enactment of laws for said territory or state.

VIII. An enforcement of the principles that no state or territory can admit other than native-born citizens to the right of suffrage, or of holding political office unless such persons shall have been naturalized according to the laws of the United States.

IX. A change in the laws of naturalization, making a continued residence of twenty-one years, of all not heretofore provided for, an indispensable requisite for citizenship hereafter, and excluding all paupers or persons convicted of crime from landing upon our shores; but no interference with the vested rights of foreigners.

X. Opposition to any union between Church and State; no interference with religious faith or worship, and no test oaths for office, except those indicated in the 5th section of this platform.

XI. Free and thorough investigation into any and all alleged abuses of public functionaries, and a strict economy in public expenditures.

XII. The maintenance and enforcement of all laws until said laws shall be repealed, or shall be declared null and void by competent judicial authority. . . .

XIV. Therefore, to remedy existing evils, and prevent the disastrous consequences otherwise resulting therefrom, we would build up the "American Party" upon the principles herein-before stated eschewing all sectional questions, and uniting upon those purely national, and admitting into said party all American citizens (referred to in the 3rd, 4th, and 5th sections) who openly avow the principles and opinions heretofore expressed, and who will subscribe their names to this platform. — *Provided nevertheless,* that a majority of those members present at any meeting of a local council where an applicant applies for membership in the American party, may, for any reason by them deemed sufficient, deny admission to such applicant.

XV. A free and open discussion of all political principles embraced in our platform.

Questions

1. What does the platform identify as the chief threat to the United States?
2. How does it propose to meet that challenge?
3. Are the sentiments expressed here part of the American character? Why or why not?

Harriet Beecher Stowe, *Uncle Tom's Cabin* (1852)

Harriet Beecher Stowe (1811–1896), a native of Litchfield, Connecticut, was the daughter of Lyman Beecher (see Chapter 10, "On the Temperance Movement") as well as the sister of Catharine (see Chapter 20, "The Christian Family") and Henry Ward Beecher. She lived with her father in Cincinnati while he served as the president of Lane Seminary. The seminary was the site of a lively debate over slavery. Cincinnati, separated by the Ohio River from the slave state of Kentucky, was a center of the turmoil associated with abolitionist agitation and efforts to aid fugitive slaves. After marrying Calvin E. Stowe, Harriet Beecher Stowe returned to New England, where in 1850 her husband began teaching biblical literature at Bowdoin College.

There, with the images of Kentucky slavery and Cincinnati abolitionism fresh in her mind, Stowe wrote Uncle Tom's Cabin, *telling the story of a loyal slave separated from his family in Kentucky by the interstate slave trade. Much of the story focuses on the kindness of little Eva and her father, St. Clare, before their deaths lead to Uncle Tom's sale to the murderous and insane Simon Legree.*

Stowe muted the abolitionists' moral repugnance for slavery with a sentimentality that offered her readers emotional release from the growing social tensions of the sectional crisis. The death of little Eva was the sentimental climax of the novel, and it became embedded in northern popular culture as the central focus of stage productions and the subject of popular songs.

The deceitful strength which had buoyed Eva up for a while was fast passing away. . . . Eva lay back on her pillows; her hair hanging loosely about her face, her crimson cheeks contrasting painfully with the intense whiteness of her complexion and the thin contour of her limbs and features. . . .

Uncle Tom was much in Eva's room. The child suffered much from nervous restlessness, and it was a relief to her to be carried; and it was Tom's greatest delight to carry her little frail form in his arms, resting on a pillow, now up and down her room, now out into the verandah; and when the fresh sea-breezes blew from the lake . . . he would sometimes . . . sing to her their favorite old hymns. . . .

The child felt no pain, — only a tranquil, soft weakness, daily and almost insensibly increasing; and she was so beautiful, so loving, so trustful, so happy, that one could not resist the soothing influence of that air of innocence and peace which seemed to breathe around her. . . .

The friend who knew most of Eva's own imaginings and foreshadowings was her faithful bearer, Tom. To him she said what she would not disturb her father by saying. To him she imparted those mysterious intimations which the soul feels; as the cords begin to unbind, ere it leaves its clay forever.

Tom, at last, would not sleep in his room, but lay all night in the outer verandah, ready to rouse to every call. . . .

"Hush!" said St. Clare, hoarsely; *"she is dying!"*

The large blue eyes unclosed, — a smile passed over her face; — she tried to raise her head, and to speak.

"Do you know me, Eva?"

"Dear papa," said the child, with a last effort throwing her arms about his neck. In a moment they dropped again. . . .

Tom had his master's hands between his own; and, with tears streaming down his dark cheeks, looked up for help where he had always been used to look. . . .

"O, bless the Lord! It's over, — it's over, dear Master!" said Tom; "look at her."

The child lay panting on her pillows, as one exhausted, — the large clear eyes rolled up and fixed. Ah, what said those eyes, that spoke so much of heaven? Earth was past, and earthly pain; but so solemn, so mysterious, was the triumphant brightness of that face, that it checked even the sobs of sorrow. They pressed around her, in breathless stillness.

"Eva," said St. Clare, gently.

She did not hear.

"O Eva, tell us what you see! What is it?" said her father.

A bright, a glorious smile passed over her face, and she said, brokenly, — "O! Love, — joy, — peace!" gave one sigh, and passed from death into life!

Questions

1. What sentiments does Stowe develop to create an emotional release at little Eva's death?
2. What relationship does Uncle Tom bear to those sentiments?
3. Does this passage suggest why *Uncle Tom* became a term of disparagement in the twentieth century? Explain.

John C. Calhoun, Defending Slavery to the British Minister in Washington (1844)

John C. Calhoun (1782–1850) resigned as vice-president in Andrew Jackson's first administration in 1833 to return to South Carolina, which he soon represented in the U.S. Senate. In 1844–1845, Calhoun briefly served as secretary of state during the Texas crisis. A conflict had developed in the Mexican province of Texas when American settlers declared their independence in 1836. Great Britain offered to mediate peace during the Texas–Mexico war that followed. The 1844–1845 Texas crisis in the United States centered on the issue of slavery in the West and the advisability of admitting Texas as a slave-holding state.

The crisis also involved what Calhoun and President John Tyler believed was a British plot to secure emancipation in Texas. Calhoun's attention focused on Lord Aberdeen, the British foreign minister, and Richard Pakenham, the British minister in Washington. Aberdeen had written to Pakenham to complain that the Tyler administration was distorting his government's views on slavery in North America. Pakenham then wrote to the State Department. He acknowledged that in general Great Britain opposed slavery while insisting that the British government was not plotting to undermine slavery in Texas or the United States. The following excerpt is drawn from Calhoun's reply to Pakenham.

The Undersigned, Secretary of State of the United States, has laid before the President the note of the Right Honorable Mr. Pakenham, Envoy Extraordinaire and Minister Plenipotentiary of Her Britannic Majesty, addressed to this Department on the 26th of February last, together with the accompanying copy of a despatch [*sic*] of Her Majesty's Principal Secretary of State for Foreign Affairs to Mr. Pakenham.

In reply, the Undersigned is directed by the President to inform the Right Honorable Mr. Pakenham that, while he regards with pleasure the disavowal of Lord Aberdeen of any intention on the part of Her Majesty's Government "to resort to any measures, either openly or secretly, which can tend to disturb the internal tranquillity of the slave-holding States, and thereby affect the tranquillity of the Union," he, at the same time, regards with deep concern, the avowal, for the first time made to this Government, "that Great Britain desires, and is constantly exerting herself to procure the general abolition of slavery throughout the world."

So long as Great Britain confined her policy to the abolition of slavery in her own possessions and colonies, no other country had a right to complain. . . . But when she goes beyond, and avows it as her settled policy, and the object of her constant exertions, to abolish it throughout the world, she makes it the duty of all other countries, whose safety or prosperity may be endangered by her policy, to adopt such measures as they may deem necessary for their protection.

It is with still deeper concern the President regards the avowal of Lord Aberdeen of the desire of Great Britain to see slavery abolished in Texas; and, as he infers, is endeavoring, through her diplomacy, to accomplish it, by making abolition of slavery one of the conditions on which Mexico should acknowledge her independence. . . . Under this conviction, it is felt to be the . . . duty of the Federal Government . . . to adopt, in self-defence, the most effectual measures to defeat it. . . .

It is well known that Texas has long desired to be annexed to this Union; that her People, at the time of the adoption of her constitution, expressed by an almost unanimous vote, her desire to that effect. . . . While they conceded to Great Britain the right of adopting whatever policy she might deem best, in reference to the African race, within her own possessions, they, on their part, claim the same right for themselves. . . . With us, it is a question to be decided, not by the Federal Government, but by each member of this Union for itself. . . . A large number of the States has [sic] decided, that it is neither wise nor humane to change the relation, which has existed from their first settlement, between the two races; while others, where the African is less numerous, have adopted the opposite policy. . . . The census and other authentic documents show that, in all instances in which the States have changed the former relation between the two races, the condition of the African, instead of being improved, has become worse. They have invariably sunk into vice and pauperism, accompanied by the bodily and mental inflictions incident thereto — deafness, blindness, insanity and idiocy, to a degree without example; while, in all other States which have retained the ancient relation between them [slavery], they have improved greatly in every respect. . . .

If such be the wretched condition of the race in their changed relation, where their number is comparatively few, and where so much interest is manifested for their improvement, what would it be in those States where the two races are nearly equal in numbers, and where, in consequence, would necessarily spring up mutual fear, jealousy, and hatred, between them. It may, in truth, be assumed as a maxim, that two races differing so greatly, and in so many respects, cannot possibly exist together in the same country. . . . Experience has proved, that the existing relation in which the one is subjected to the other in the slave-holding States, is consistent with the peace and safety of both, with great improvement to the inferior; while the same experience proves, that the relation which it is the desire and object of Great Britain to substitute in its stead, in this and all other countries, under the plausible name of the abolition of slavery, would (if it did not destroy the inferior by conflicts to which it would lead), reduce it to the extremes of vice and wretchedness. In this view of the subject, it may be asserted that what is called Slavery, is, in reality, a political institution, essential to the peace, safety, and prosperity of those States of the Union in which it exists.

Questions

1. What is Calhoun's criticism of the northern states?
2. How does Calhoun invoke both the idea of states' rights and the Monroe Doctrine? Is there a contradiction?
3. Calhoun is sending several implied messages to Great Britain. What are they?

Connections Questions

1. Why do Thomas R. Dew ("The Virtues of Slavery") and John C. Calhoun ("Defending Slavery") stress a moral defense of slavery?
2. How might cultural and economic factors have played a role in the influence of *Uncle Tom's Cabin* on the debate about slavery? How might those factors have differed in a country such as Russia, which was contending with its own form of slavery (serfdom) at the time?
3. What connection, if any, is there between the Know-Nothing platform and Calhoun's defense of slavery?

CHAPTER 14

The Crisis of the Union 1845–1860

Salmon P. Chase, *Union and Freedom without Compromise* (1850)

Born in New Hampshire and educated at Dartmouth College, Salmon P. Chase (1808–1873) studied law with President John Quincy Adams's attorney general, William Wirt, before moving west to establish himself as a successful young lawyer in Cincinnati. Chase voted for William Henry Harrison in 1840 but soon thereafter joined the fledgling abolitionist Liberty party. Chase volunteered to be the defense attorney in a celebrated 1836 fugitive slave case involving a woman named Matilda and James G. Birney (the Liberty party's presidential candidate in 1840 and 1844), who employed her in his home.

Although Chase lost the case, the state supreme court ordered his argument printed, thus securing for Chase the title "attorney general of the fugitive slave" in antislavery circles. Chase took a leading role in the formation of the Free Soil party in 1848 and forged a Free Soil–Democratic coalition in Ohio that won him election to the United States Senate. In the Senate, Chase opposed the compromise measures on slavery crafted by Henry Clay, Daniel Webster, and Stephen Douglas. The argument he developed became the central tenet of the Republican party.

I think, Mr. President, that two facts may now be regarded as established: First that in 1787 the national policy in respect to slavery was one of restriction, limitation, and discouragement. Second that it was generally expected that under the action of the State Governments slavery would gradually disappear from the States.

Such was the state of the country when the Convention met to frame the Constitution of the United States. . . . The framers of the Constitution acted under the influence of the general sentiment of the country. Some of them had contributed in no small measure to form that sentiment. Let us examine the instrument [the Constitution] in its light, and ascertain the original import of its language.

What, then, shall we find in it? The guaranties so much talked of? Recognition of property in men? Stipulated protection for that property in national territories and by national law? No, sir: nothing like it.

We find, on the contrary, extreme care to exclude these ideas from the Constitution. Neither the word "slave" nor "slavery" is to be found in any provision. There is not a single expression which charges the National Government with any responsibility in regard to slavery. No power is conferred on Congress either to establish or sustain it. The framers of the Constitution left it where they found it, exclusively within and under the jurisdiction of the States. Wherever slaves are referred to at all in the Constitution, whether in the clause providing for the apportionment of representation and direct taxation [Article I, section 2], or in that stipulating for the extradition of fugitive from service [the "fugitive slave" clause, Article IV, section 2], or in that restricting Congress as to the prohibition of importation or migration [Article I, section 9], they are spoken of, not as persons held as property, but as persons held to service, or having their condition determined, under State laws. We learn, indeed from the debates in the Constitutional Convention that the idea of property in men was excluded with special solicitude. . . .

Unhappily . . . the original policy of the Government and the original principles of the Government in respect to slavery did not permanently control its action. A change occurred — almost imperceptible at first but becoming more and more marked and decided until nearly total. . . . It was natural, though it does [not] seem to have been anticipated, that the unity of the slave interest strengthened by this accession of political power, should gradually weaken the public sentiment and modify the national policy against slavery. . . . Mr. President, I have spoken freely of slave State ascendency in the affairs of this Government, but I desire not to be misunderstood. I take no sectional position. The supporters of slavery are the sectionalists. . . . Freedom is national; slavery only is local and sectional. . . .

What have been the results . . . of the subversion of the original policy of slavery restriction and discouragement . . . instead of slavery being regarded as a curse, a reproach, a blight, an evil, a wrong, a sin, we are now told that it is the most stable foundation of our institutions; the happiest relation that labor can sustain to capital; a blessing to both races . . . this is a great change, and a sad change. If it goes on, the spirit of liberty must at length become extinct, and a despotism will be established under the forms of free institutions. . . . There can be no foundation whatever for the doctrine advanced . . . that an equilibrium between the slaveholding and non-slaveholding sections of our country has been, is, and ought to be, an approved feature of our political system. . . . I shall feel myself supported by the precepts of the sages of the Revolutionary era, by the example of the founders of the Republic, by the original policy of the Government, and by the principles of the Constitution.

Questions

1. How does Chase invoke a sense of patriotism to his side of the argument?
2. Why does he believe it important that slavery is not explicitly mentioned in the Constitution?
3. What supposedly changed the slavery issue for the worse?

The Fugitive Slave Act of 1850

Article IV, section 2 of the Constitution obligated states to surrender escaped slaves back to their owners. Yet growing antislavery sentiment in the North had led most states to ignore that provision. As tensions mounted, the South insisted that the northern states live up to their constitutional obligation. As part of the Compromise of 1850, Congress enacted a tougher fugitive slave statute to satisfy southern demands.

Be it enacted by the Senate and House of Representatives of the United States of America in congress assembled, . . .

SEC. 6. *And be it further enacted,* That when a person held to service or labor in any State or Territory of the United States, has heretofore or shall hereafter escape into another State or Territory of the United States, the person or persons to whom such service or labor may be due, or his, her, or their agent or attorney, duly authorized, by power of attorney, in writing, acknowledged and certified under the seal of some legal officer or court of the State or Territory in which the same may be executed, may pursue and reclaim such fugitive person, either by procuring a warrant from some one of the courts, judges, or commissioners aforesaid, of the proper circuit, district, or county, for the apprehension of such fugitive from service or labor, or by seizing and arresting such fugitive, where the same can be done without process, and by taking, or causing such person to be taken, forthwith before such court, judge, or commissioner, whose duty it shall be to hear and determine the case of such claimant in a summary manner. . . . In no trial or hearing under this act shall the testimony of such alleged fugitive be admitted in evidence; and the certificates in this and the first [fourth] section be mentioned, shall be conclusive of the right of the person or persons in whose favor granted, to remove such fugitive to the State or Territory from which he escaped, and shall prevent all molestation of such person or persons by any process issued by any court, judge, magistrate, or other person whomsoever.

SEC. 7. *And be it further enacted,* That any person who shall knowingly and willingly obstruct, hinder, or prevent such claimant, his agent or attorney, or any person or persons lawfully assisting him, her, or them, from arresting such a fugitive from service or labor, either with or without process as aforesaid, or shall rescue, or attempt to rescue, such fugitive from service or labor, from the custody of such claimant, his or her agent or attorney, or other person or persons lawfully assisting as aforesaid, when so arrested, pursuant to the authority herein given and declared; or shall aid, abet, or assist such person so owing service or labor as aforesaid, directly or indirectly, to escape from such claimant, his agent or attorney, or other person or persons legally authorized as aforesaid; or shall harbor or conceal such fugitive, so as to prevent the discovery and arrest of such person, after notice or knowledge of the fact that such person was a fugitive from service or labor as aforesaid, shall, for either of said offences, be subject to a fine not exceeding one thousand dollars, and imprisonment not exceeding six months . . . and shall moreover forfeit and pay, by way of civil damages to the party injured by such illegal conduct, the sum of one thousand dollars, for each fugitive so lost as aforesaid. . . .

SEC. 9. *And be it further enacted*, That, upon affidavit made by the claimant of such fugitive, his agent or attorney, after such certificate has been issued, that he has reason to apprehend that such fugitive will be rescued by force from his or their possession before he can be taken beyond the limits of the State in which the arrest is made, it shall be the duty of the officer making the arrest to retain such fugitive in his custody, and to remove him to the State whence he fled, and there to deliver him to said claimant, his agent, or attorney. And to this end, the officer aforesaid is hereby authorized and required to employ so many persons as he may deem necessary to overcome such force, and to retain them in his service so long as circumstances may require. The said officer and his assistants, while so employed, to receive the same compensation, and to be allowed the same expenses, as are now allowed by law for transportation of criminals, to be certified by the judge of the district within which the arrest is made, and paid out of the treasury of the United States.

Questions

1. Why does the act use the term *fugitive person*?
2. What civil liberty is the accused denied?
3. Is southern support for this statute consistent with the doctrine of states' rights? Why or why not?

The Rescue of a Slave (1855)

The South's demand for a stronger fugitive slave law grew out of increased efforts by northern abolitionists to help slaves escape and to assist runaway slaves in reaching safe havens in the North and Canada. After passage of the Fugitive Slave Act, such attempts increased.

In 1855 Colonel John Wheeler, the American minister to Nicaragua, was traveling by boat to New York with three slaves. At a stopover in Philadelphia, a member of the Vigilance Committee came aboard and informed Jane Johnson, Wheeler's slave, that under Pennsylvania law she was free. Johnson left the boat with her children, after which Wheeler unsuccessfully tried to secure her return. Following is the affidavit Jane Johnson filed with a New York magistrate.

Jane Johnson being sworn, makes oath and says —

My name is Jane — Jane Johnson: I was the slave of Mr. Wheeler of Washington; he bought me and my two children, about two years ago, from Mr. Cornelius Crew, of Richmond, Va.; my youngest child is between six and seven years old, the other between ten and eleven; I have one other child only, and he is in Richmond; I have not seen him for about two years; never expect to see him again; Mr. Wheeler brought me and my two children to Philadelphia, on the way to Nicaragua, to wait on his wife; I didn't want to go without my two children, and he consented to take them; we came to Philadelphia by the cars; stopped at Mr. Sully's, Mr. Wheeler's father-in-law, a few moments; then went to the steamboat for New York at 2 o'clock, but were too late; we went into Bloodgood's Hotel; Mr. Wheeler went to dinner; Mr. Wheeler had told me in Washington to have nothing to say to colored persons, and if any of them spoke to me, to say I was a free woman traveling with a minister; we staid at Bloodgood's till 5 o'clock; Mr. Wheeler kept his eye on me all the time except when he was at dinner; he left his dinner to come and see if I was safe, and then went back again; while he was at dinner, I saw a colored woman and told her I was a slave woman, that my master had told me not to speak to colored people, and that if any of them spoke to me to say that I was free; but I am not free; but I want to be free; she said: 'poor thing, I pity you;' after that I saw a colored man and said the same thing to him, he said he would telegraph to New York, and two men would meet me at 9 o'clock and take me with them; after that we went on board the boat, Mr. Wheeler sat beside me on the deck; I saw a colored gentleman come on board, he beckoned to me; I nodded my head, and could not go; Mr. Wheeler was beside me and I was afraid; a white gentleman then came and said to Mr. Wheeler, 'I want to speak

to your servant, and tell her of her rights;' Mr. Wheeler rose and said, 'If you
have anything to say, say it to me — she knows her rights;' the white gentleman asked me if I wanted to be free; I said 'I do, but I belong to this gentleman and I can't have it;' he replied, 'Yes, you can, come with us, you are as free
[as] your master, if you want your freedom come now; if you go back to Washington you may never get it;' I rose to go, Mr. Wheeler spoke, and said, 'I will
give you your freedom,' but he had never promised it before, and I knew he
would never give it to me; the white gentleman held out his hand and I went
toward him; I was ready for the word before it was given me; I took the children by the hands, who both cried, for they were frightened, but both stopped
when they got on shore; a colored man carried the little one, I led the other
by the hand. We walked down the street till we got to a hack; nobody forced
me away; nobody pulled me, and nobody led me; I went away of my own free
will; I always wished to be free and meant to be free when I came North; I
hardly expected it in Philadelphia, but I thought I should get free in New
York; I have been comfortable and happy since I left Mr. Wheeler, and so are
the children; I don't want to go back; I could have gone in Philadelphia if I had
wanted to; I could go now; but I had rather die than go back. I wish to make
this statement before a magistrate, because I understand that Mr. Williamson
is in prison on my account, and I hope the truth may be of benefit to him.

her
Jane × Johnson
mark

Questions

1. How has slavery changed the family life of Jane Johnson?
2. When does Mr. Wheeler become aware that he might lose his slave? How
does he try to prevent the escape?
3. What were the consequences of this slave rescue?

Charles Sumner, "The Crime against Kansas" (1856)

Born in Boston and educated at Harvard, Charles Sumner (1811–1874) en-
tered the world of New England social reform in the 1840s and moved quickly
into antislavery political activity after the organization of the Free Soil party
in 1848. A political coalition of Free-Soilers and Democrats in Massachusetts
sent Sumner to the United States Senate in 1851. There he replaced Daniel
Webster, whose authorship of and support for the Compromise of 1850 and
the Fugitive Slave Act outraged those of growing antislavery sentiment in
Massachusetts.

Sumner's purpose in the Senate was first and foremost to fight the "Slave
Power," which he blamed for the outbreak of violence in Kansas (see text pp.
381–82). Sumner took the floor of the Senate over two days (May 19–20,
1856) to defend the free-soil settlers and denounce as barbarians the pro-
slavery forces attempting to seize control of the territory. In the course of that
speech, "The Crime against Kansas," Sumner made derogatory personal ref-
erences to South Carolina's elderly senator, Andrew Butler, who had recently
suffered a stroke. Two days later Representative Preston Brooks of South Car-
olina (Butler's nephew) viciously beat Sumner with a cane. Brooks became a
hero in South Carolina, and Sumner — revered as a martyr to the cause of
freedom — won re-election to the Senate for every term until he died.

Mr. President — You are now called to redress a great wrong. Seldom in
the history of nations is such a question presented. Tariffs, army bills, navy
bills, land bills, are important, and justly occupy your care; but these all belong to the course of ordinary legislation. . . . Far otherwise is it with the eminent question now before you, involving, as it does, Liberty in a broad Territory, and also involving the peace of the whole country, with our good name
in history forevermore. . . .

The wickedness which I now begin to expose is immeasurably aggravated
by the motive which prompted it. Not in any common lust for power did this
uncommon tragedy have its origin. It is the rape of a virgin Territory, compelling it to the hateful embrace of Slavery; and it may be clearly traced to a
depraved desire for a new Slave State, hideous offspring of such a crime, in
the hope of adding to the power of Slavery in the National Government. Yes,
Sir, when the whole world alike . . . is rising up to condemn this wrong . . . here
in our Republic, *force* — ay, Sir, FORCE — is openly employed in compelling Kansas to this pollution, and all for the sake of political power. . . .

Before entering upon the argument, I must say something of a general
character, particularly in response to what has fallen from Senators who have

raised themselves to eminence on this floor in championship of human wrong: I mean the Senator from South Carolina [Mr. Butler]. . . . The Senator from South Carolina has read many books of chivalry, and believes himself a chivalrous knight, with sentiments of honor and courage. Of course he has chosen a mistress to whom he has made his vows, and who, though ugly to others, is always lovely to him, — though polluted in the sight of the world, is chaste in his sight: I mean the harlot Slavery. For her his tongue is always profuse with words. Let her be impeached in character, or any proposition be made to shut her out from the extension of her wantonness, and no extravagance of manner or hardihood of assertion is then too great for this Senator. . . .

I undertake, in the first place, to expose the CRIME AGAINST KANSAS, in origin and extent. . . . The debate [over the Kansas-Nebraska bill], which convulsed Congress, stirred the whole country. From all sides attention was directed upon Kansas, which at once became the favorite goal of emigration. The bill loudly declares that its object is "to leave the people perfectly free to form and regulate their domestic institutions in their own way"; and its supporters everywhere challenge the determination of the question between Freedom and Slavery by a competition of emigration. . . . The populous North, stung by a sense of outrage, and inspired by a noble cause, are pouring into the debatable land, and promise soon to establish a supremacy of Freedom.

Then was conceived the consummation of the Crime against Kansas. What could not be accomplished peaceably was to be accomplished forcibly. . . . The violence, for some time threatened, broke forth on the 29th of November, 1854, at the first election of a Delegate to Congress, when companies from Missouri, amounting to upwards of one thousand, crossed into Kansas, and with force and arms proceeded to vote for . . . the candidate of Slavery. . . . Five . . . times and more have these invaders entered Kansas in armed array, and thus five . . . times and more have they trampled upon the organic law of the Territory. These extraordinary expeditions are simply the extraordinary witnesses to successive, uninterrupted violence. . . . Border incursions, which in barbarous ages or barbarous lands fretted and harried an exposed people, are here renewed, with this peculiarity, that our border robbers do not simply levy blackmail and drive off a few cattle . . . they commit a succession of deeds in which . . . the whole Territory is enslaved.

Private griefs mingle their poignancy with public wrongs. I do not dwell on the anxieties of families exposed to sudden assault, and lying down to rest with the alarms of war ringing in the ears, not knowing that another day may be spared to them. . . . Our souls are wrung by individual instances. . . .

Thus was the Crime consummated. Slavery stands erect, clanking its chains on the Territory of Kansas, surrounded by a code of death, and trampling upon all cherished liberties. . . . Emerging from all the blackness of this Crime . . . I come now to the APOLOGIES which the Crime has found. . . .

With regret I come again upon the Senator from South Carolina [Butler. His speech slurred by a stroke, Butler had interjected critical comments on more than thirty occasions while Sumner spoke] who, omnipresent in this debate, overflows with rage at the simple suggestion that Kansas has applied for admission as a State, and, with incoherent phrase, discharges the loose expectoration of his speech, now upon her representative, and then upon her people. . . . [I]t is against the [free-soil majority in] . . . Kansas that sensibilities of the Senator are particularly aroused. . . .

The contest, which, beginning in Kansas, reaches us will be transferred soon from Congress to that broader stage, where every citizen is not only spectator, but actor; and to their judgment I confidently turn. To the people, about to exercise the electoral franchise, in choosing a Chief Magistrate of the Republic, I appeal, to vindicate the electoral franchise in Kansas. Let the ballot-box of the Union . . . protect the ballot-box in that Territory.

Questions

1. Is the "crime" discussed here political or moral in nature? Explain.
2. What is Sumner's view of popular sovereignty?
3. What does Sumner fear will happen next?

U.S. Supreme Court,
Dred Scott v. Sandford (1857)

In his inaugural address on March 4, 1857, President James Buchanan announced that the constitutional issues argued among the pro- and antislavery forces in Kansas would soon be "speedily and finally settled" in court. Two days later the Supreme Court announced its decision in the case of Dred Scott v. Sandford.

Dred Scott (c. 1795–1858) had been the slave of Dr. John Emerson, a surgeon in the U.S. Army. While on active duty, Emerson had taken Scott to Illinois in 1834 and to the upper Louisiana Purchase territory in 1836 before returning to Missouri. Slavery had been excluded in Illinois by the Northwest Ordinance of 1787 and from the upper Louisiana Purchase territory by the Missouri Compromise of 1820.

In his suit Scott claimed to have been freed by reason of his residence in free territory. The Supreme Court's decision came in nine separate decisions, two in dissent. But the wide-ranging opinion of Chief Justice Roger B. Taney (1777–1864) was popularly considered the official Court decision. (Taney had

been in correspondence with Buchanan before his inaugural address.) The de-
cision attempted — and failed — to resolve the legal status of slavery.

Chief Justice Taney delivered the opinion of the Court.

The question is simply this: Can a negro, whose ancestors were imported into this country, and sold as slaves, become a member of the political community formed and brought into existence by the Constitution of the United States, and as such become entitled to all the rights, and privileges, and immunities, guarantied by that instrument to the citizen? One of which rights is the privilege of suing in a court of the United States in the cases specified in the Constitution. . . .

The words "people of the United States" and "citizens" are synonymous terms, and mean the same thing. They both describe the political body who, according to our republican institutions, form the sovereignty, and who hold the power and conduct the government through their representatives. They are what we familiarly call the "sovereign people," and every citizen is one of this people, and a constituent member of this sovereignty. The question before us is, whether the class of persons described in the plea in abatement compose a portion of this people, and are constituent members of this sovereignty? We think they are not, and that they are not included, and were not intended to be included, under the word "citizens" in the Constitution, and can therefore claim none of the rights and privileges which that instrument provides for and secures to citizens of the United States. On the contrary, they were at that time considered as a subordinate and inferior class of beings, who had been subjugated by the dominant race, and, whether emancipated or not, yet remained subject to their authority, and had no rights or privileges but such as those who held the power and the government might choose to grant them. . . .

In discussing this question, we must not confound the rights of citizenship which a State may confer within its own limits, and the rights of citizenship as a member of the Union. It does not by any means follow, because he [Scott] has all the rights and privileges of a citizen of a State, that he must be a citizen of the United States. He may have all of the rights and privileges of the citizen of a State, and yet not be entitled to the rights and privileges of a citizen in any other State. For, previous to the adoption of the Constitution of the United States, every State had the undoubted right to confer on whomsoever it pleased the character of citizen, and to endow him with all its rights. But this character of course was confined to the boundaries of the State, and gave him no rights or privileges in other States beyond those secured to him by the laws of nations and the comity of States. Nor have the several States surrendered the power of conferring these rights and privileges by adopting the Constitution of the United States. . . .

It is very clear, therefore, that no State can, by any act or law of its own, passed since the adoption of the Constitution, introduce a new member into the political community created by the Constitution of the United States. It cannot make him a member of this community by making him a member of its own. And for the same reason it cannot introduce any person, or description of persons, who were not intended to be embraced in this new political family, which the Constitution brought into existence, but were intended to be excluded from it.

The question then arises, whether the provisions of the Constitution, in relation to the personal rights and privileges to which the citizen of a State should be entitled, embraced the negro African race, at that time in this country, or who might afterwards be imported, who had then or should afterwards be made free in any State; and to put it in the power of a single State to make him a citizen of the United States, and endue him with the full rights of citizenship in every other State without their consent? Does the Constitution of the United States act upon him whenever he shall be made free under the laws of a State, and raised there to the rank of a citizen, and immediately clothe him with all the privileges of a citizen in every other State, and in its own courts?

In the opinion of the court, the legislation and histories of the times, and the language used in the Declaration of Independence, show, that neither the class of persons who had been imported as slaves, nor their descendants, whether they had become free or not, were then acknowledged as a part of the people, nor intended to be included in the general words used in that memorable instrument. . . .

It is too clear for dispute, that the enslaved African race were not intended to be included, and formed no part of the people who framed and adopted this declaration; for if the language, as understood in that day, would embrace them, the conduct of the distinguished men who framed the Declaration of Independence would have been utterly and flagrantly inconsistent with the principles they asserted; and instead of the sympathy of mankind, to which they so confidently appealed, they would have deserved and received universal rebuke and reprobation.

We proceed . . . to inquire whether the facts relied on by the plaintiff entitled him to his freedom. . . .

The act of Congress, upon which the plaintiff relies, declares that slavery and involuntary servitude, except as a punishment for crime, shall be forever prohibited in all that part of the territory ceded by France, under the name of Louisiana, which lies north of thirty-six degrees thirty minutes north latitude and not included within the limits of Missouri. And the difficulty which meets us at the threshold of this part of the inquiry is whether Congress was authorized to pass this law under any of the powers granted to it by the Constitution; for, if the authority is not given by that instrument, it is the duty of this Court to declare it void and inoperative and incapable of conferring freedom upon anyone who is held as a slave under the laws of any one of the states.

The counsel for the plaintiff has laid much stress upon that article in the Constitution which confers on Congress the power "to dispose of and make all needful rules and regulations respecting the territory or other property belonging to the United States"; but, in the judgment of the Court, that provision has no bearing on the present controversy, and the power there given, whatever it may be, is confined, and was intended to be confined, to the territory which at that time belonged to, or was claimed by, the United States and was within their boundaries as settled by the [1783] treaty with Great Britain and can have no influence upon a territory afterward acquired from a foreign government. It was a special provision for a known and particular territory, and to meet a present emergency, and nothing more. . . .

. . . It may be safely assumed that citizens of the United States who migrate to a territory belonging to the people of the United States cannot be ruled as mere colonists, dependent upon the will of the general government, and to be governed by any laws it may think proper to impose. The principle upon which our governments rest, and upon which alone they continue to exist, is the union of states, sovereign and independent within their own limits in their internal and domestic concerns, and bound together as one people by a general government, possessing certain enumerated and restricted powers, delegated to it by the people of the several states, and exercising supreme authority within the scope of the powers granted to it, throughout the dominion of the United States. A power, therefore, in the general government to obtain and hold colonies and dependent territories, over which they might legislate without restriction, would be inconsistent with its own existence in its present form. Whatever it acquires, it acquires for the benefit of the people of the several states who created it. It is their trustee acting for them and charged with the duty of promoting the interests of the whole people of the Union in the exercise of the powers specifically granted. . . .

But the power of Congress over the person or property of a citizen can never be a mere discretionary power under our Constitution and form of government. The powers of the government and the rights and privileges of the citizen are regulated and plainly defined by the Constitution itself. And, when the territory becomes a part of the United States, the federal government enters into possession in the character impressed upon it by those who created it. It enters upon it with its powers over the citizen strictly defined and limited by the Constitution, from which it derives its own existence, and by virtue of which alone it continues to exist and act as a government and sovereignty. . . .

Upon these considerations it is the opinion of the Court that the act of Congress which prohibited a citizen from holding and owning property of this kind in the territory of the United States north of the line therein mentioned is not warranted by the Constitution and is therefore void; and that neither Dred Scott himself, nor any of his family, were made free by being carried into this territory; even if they had been carried there by the owner with the intention of becoming a permanent resident.

Questions

1. What historic document does Taney ignore? What might be his reasons?
2. Does Taney view slaves as human? Explain.
3. How might an opinion favoring Scott be constructed?

The Lincoln-Douglas Debates (1858)

Stephen Douglas (1813–1861) had tried to address the issue of slavery in the territories with his theory of popular sovereignty, by which the people could decide. But the Dred Scott *decision seemed to cut the ground out from under his argument. When Douglas and Abraham Lincoln competed for a Senate seat in Illinois in 1858, they engaged in a series of debates. At Freeport, Lincoln (1809–1865) put the issue to him squarely, and Douglas attempted to resolve the seeming inconsistencies between the Court's ruling and his own political views.*

LINCOLN'S OPENING SPEECH

As to the first one, in regard to the fugitive slave law, I have never hesitated to say, and I do not now hesitate to say, that I think, under the Constitution of the United States, the people of the southern states are entitled to a congressional fugitive slave law. Having said that, I have had nothing to say in regard to the existing fugitive slave law further than that I think it should have been framed so as to be free from some of the objections that pertain to it, without lessening its efficiency. And inasmuch as we are not now in an agitation in regard to an alteration or modification of that law, I would not be the man to introduce it as a new subject of agitation upon the general question of slavery.

In regard to the other question of whether I am pledged to the admission of any more slave states into the Union, I state to you very frankly that I would be exceedingly sorry ever to be put in a position of having to pass upon that question. I should be exceedingly glad to know that there would never be another slave state admitted into the Union; . . . but I must add, that if slavery shall be kept out of the territories during the territorial existence of any one given territory, and then the people shall, having a fair chance and a clear field, when they come to adopt the constitution, do such an extraordinary thing as to adopt a slave constitution, uninfluenced by the actual presence of the institution among them, I see no alternative, if we own the country, but to admit them into the Union. . . .

The fourth one is in regard to the abolition of slavery in the District of Columbia. In relation to that, I have my mind very distinctly made up. I should be exceedingly glad to see slavery abolished in the District of Columbia. . . . I believe that Congress possesses the constitutional power to abolish it. Yet as a member of Congress, I should not with my present views, be in favor of *endeavoring* to abolish slavery in the District of Columbia, unless it would be upon these conditions. *First,* that the abolition should be gradual. *Second,* that it should be on a vote of the majority of qualified voters in the District, and *third,* that compensation should be made to unwilling owners. With these three conditions, I confess I would be exceedingly glad to see Congress abolish slavery in the District of Columbia, and, in the language of Henry Clay, "sweep from our Capital that foul blot upon our nation." . . .

My answer as to whether I desire that slavery should be prohibited in all the territories of the United States is full and explicit within itself, and cannot be made clearer by any comments of mine. So I suppose in regard to the question of whether I am opposed to the acquisition of any more territory unless slavery is first prohibited therein, my answer is such that I could add nothing by way of illustration, or making myself better understood, than the answer which I have placed in writing. . . .

I now proceed to propound to the Judge the interrogatories, as far as I have framed them. . . . The first one is —

Question 1. If the people of Kansas shall, by means entirely unobjectionable in all other respects, adopt a state constitution, and ask admission into the Union under it, *before* they have the requisite number of inhabitants according to the English Bill — some ninety-three thousand — will you vote to admit them? . . .

Q. 2. Can the people of a United States territory, in any lawful way, against the wish of any citizen of the United States, exclude slavery from its limits prior to the formation of a state constitution? . . .

Q. 3. If the Supreme Court of the United States shall decide that states can not exclude slavery from their limits, are you in favor of acquiescing in, adopting and following such decision as a rule of political action? . . .

Q. 4. Are you in favor of acquiring additional territory, in disregard of how such acquisition may affect the nation on the slavery question? . . .

DOUGLAS'S REPLY

In a few moments I will proceed to review the answers which he has given to these interrogatories; but in order to relieve his anxiety I will first respond to those which he has presented to me. . . .

First, he desires to know if the people of Kansas shall form a constitution by means entirely proper and unobjectionable and ask admission into the Union as a state, before they have the requisite population for a member of Congress, whether I will vote for that admission. . . . In reference to Kansas; it is my opinion, that as she has population enough to constitute a slave state, she has people enough for a free state. . . . I will not make Kansas an exceptional case to the other states of the Union. ("Sound," and "hear, hear.") I hold it to be a sound rule of universal application to require a territory to contain the requisite population for a member of Congress, before it is admitted as a state into the Union. I made that proposition in the Senate in 1856, and I renewed it during the last session, in a bill providing that no territory of the United States should form a constitution and apply for admission until it had the requisite population. . . .

The next question propounded to me by Mr. Lincoln is, can the people of a territory in any lawful way against the wishes of any citizen of the United States; [sic] exclude slavery from their limits prior to the formation of a state constitution? I answer emphatically, as Mr. Lincoln has heard me answer a hundred times from every stump in Illinois, that in my opinion the people of a territory can, by lawful means, exclude slavery from their limits prior to the formation of a state constitution. . . . Mr. Lincoln knew that I had answered that question over and over again. He heard me argue the Nebraska Bill on that principle all over the state in 1854, in 1855 and in 1856, and he has no excuse for pretending to be in doubt as to my position on that question. It matters not what way the Supreme Court may hereafter decide as to the abstract question whether slavery may or may not go into a territory under the Constitution, the people have the lawful means to introduce it or exclude it as they please, for the reason that slavery cannot exist a day or an hour anywhere, unless it is supported by local police regulations. . . . Those police regulations can only be established by the local legislature, and if the people are opposed to slavery they will elect representatives to that body who will by unfriendly legislation effectually prevent the introduction of it into their midst. If, on the contrary, they are for it, their legislation will favor its extension. Hence, no matter what the decision of the Supreme Court may be on that abstract question, still the right of the people to make a slave territory or a free territory is perfect and complete under the Nebraska Bill. I hope Mr. Lincoln deems my answer satisfactory on that point. . . .

The third question which Mr. Lincoln presented is, if the Supreme Court of the United States shall decide that a state of this Union cannot exclude slavery from its own limits will I submit to it? I am amazed that Lincoln should ask such a question. . . . Yes, a school boy does know better. Mr. Lincoln's object is to cast an imputation upon the Supreme Court. He knows that there never was but one man in America, claiming any degree of intelligence or decency, who ever for a moment pretended such a thing. It is true that the Washington *Union,* in an article published on the 17th of last December, did put forth that doctrine, and I denounced the article on the floor of the Senate. . . .

The fourth question of Mr. Lincoln is, are you in favor of acquiring additional territory in disregard as to how such acquisition may affect the Union on the slavery question? This question is very ingeniously and cunningly put. . . .

The Black Republican creed lays it down expressly, that under no circumstances shall we acquire any more territory unless slavery is first prohibited in the country. I ask Mr. Lincoln whether he is in favor of that proposition. Are you (addressing Mr. Lincoln) opposed to the acquisition of any more territory, under any circumstances, unless slavery is prohibited in it? That he does not like to answer. When I ask him whether he stands up to that article in the platform of his party, he turns, Yankee-fashion, and without answering it, asks me whether I am in favor of acquiring territory without regard to how it may affect the Union on the slavery question. . . . I answer that whenever it becomes necessary, in our growth and progress to acquire more territory, that I am in favor of it, without reference to the question of slavery, and when we have acquired it, I will leave the people free to do as they please, either to make it slave or free territory, as they prefer. . . . It is idle to tell me or you that we have territory enough. Our fathers supposed that we had enough when our territory extended to the Mississippi River, but a few years' growth and expansion satisfied them that we needed more, and the Louisiana territory, from the west branch of the Mississippi, to the British possessions, was acquired. Then we acquired Oregon, then California and New Mexico. We have enough now for the present, but this is a young and a growing nation. It swarms as often as a hive of bees, and as new swarms are turned out each year, there must be hives in which they can gather and make their honey.

Questions

1. How is the tone of Abraham Lincoln's speech one of antislavery rather than abolitionism?
2. What is the purpose of Lincoln's questions to Douglas?
3. Why does Douglas talk about the "Black Republican creed"?

The Trial of John Brown (1859)

Lincoln and the Republicans tried to reassure the South that they did not want to disturb slavery where it existed but only halt its spread. Then John Brown attempted to raid the government arsenal at Harpers Ferry, Virginia, and trigger a massive slave rebellion (see text pp. 389–90). Although Republican leaders disavowed his action, private letters show that he had support from prominent abolitionists. Brown was tried and convicted of treason, and his statement before hanging has become a classic. He was executed on December 2, 1859; abolitionists, as Ralph Waldo Emerson said, now had a "new saint." Slaveholders blamed Republican ideas for the raid and more than ever feared a Republican presidential victory.

The clerk then asked Mr. Brown whether he had anything to say why sentence should not be pronounced upon him.

Mr. Brown immediately rose, and in a clear, distinct voice, said:

I have, may it please the Court, a few words to say. In the first place, I deny everything but what I have all along admitted, of a design on my part to free slaves. I intended certainly to have made a clean thing of that matter, as I did last winter when I went into Missouri, and there took slaves without the snapping of a gun on either side, moving them through the country, and finally leaving them in Canada. I designed to have done the same thing again on a larger scale. That was all I intended to do. I never did intend murder or treason, or the destruction of property, or to excite or incite the slaves to rebellion, or to make insurrection. I have another objection, and that is that it is unjust that I should suffer such a penalty. Had I interfered in the manner which I admit, and which I admit has been fairly proved — for I admire the truthfulness and candor of the greater portion of the witnesses who have testified in this case — had I so interfered in behalf of the rich, the powerful, the intelligent, the so-called great, or in behalf of any of their friends, either father, mother, brother, sister, wife, or children, or any of that class, and suffered and sacrificed what I have in this interference, it would have been all right, and every man in this Court would have deemed it an act worthy of reward rather than punishment. This Court acknowledges, too, as I suppose, the validity of the law of God. I see a book kissed, which I suppose to be the Bible, or at least the New Testament, which teaches me that all things whatsoever I would that men should do to me, I should do even so to them. It teaches me further to remember them that are in bonds as bound with them. I endeavored to act up to that instruction. I say I am yet too young to understand that God is any respecter of persons. I believe that to have interfered as I have done, as I have always freely admitted I have done in behalf of His despised poor, is no wrong, but right. Now, if it is deemed necessary that I should forfeit my life for the furtherance of the ends of justice, and mingle my blood further with the blood of my children and with the blood of millions in this slave country whose rights are disregarded by wicked, cruel, and unjust enactments, I say let it be done. Let me say one word further. I feel entirely satisfied with the treatment I have received on my trial. Considering all the circumstances, it has been more generous than I expected. But I feel no consciousness of guilt. I have stated from the first what was my intention, and what was not. I never had any design against the liberty of any person, nor any disposition to commit treason or excite slaves to rebel or make any general insurrection. I never encouraged any man to do so, but always discouraged any idea of that kind. Let me say also in regard to statements made by some of those who were connected with me, I fear it has been stated by some of them that I have induced them to join me, but the contrary is true. I do not say this to injure them, but as regretting their weakness. Not one but joined me of his own accord, and the greater part at their own expense. A number of them I never saw, and never had a word of conversation with till the day they came to me, and that was for the purpose I have stated. Now, I am done.

While Mr. Brown was speaking, perfect quiet prevailed, and when he had finished the Judge proceeded to pronounce sentence upon him. After a few primary remarks, he said, that no reasonable doubt could exist of the guilt of the prisoner, and sentenced him to be hung in public, on Friday, the 2d of December next.

Mr. Brown received his sentence with composure.

Questions

1. What is Brown's defense?
2. Does he admit guilt? Why or why not?
3. Did Brown's career and death benefit the abolitionist cause? Explain your answer.

Connections Questions

1. How does Salmon Chase's view of the Constitution ("Union and Freedom") differ from Roger Taney's ("*Dred Scott v. Sandford*")?
2. Do the documents in this section suggest that there was a middle way not taken in regard to slavery? Why or why not?
3. Construct a debate between Abraham Lincoln and John Brown. What, if any, would be their points of agreement? their strongest points of disagreement?

CHAPTER 15

Two Societies at War 1861–1865

Anna Elizabeth Dickinson,
The New York City Draft Riots (1863)

When the Union instituted conscription in 1863, it allowed men to avoid the draft if they could provide a substitute or pay a $300 fee — over half the annual income of an average worker. Lincoln's Democratic opponents exploited resentment over the high fee to win support from recent immigrants and the urban poor. In July 1863 riots against the draft broke out in New York City (see text p. 401). The following description of the riots is by Anna Dickinson, who was involved in the antislavery and women's rights movements. Her account is no exaggeration; the rioting was finally suppressed on the fourth day by troops from the Army of the Potomac.

On the morning of Monday, the thirteenth of July, began this outbreak, unparalleled in atrocities by anything in American history, and equalled only by the horrors of the worst days of the French Revolution. Gangs of men and boys, composed of railroad *employees,* workers in machine-shops, and a vast crowd of those who lived by preying upon others, thieves, pimps, professional ruffians, — the scum of the city, — jail-birds, or those who were running with swift feet to enter the prison-doors, began to gather on the corners, and in streets and alleys where they lived; from thence issuing forth they visited the great establishments on the line of their advance, commanding their instant clos[ing] and the companionship of the workmen, — many of them peaceful and orderly men, — on pain of the destruction of one and a murderous assault upon the other, did not their orders meet with instant compliance.

A body of these, five or six hundred strong, gathered about one of the enrolling-offices in the upper part of the city, where the draft was quietly proceeding, and opened the assault upon it by a shower of clubs, bricks, and paving-stones torn from the streets, following it up by a furious rush into the office. Lists, records, books, the drafting-wheel, every article of furniture or work in the room was rent in pieces, and strewn about the floor or flung into the street; while the law officers, the newspaper reporters, — who are expected to be everywhere, — and the few peaceable spectators, were compelled to make a hasty retreat through an opportune rear exit, accelerated by the curses and blows of the assailants.

A safe in the room, which contained some of the hated records, was fallen upon by the men, who strove to wrench open its impregnable lock with their naked hands, and, baffled, beat them on its iron doors and sides till they were stained with blood, in a mad frenzy of senseless hate and fury. And then, finding every portable article destroyed, — their thirst for ruin growing by the little drink it had had, — and believing, or rather hoping, that the officers had taken refuge in the upper rooms, set fire to the house, and stood watching the slow and steady lift of the flames, filling the air with demoniac shrieks and yells, while they waited for the prey to escape from some door or window, from the merciless fire to their merciless hands. One of these, who was on the other side of the street, courageously stepped forward, and, telling them that they had utterly demolished all they came to seek, informed them that helpless women and little children were in the house, and besought them to extinguish the flames and leave the ruined premises; to disperse, or at least to seek some other scene.

By his dress recognizing in him a government official, so far from hearing or heeding his humane appeal, they set upon him with sticks and clubs, and beat him till his eyes were blind with blood, and he — bruised and mangled — succeeded in escaping to the handful of police who stood helpless before this howling crew, now increased to thousands. With difficulty and pain the inoffensive tenants escaped from the rapidly spreading fire, which, having devoured the house originally lighted, swept across the neighboring buildings till the whole block stood a mass of burning flames. The firemen came up tardily and reluctantly, many of them of the same class as the miscreants who surrounded them, and who cheered at their approach, but either made no attempt to perform their duty, or so feeble and farcical a one, as to bring disgrace upon a service they so generally honor and ennoble.

At last, when there was nothing more to accomplish, the mob, swollen to a frightful size, including myriads of wretched, drunken women, and the half-grown, vagabond boys of the pavements, rushed through the intervening streets, stopping cars and insulting peaceable citizens on their way, to an armory where were manufactured and stored carbines and guns for the government. In anticipation of the attack, this, earlier in the day, had been fortified by a police squad capable of coping with an ordinary crowd of ruffians, but as chaff before fire in the presence of these murderous thousands. Here, as before, the attack was begun by a rain of missiles gathered from the streets; less fatal, doubtless, than more civilized arms, but frightful in the ghastly wounds and injuries they inflicted. Of this no notice was taken by those who were stationed within; it was repeated. At last, finding they were treated with contemptuous silence, and that no sign of surrender was offered, the crowd swayed back, — then forward, — in a combined attempt to force the wide entrance-doors. Heavy hammers and sledges, which had been brought from forges and workshops, caught up hastily as they gathered the mechanics into their ranks, were used with frightful violence to beat them in, — at last successfully. The foremost assailants began to climb the stairs, but were checked, and for the moment driven back by the fire of the officers, who at last had been commanded to resort to their revolvers. A half-score fell wounded; and one, who had been acting in some sort as their leader, — a big, brutal, Irish ruffian, — dropped dead. . . .

Late in the afternoon a crowd which could have numbered not less than ten thousand, the majority of whom were ragged, frowzy, drunken women, gathered about the Orphan Asylum for Colored Children, — a large and beautiful building, and one of the most admirable and noble charities of the city. When it became evident, from the menacing cries and groans of the multitude, that danger, if not destruction, was meditated to the harmless and inoffensive inmates, a flag of truce appeared, and an appeal was made in their behalf, by the principal, to every sentiment of humanity which these beings might possess, — a vain appeal! Whatever human feeling had ever, if ever, filled these souls was utterly drowned and washed away in the tide of rapine and blood in which they had been steeping themselves. The few officers who stood guard over the doors, and manfully faced these demoniac legions, were beaten down and flung to one side, helpless and stunned, whilst the vast crowd rushed in. All the articles upon which they could seize — beds, bedding, carpets, furniture, — the very garments of the fleeing inmates, some of these torn from their persons as they sped by — were carried into the streets, and hurried off by the women and children who stood ready to receive the goods which their husbands, sons, and fathers flung to their care. The little ones, many of them, assailed and beaten; all, — orphans and care-takers, — exposed to every indignity and every danger, driven on to the street, — the building was fired. This had been attempted whilst the helpless children — some of them scarce more than babies — were still in their rooms. . . .

By far the most infamous part of these cruelties was that which wreaked every species of torture and lingering death upon the colored people of the city, — men, women, and children, old and young, strong and feeble alike. Hundreds of these fell victims to the prejudice fostered by public opinion, incorporated in our statute-books, sanctioned by our laws, which here and thus found legitimate out-growth and action. . . .

It was absurd and futile to characterize this new Reign of Terror as anything but an effort on the part of Northern rebels to help Southern ones, at the most critical moment of the war, — with the State militia and available troops absent in a neighboring Commonwealth, — and the loyal people unprepared. These editors [of Democratic newspapers] and their coadjutors, men of brains and ability, were of that most poisonous growth, — traitors to the Government and the flag of their country, — renegade Americans. Let it, however, be written plainly and graven deeply, that the tribes of savages —the hordes of ruffians — found ready to do their loathsome bidding, were not of native growth, nor American born. . . .

Questions

1. To what does Dickinson compare the riot? Why?
2. Who does she blame for the violence?
3. What prejudices of her own does she reveal?

The Work of the United States
Sanitary Commission (1864)

The United States Sanitary Commission represented the largest and most successful volunteer wartime activity in the North. The commission's founders intended to bring modern methods of sanitation to the treatment of sick and wounded soldiers and thereby avoid the devastating health problems that had plagued British and French troops during the Crimean War (1854–1856). In June 1861 the Sanitary Commission received official recognition from the War Department as a civilian agency supporting the Army Medical Bureau.

Sharply critical of traditional army methods, Sanitary Commission inspectors visited military encampments to direct latrine construction, food preparation, and hospital design. Sanitary Commission needs dominated the home-front activities of northern women. Hundreds of volunteers organized "sanitary fairs" in northern cities to raise funds to provide soldiers with medical supplies, fresh fruit and vegetables, and nurses and doctors to assist in the care and evacuation of the wounded. Although the intrusion of civilians into military matters disturbed some commanders, the commission's popularity among the troops and its influence with Congress ensured the success of its efforts.

The proclamation of the President [following the fall of Fort Sumter] . . . evoked the patriotic and earnest sympathies of the women of the nation, as well as those of the sterner sex. Everywhere fair hands were at work, and fair brows grew grave with thought, of what could be done for those who were going forth to fight the nation's battles. With the characteristic national fondness for organization, Ladies' Aid and Relief Societies were formed everywhere. One, "The Soldiers' Aid Society," at Cleveland, Ohio, bearing the date April 20, 1861, only five days after the President's proclamation; another at Philadelphia, "The Ladies' Aid Society," adopting its constitution on the 26th of April, and a third, "The Woman's Central Association of Relief, of New

York," on the 30th of the same month. By the middle of May there were hundreds of these associations formed. As yet, however, they hardly knew what was to be done, or how, when, and where to do it. . . . The Woman's Central Association of Relief had among its officers some gentlemen of large experience in sanitary science, and of considerable knowledge of military hygiene, and they wisely gave a practical turn to its labors from the first. . . . Other organizations of gentlemen were attempting by . . . similar measures, to render assistance to the Government. . . . Fraternizing with each other . . . these associations resolved to send a joint delegation to Washington. . . .

On the 18th of May, 1861 . . . representatives of these . . . associations drew up and forwarded to the Secretary of War a communication setting forth the propriety of creating an organization which should unite the duties and labors of [these] associations, and co-operate with the Medical Bureau of the War Department . . . in securing the welfare of the army. For this purpose they asked that a mixed commission of civilians, military officers, and medical men, might be appointed by the Government, charged with the duty of methodizing and reducing to practical service the already active but undirected benevolence of the people. . . .

The President and Secretary of War were not at first disposed to look with any great favor upon this plan, which they regarded rather as a sentimental scheme concocted by women, clergymen, and humane physicians, than as one whose practical workings would prove of incalculable benefit to the army. . . . [But] when the Acting Surgeon-General asked for it, as a needed adjuvant to the Medical Bureau, likely soon to be overwhelmed by its new duties, they finally decided, though reluctantly, to permit its organization.

Accordingly the Secretary of War, on the 9th of June, decided on the creation of . . . "The United States Sanitary Commission." . . . After the Government had established its own permanent hospitals . . . a considerable number of the supplies were furnished by the Sanitary Commission. The value of these supplies furnished by private hands . . . has been carefully ascertained . . . [and] could not have been less in value than $2,200,000.

One of these hospitals, now under the charge of the Government, originated in the philanthropic spirit of the citizens of . . . Philadelphia. . . . After the great battles before Washington, in the summer of 1862 [the Second Battle of Bull Run], trains, freighted with the wounded, poured into Philadelphia, and no provisions having been made for their quiet and speedy transfer to the hospitals, most of which were at considerable distance, they were temporarily placed in churches. . . . The citizens of the vicinity, a large portion of them mechanics, laboring by day in the busy manufactories of that vicinity, were greatly distressed at witnessing this suffering, and resolved . . . to erect near the station-house a hospital for the temporary accommodation of sick and wounded soldiers. A landowner generously gave them the use of some vacant lots . . . others contributed lumber, furniture, heating apparatus, bath-tubs, and some, money. One poor Irishman wheeled a half-worn stove to the new hospital. "He had nothing else to give," he said, "and must do something for the sogers." The hospital was erected, and furnished with five hundred beds in fifteen days. . . .

The feeling of sympathy and patriotism which has actuated the masses of the people, manifested itself in numberless instances of thoughtfulness and tenderness, even from classes, among whom it was hardly to be looked for.

Questions

1. Why did government leaders initially oppose the Sanitary Commission?
2. What happened to Union soldiers wounded in the Second Battle of Bull Run?
3. How does gender figure in the work of the commission?

William Howard Russell,
My Diary North and South (1863)

William Howard Russell was a special correspondent for the London Times. *He began his career in journalism in the early 1840s with reports on events in Ireland. He wrote in a style that appeared to be unbiased, objective, and informative. During the Crimean War, many of Russell's letters to the* Times *also appeared in American papers. As civil war loomed in the United States, Russell — by now well known to Americans as a war correspondent — arrived in New York in March 1861.*

Russell toured the South, arriving in Charleston shortly after the fall of Fort Sumter in April. His southern tour ended in Washington, D.C., in July as the North and South prepared for the first battle of the war. Russell's coverage of the Union defeat at Bull Run (see text p. 397) angered many in the North, and the pro-Confederate sympathies of the London Times *led President Lincoln to deny Russell any special privileges. Unable to write the kind of eyewitness accounts that had made him famous, Russell soon returned to England, where he published the diary of his American journey.*

July 20th. The great battle which is to arrest rebellion, or to make it a power in the land, is no longer distant or doubtful. [General Irvin] McDow-

ell has completed his reconnaissance of the country in front of the enemy and
General [Winfield] Scott anticipates that he will be in possession of Manas-
sas tomorrow night. All the statements of officers concur in describing the
Confederates as strongly entrenched along the line of Bull's Run covering the
railroad. . . . July 21st. . . . I swallowed a cup of tea and a morsel of bread . . .
got a flask of light Bordeaux, a bottle of water, a paper of sandwiches, and having replenished my small flask with brandy, stowed them all away in the bottom of the gig . . . and thus through the deserted city we proceeded [across the
Potomac into Virginia]. . . . [About] nine o'clock . . . I thought I heard . . . the
well-known boom of a gun, followed by two or three in rapid succession. . . .
"They are at it! We shall be late! Drive on as fast as you can!" . . . the sounds
which came upon the breeze, and the fights which met our eyes, were in terrible variance with the tranquil character of the landscape. The woods far and
near echoed to the roar of cannon, and then frayed lines of blue smoke
marked the spots whence came the muttering sound of rolling musketry; the
white puffs of smoke burst high above the tree tops, and the gunners' rings
from shell and howitzer marked the fire of the artillery. . . .

On the hill beside me there was a crowd of civilians on horseback and in
all sorts of vehicles, with a few of the fairer, if not gentler sex. A few officers
and some soldiers . . . from the regiments in reserve, moved about among the
spectators and pretended to explain the movements of the troops below, of
which they were profoundly ignorant. . . .

Loud cheers suddenly burst from the spectators as a man dressed in the
uniform of an officer . . . galloped along the front . . . shouting at the top of
his voice. . . . "We've whipped them on all points," he cried. "We have taken
all their batteries. They are retreating as fast as they can, and we are after
them." . . . I had ridden between three and a half and four miles [further] . . .
when my attention was attracted by loud shouts in advance. . . . My first impression was that the wagons were returning for fresh supplies of ammunition.
But every moment the crowd increased, drivers and men cried out with the
most vehement gestures, "Turn back! Turn back! We are whipped." . . . A[n] . . .
officer . . . confirmed the report that the whole army was in retreat and that
the Federals were beaten on all points. . . . All these things took place in a few
seconds. I got up out of the road into a cornfield, through which men were
hastily walking or running, their faces streaming with perspiration, and generally without arms, and worked my way for about half a mile or so . . . against
an increasing stream of fugitives, the ground being strewed with coats, blankets, firelocks, cooking tins, caps, belts, bayonets. . . . [Then] the dreaded cry,
"The cavalry! cavalry are coming!" rang through the crowd, and looking back
to Centreville I perceived coming down the hill, between me and the sky, a
number of mounted men, who might at a hasty glance be taken for horsemen
in the act of sabering the fugitives. In reality they were soldiers and civilians
with, I regret to say, some officers among them. . . . [To a] fellow who,

shouting out, "Run! run!" as loud as he could beside me . . . I said, "What on earth are you running for? What are you afraid of?" He was in the roadside below me, and at once turning on me exclaimed, "I'm not afraid of you," presented his piece and pulled the trigger so instantaneously, that had it gone off I could not have swerved from the ball. As the scoundrel deliberately drew up to examine the [gun] . . . I judged it best not to give him another chance and spurred on through the crowd. . . .

And I continued through the wood till I got a clear space in front on the road, along which a regiment of infantry was advancing towards me. They halted ere I came up, and with leveled firelocks arrested the men on horses and the carts and wagons galloping towards them, and blocked the road to stop their progress. . . . [A] soldier pointed his firelock at my head from the higher ground on which he stood . . . and sung out, "Halt! Stop — or I fire!" . . . Bowing to the officer who was near me, I said . . . "I am a civilian going to Washington; will you be kind enough to look at this pass, specially given to me by General Scott." The officer looked at it . . . [a]nd with a cry of "Pass that man!" . . . I . . . very leisurely . . . got out on the road. . . . July 22nd. I awoke from a deep sleep this morning, about six o'clock. The rain was falling in torrents . . . but louder than all came a strange sound . . . I saw a steady stream of men covered with mud, soaked through with rain, who were pouring irregularly, without any semblance of order up Pennsylvania Avenue towards the Capitol. A dense steam of vapour rose from the multitude. . . . Many of them were without knapsacks, crossbelts, and firelocks. Some had neither greatcoats nor shoes, others were covered with blankets. . . . I ran down stairs and asked an "officer" . . . where the men were coming from. "Where from? Well, sir, I guess we're all coming out of Verginny as far as we can, and pretty well whipped too."

Questions

1. What do Russell and the spectators expect to see?
2. How do those expectations play out?
3. Does Russell act as you might expect a war correspondent to behave? Why or why not?

James B. Griffin, A Soldier's
Letter to His Wife (1862)

*In 1861 James B. Griffin rode off to Virginia from Edgefield, South Car-
olina, in a style befitting a southern gentleman: with a fine horse, two slaves
to wait on him, two trunks, and his favorite hunting dog. Griffin joined the
Army of Northern Virginia, where he served under P. G. T. Beauregard and
Joseph E. Johnson. Griffin was thirty-five years old, a wealthy planter, and the
owner of sixty-one slaves when he joined Wade Hampton's elite legion as a
major of cavalry.*

*Griffin left behind seven children, the eldest of whom was only twelve, and
a wife who was eight and a half months pregnant. ("Little Jimmie," referred
to in the letter, was born while Griffin was away at war.) This letter home
came from the Virginia front and refers to the surrender of Fort Donelson by
General Simon Bolivar Buckner to Ulysses S. Grant. It is one of eighty-seven
letters Griffin wrote to his wife between June 1861 and February 1865.*

Camp of the Legion
February 26th 1862

My Darling Leila
    I am delighted, my Darling to learn by your last letter that Minnie has at
last "Come through." And I am also pleased, and tender my congratulations
that she has another Boy. Notwithstanding you all were anxious for her to have
a daughter. I really think she should be proud that she has another Boy. This
is the time, above all others, that *men* should be raised. And this too, is the
time above all others when females deserve sympathy. I assure you, I feel, far
more anxiety about my dear little daughters, than I do about my Boys. For
while men can manage to work for themselves, and can fight the battles of
their Country if necessary, Females are very dependent. True, they too can do
a great deal, and, 'tis true that our Southern Ladies have done and are still acting a conspicuous part in this war[.] In many instances (to the same of our Sex
be it said) a much bolder and more *manly* part than many men. But still,
when it comes to the physical test, of course, they are helpless. It is on this account, that I think the Parents should congratulate themselves on the birth of
a son rather than a daughter. We cannot see, My Darling, into the future, but
I trust & have confidence in our people to believe, that if the unprincipled
North shall persist in her policy of Subjugating the South, that we, who are
able to resist them, will continue to do so, until we grow old and worn out in
the service, and that then, our Sons will take the arms from our hands, and
spend their lives, if necessary, in battling for Liberty and independence. As for

my part, If this trouble should not be settled satisfactorily to us sooner — I would be proud of the thought that our youngest Boy — Yes Darling little Jimmie, will after awhile be able and I trust willing to take his Father's place in the field, and fight until he dies, rather than, be a Slave, *Yea* worse than a Slave to Yankee Masters — Have you ever anticipated, My Darling, what would be our probable condition, if we should be conquered in this war? The picture is really too horrible to contemplate. In the first place, the tremendous war tax, which will have accumulated, on the northern Government, would be paid entirely and exclusively by the property belonging to the Southerners. And more than this we would be an humbled, down trodden and disgraced, people. Not entitled to the respect of any body, and have no respect for ourselves. In fact we would be the most wretched and abject people on the face of the Earth. Just be what our Northern Masters say we may be. Would you, My Darling, desire to live, if this was the case? Would you be willing to leave your Children under such a government? No — I know you would sacrifice every comfort on earth, rather than submit to it. Excuse me, My Darling, I didn't intend to, run off in this strain. You might think, from my painting this horrid picture to you, that I had some doubts as to whether we might not have to experience it. But No, I heaven't the most remote idea that we will. I think our people will arouse themselves, shake off the lethargy, which seems now to have possession of them, and will meet the issue like *men*. We must see that we have *all* — Yes our all — staked upon the result — And we are obliged to succeed and we will do it. Just at this time the Enemy appears to have advantage of us. But this is no more than we have, all along, had of him, until lately. He did not succombe and give up for it — and shall we, Who have so much more to fight for than he has, do so? I am completely surprised and mortified at the feeling manifested by our people at this time. But they will soon rally and come with redoubled energy. Our Soldiers too, or rather our Generals have got to learn to fight better. The idea, of a Genl surrendering with 12000 men under his command, is a species of bravery and Generalship, which I do not understand. I wish Congress would pass a law breaking an officer of his commission who surrenders. I received a letter last night from your Uncle Billy — was very glad to hear from him. If you haven't sent my holsters and boot legs — you neednt send them as I dont now need them. I also received a letter last night from Sue, will write to her soon. My Darling tell Spradley, not to commence planting corn early[.] My land will not admit of early planting, of either corn or cotton. I generally, commence planting corn from the 15th to the 20th of March, and cotton about the same time in April. I see that Congress is about passing a bill, to impose a heavy tax on cotton raised this year. If they pass it — I wish no land planted in cotton except the new ground, and the field next to the overseers house, all the ballance planted in corn. I will write you, however in time. My Darling, Now is the time to bring out all your courage — Do not become despondent — Dont matter what *alarmists* and Croakers may say — take advice from him whom you *know* will advise you for the best. Keep up your spirits and your courage, and the clouds will soon pass away, and sun shine will return — My sheet is full — and I will close by begging to be remembered to all — My love to My Children and My Darling Leila

from Your Husband

I enclose a few Virginia Cabbage seed — and a sprig of spruce pine. It grows here beautifully. G — Tell Willie to write often [.]

Questions

1. Why is Griffin so preoccupied with the birth of boys rather than girls?
2. What is the irony in his fears of a Union victory?
3. What does Griffin regard as the South's weakness? Why are his comments about the proposed cotton tax more important?

Abraham Lincoln, The Gettysburg Address (1863)

The Battle of Gettysburg in July 1863 was the bloodiest of the Civil War. But the costly Union victory strengthened northern resolve and ended any hopes that the Confederacy had of winning foreign recognition (see text p. 410). Later that year, in a speech dedicating a cemetery at Gettysburg, Abraham Lincoln helped define the modern concept of the American nation.

Four score and seven years ago our fathers brought forth on this continent, a new nation, conceived in Liberty, and dedicated to the proposition that all men are created equal.

Now we are engaged in a great civil war, testing whether that nation, or any nation so conceived and so dedicated, can long endure. We are met on a great battle-field of that war. We have come to dedicate a portion of that field, as a final resting place for those who here gave their lives that that nation might live. It is altogether fitting and proper that we should do this.

But, in a larger sense, we can not dedicate — we can not consecrate — we can not hallow — this ground. The brave men, living and dead, who struggled here, have consecrated it, far above our poor power to add or detract. The world will little note, nor long remember what we say here, but it can never forget what they did here. It is for us the living, rather, to be dedicated here to the unfinished work which they who fought here have thus far so nobly advanced. It is rather for us to be here dedicated to the great task remaining before us — that from these honored dead we take increased devotion to that cause for which they gave the last full measure of devotion — that we here highly resolve that these dead shall not have died in vain — that this nation, under God, shall have a new birth of freedom — and that government of the people, by the people, for the people, shall not perish from the earth.

Questions
1. How does Lincoln redefine American history here? Why?
2. What is his purpose in focusing on the dead rather than in discussing his war aims?
3. What aspects of the Gettysburg Address prove Lincoln wrong about his remarks being soon forgotten?

Black Soldiers in Missouri
Bring Families to Freedom (1864)

When President Lincoln issued the final Emancipation Proclamation on January 1, 1863, he exempted areas in eastern and western Virginia and lower Louisiana as well as the states of Delaware, Maryland, Kentucky, Tennessee, and Missouri. But Lincoln had also decided to end his longstanding opposition to the recruitment of black soldiers. Now the federal army admitted blacks and offered freedom to those who still remained slaves.

Despite desultory recruitment efforts in Missouri, nearly 40 percent of the black men of military age — well over 8,000 — joined the federal army, for the most part in late 1863 and early 1864. Although the status of freedom was not automatically passed on to the wives and children of black soldiers, the protection of the federal government was. In a striking reversal of social relationships, former slaves, now Union soldiers, were willing to confront former masters.

Glasgow, March 6, '64
Some negroes who were enlisted in this county and sent to St. Louis, have come back to Booneville and crossed into Howard County with some white

soldiers and are hauling off tobacco from their former masters and owners and taking their wives and children.

Is this to be allowed.

(Signed) J. P. Lewis
Asst Prov. Ml.

Benton Barracks Post Hospital Mo St. Louis
May the 10, 1864

Dear Wife It is with pleasure that I am allowed this morning to write to you and inform you that by the tender mercies of that God who has been my Protector and keeper thus far and still watches over me with paternal care & Love — and it is my prayer that when this comes to you it may find You in the enjoyment of good health and in the Love of God. . . . General Piles [William A. Pile] has given orders if I want you to come here that it shall be granted & determined by the Provost at Tipton. So it lays to your own choice to stay or come. . . . If You do not want to stay tell Mr. Wilson in a decent manner . . . and General Pile says if You Mr. Wilson is . . . a good . . . Union man . . . you will let her come on good terms and give her a piece of writing to shew that You are what you profess to be, and if you do not . . . we will shew You what we intend to do. — We are not expecting that this will insult a Union man. . . . I will find out whether this has been read to her . . . or not, and if I should find out that she has never heard her deliverance I will undoubtedly punish you. . . . [R]ecollect I am writing to Your interest if You look at it right. You can See I have power and You know that on the 10 day of May I write to You with this determination that by the 20th day of May this matter must & will be closed so you can rest till Then or do it sooner as it will be better for You. . . . I want you to understand that we have laboured in the field to Subdue Slavery and now we mean to protect them. . . .

P.S. please read this to my wife and then if you please answer it Immediately so I may know what Steps to take.

Your Friend Sam Bowmen

Questions

1. How does the enlistment of black troops undermine slavery in Missouri?
2. What factors might delay Mrs. Bowmen's freedom?
3. How does the letter suggest to Mr. Wilson that postwar Missouri may be considerably different from the Missouri he used to know?

Connections Questions

1. Compare the depictions of the Irish in the first two documents (Anna Elizabeth Dickinson, "The New York City Draft Riots"; "The Work of the United States Sanitary Commission"). Why is there a difference?

2. Is the Gettysburg Address propaganda or something else? Frame your answer within the context of other historic documents, e.g., the Declaration of Independence and the U.S. Constitution.

3. The letters of James Griffin ("A Soldier's Letter") and Sam Bowmen ("Black Soldiers") both offer glimpses of postwar American society. How do they compare? Are there any similarities? What is their greatest difference?

CHAPTER 16

Reconstruction 1865–1877

Carl Schurz, Report on Conditions
in the South (1865)

*By December 1865, when Congress was gathering in Washington for a
new session, President Andrew Johnson had declared that all the Confederate states but Texas had met his requirements for restoration. Newly elected
senators and representatives from the former Confederacy were arriving to
take seats in Congress.*

*But Johnson's efforts to restore the South stalled. Congress exercised its
constitutional authority to deny seats to delegations from the South and
launched an investigation into conditions there. In response to a Senate resolution requesting "information in relation to the States of the Union lately in
rebellion," Johnson responded with more wish than reality: "In 'that portion
of the Union lately in rebellion' the aspect of affairs is more promising than,
in view of all the circumstances, could well have been expected. The people
throughout the entire south evince a laudable desire to renew their allegiance
to the government, and to repair the devastations of war by a prompt and
cheerful return to peaceful pursuits. An abiding faith is entertained that their
actions will conform to their professions, and that, in acknowledging the supremacy of the Constitution and the laws of the United States, their loyalty
will be unreservedly given to the government, whose leniency they cannot
fail to appreciate, and whose fostering care will soon restore them to a condition of prosperity."*

*Johnson's message to the Senate was accompanied by a report from Major
General Carl Schurz (see Chapter 13, "A German Immigrant"). Among the
subjects Schurz considered were the level of white acceptance of defeat and
emancipation and the condition of former slaves and southern Unionists.
Since he had chosen Schurz for the task, Johnson did not expect to read a report that plainly contradicted him.*

SIR: . . . You informed me that your "policy of reconstruction" was merely
experimental, and that you would change it if the experiment did not lead to
satisfactory results. To aid you in forming your conclusions upon this point I
understood to be the object of my mission, . . .

CONDITION OF THINGS IMMEDIATELY AFTER THE CLOSE
OF THE WAR

In the development of the popular spirit in the south since the close of the war
two well-marked periods can be distinguished. The first commences with the

sudden collapse of the confederacy and the dispersion of its armies, and the second with the first proclamation indicating the "reconstruction policy" of the government. . . . When the news of Lee's and Johnston's surrenders burst upon the southern country the general consternation was extreme. People held their breath, indulging in the wildest apprehensions as to what was now to come. . . . Prominent Unionists told me that persons who for four years had scorned to recognize them on the street approached them with smiling faces and both hands extended. Men of standing in the political world expressed serious doubts as to whether the rebel States would ever again occupy their position as States in the Union, or be governed as conquered provinces. The public mind was so despondent that if readmission at some future time under whatever conditions had been promised, it would then have been looked upon as a favor. The most uncompromising rebels prepared for leaving the country. The masses remained in a state of fearful expectancy. . . .

Such was, according to the accounts I received, the character of that first period. The worst apprehensions were gradually relieved as day after day went by without bringing the disasters and inflictions which had been vaguely anticipated, until at last the appearance of the North Carolina proclamation substituted new hopes for them. The development of this second period I was called upon to observe on the spot, and it forms the main subject of this report.

RETURNING LOYALTY

. . . [T]he white people at large being, under certain conditions, charged with taking the preliminaries of "reconstruction" into their hands, the success of the experiment depends upon the spirit and attitude of those who either attached themselves to the secession cause from the beginning, or, entertaining originally opposite views, at least followed its fortunes from the time that their States had declared their separation from the Union. . . .

I may group the southern people into four classes, each of which exercises an influence upon the development of things in that section:

1. Those who, although having yielded submission to the national government only when obliged to do so, have a clear perception of the irreversible changes produced by the war, and honestly endeavor to accommodate themselves to the new order of things. Many of them are not free from traditional prejudice but open to conviction, and may be expected to act in good faith whatever they do. This class is composed, in its majority, of persons of mature age—planters, merchants, and professional men; some of them are active in the reconstruction movement, but boldness and energy are, with a few individual exceptions, not among their distinguishing qualities.

2. Those whose principal object is to have the States without delay restored to their position and influence in the Union and the people of the

States to the absolute control of their home concerns. They are ready, in order to attain that object, to make any ostensible concession that will not prevent them from arranging things to suit their taste as soon as that object is attained. This class comprises a considerable number, probably a large majority, of the professional politicians who are extremely active in the reconstruction movement. They are loud in their praise of the President's reconstruction policy, and clamorous for the withdrawal of the federal troops and the abolition of the Freedmen's Bureau.

3. The incorrigibles, who still indulge in the swagger which was so customary before and during the war, and still hope for a time when the southern confederacy will achieve its independence. This class consists mostly of young men, and comprises the loiterers of the towns and the idlers of the country. They persecute Union men and negroes whenever they can do so with impunity, insist clamorously upon their "rights," and are extremely impatient of the presence of the federal soldiers. A good many of them have taken the oaths of allegiance and amnesty, and associated themselves with the second class in their political operations. This element is by no means unimportant; it is strong in numbers, deals in brave talk, addresses itself directly and incessantly to the passions and prejudices of the masses, and commands the admiration of the women.

4. The multitude of people who have no definite ideas about the circumstances under which they live and about the course they have to follow; whose intellects are weak, but whose prejudices and impulses are strong, and who are apt to be carried along by those who know how to appeal to the latter. . . .

FEELING TOWARDS THE SOLDIERS AND THE PEOPLE OF THE NORTH

. . . [U]pon the whole, the soldier of the Union is still looked upon as a stranger, an intruder—as the "Yankee," "the enemy." . . .

It is by no means surprising that prejudices and resentments, which for years were so assiduously cultivated and so violently inflamed, should not have been turned into affection by a defeat; nor are they likely to disappear as long as the southern people continue to brood over their losses and misfortunes. They will gradually subside when those who entertain them cut resolutely loose from the past and embark in a career of new activity on a common field with those whom they have so long considered their enemies. . . . [A]s long as these feelings exist in their present strength, they will hinder the growth of that reliable kind of loyalty which springs from the heart and clings to the country in good and evil fortune.

SITUATION OF UNIONISTS

. . . It struck me soon after my arrival in the south that the known Unionists—I mean those who during the war had been to a certain extent identified with the national cause—were not in communion with the leading social and political circles; and the further my observations extended the clearer it became to me that their existence in the south was of a rather precarious nature. . . . Even Governor [William L.] Sharkey, in the course of a conversation I had with him in the presence of Major General Osterhaus, admitted that, if our troops were then withdrawn, the lives of northern men in Mississippi would not be safe. . . . [General Osterhaus said]: "There is no doubt whatever that the state of affairs would be intolerable for all Union men, all recent immigrants from the north, and all negroes, the moment the protection of the United States troops were withdrawn." . . .

NEGRO INSURRECTIONS AND ANARCHY

. . . [I do] not deem a negro insurrection probable as long as the freedmen were assured of the direct protection of the national government. Whenever they are in trouble, they raise their eyes up to that power, and although they may suffer, yet, as long as that power is visibly present, they continue to hope. But when State authority in the south is fully restored, the federal forces withdrawn, and the Freedmen's Bureau abolished, the colored man will find himself turned over to the mercies of those whom he does not trust. If then an attempt is made to strip him again of those rights which he justly thought he possessed, he will be apt to feel that he can hope for no redress unless he procure it himself. If ever the negro is capable of rising, he will rise then. . . .

There is probably at the present moment no country in the civilized world which contains such an accumulation of anarchical elements as the south. The strife of the antagonistic tendencies here described is aggravated by the passions inflamed and the general impoverishment brought about by a long and exhaustive war, and the south will have to suffer the evils of anarchical disorder until means are found to effect a final settlement of the labor question in accordance with the logic of the great revolution.

THE TRUE PROBLEM — DIFFICULTIES AND REMEDIES

In seeking remedies for such disorders, we ought to keep in view, above all, the nature of the problem which is to be solved. As to what is commonly termed "reconstruction," it is not only the political machinery of the States and their constitutional relations to the general government, but the whole organism of southern society that must be reconstructed, or rather constructed anew, so as to bring it in harmony with the rest of American society. The difficulties of this task are not to be considered overcome when the people of the south take the oath of allegiance and elect governors and legislatures and members of Congress, and militia captains. That this would be done had become certain as soon as the surrenders of the southern armies had made further resistance impossible, and nothing in the world was left, even to the most uncompromising rebel, but to submit or to emigrate. It was also natural that they should avail themselves of every chance offered them to resume control of their home affairs and to regain their influence in the Union. But this can hardly be called the first step towards the solution of the true problem, and it is a fair question to ask, whether the hasty gratification of their desire to resume such control would not create new embarrassments.

The true nature of the difficulties of the situation is this: The general government of the republic has, by proclaiming the emancipation of the slaves, commenced a great social revolution in the south, but has, as yet, not completed it. Only the negative part of it is accomplished. The slaves are emancipated in point of form, but free labor has not yet been put in the place of slavery in point of fact. And now, in the midst of this critical period of transition, the power which originated the revolution is expected to turn over its whole future development to another power which from the beginning was hostile to it and has never yet entered into its spirit, leaving the class in whose favor it was made completely without power to protect itself and to take an influential part in that development. The history of the world will be searched in vain for a proceeding similar to this which did not lead either to a rapid and violent reaction, or to the most serious trouble and civil disorder. It cannot be said that the conduct of the southern people since the close of the war has exhibited such extraordinary wisdom and self-abnegation as to make them an exception to the rule.

In my despatches from the south I repeatedly expressed the opinion that the people were not yet in a frame of mind to legislate calmly and understandingly upon the subject of free negro labor. And this I reported to be the opinion of some of our most prominent military commanders and other observing men. It is, indeed, difficult to imagine circumstances more unfavorable for the development of a calm and unprejudiced public opinion than those under which the southern people are at present laboring. The war has not only defeated their political aspirations, but it has broken up their whole social organization. . . .

In which direction will these people be most apt to turn their eyes? Leaving the prejudice of race out of the question, from early youth they have been acquainted with but one system of labor, and with that one system they have been in the habit of identifying all their interests. They know of no way to help themselves but the one they are accustomed to. . . .

It is certain that every success of free negro labor will augment the number of its friends, and disarm some of the prejudices and assumptions of its opponents. I am convinced one good harvest made by unadulterated free labor in the south would have a far better effect than all the oaths that have been taken, and all the ordinances that have as yet been passed by southern conventions. But how can such a result be attained? The facts enumerated in this report, as well as the news we receive from the south from day to day, must make it evident to every unbiased observer that unadulterated free labor cannot be had at present, unless the national government holds its protective and controlling hand over it. . . . One reason why the southern people are so slow in accommodating themselves to the new order of things is, that they confidently expect soon to be permitted to regulate matters according to their own notions. Every concession made to them by the government has been taken as an encouragement to persevere in this hope, and, unfortunately for them, this hope is nourished by influences from other parts of the country. Hence their anxiety to have their State governments restored *at once,* to have the troops withdrawn, and the Freedmen's Bureau abolished, although a good many discerning men know well that, in view of the lawless spirit still prevailing, it would be far better for them to have the general order of society firmly maintained by the federal power until things have arrived at a final settlement. Had, from the beginning, the conviction been forced upon them that the adulteration of the new order of things by the admixture of elements belonging to the system of slavery would under no circumstances be permitted, a much larger number would have launched their energies into the new channel, and, seeing that they could do "no better," faithfully co-operated with the government. It is hope which fixes them in their perverse notions. That hope nourished or fully gratified, they will persevere in the same direction. That hope destroyed, a great many will, by the force of necessity, at once accommodate themselves to the logic of the change. If, therefore, the national government firmly and unequivocally announces its policy not to give up the control of the free-labor reform until it is finally accomplished, the progress of that reform will undoubtedly be far more rapid and far less difficult than it will be if the attitude of the government is such as to permit contrary hopes to be indulged in. . . .

IMMIGRATION [AND CAPITAL]

[The south would benefit] from immigration of northern people and Europeans. . . . The south needs capital. But capital is notoriously timid and averse to risk. . . . Capitalists will be apt to consider—and they are by no means wrong in doing so—that no safe investments can be made in the south as long as southern society is liable to be convulsed by anarchical disorders. No greater encouragement can, therefore, be given to capital to transfer itself to the south than the assurance that the government will continue to control the development of the new social system in the late rebel States until such dangers are averted by a final settlement of things upon a thorough free-labor basis.

How long the national government should continue that control depends upon contingencies. It ought to cease as soon as its objects are attained; and its objects will be attained sooner and with less difficulty if nobody is permitted to indulge in the delusion that it will cease *before* they are attained. This is one of the cases in which a determined policy can accomplish much, while a half-way policy is liable to spoil things already accomplished. . . .

NEGRO SUFFRAGE

It would seem that the interference of the national authority in the home concerns of the southern States would be rendered less necessary, and the whole problem of political and social reconstruction be much simplified, if, while the masses lately arrayed against the government are permitted to vote, the large majority of those who were always loyal, and are naturally anxious to see the free labor problem successfully solved, were not excluded from all influence upon legislation. In all questions concerning the Union, the national debt, and the future social organization of the south, the feelings of the colored man are naturally in sympathy with the views and aims of the national government. While the southern white fought against the Union, the negro did all he could to aid it; while the southern white sees in the national government his conqueror, the negro sees in it his protector; while the white owes to the national debt his defeat, the negro owes to it his deliverance; while the white considers himself robbed and ruined by the emancipation of the slaves, the negro finds in it the assurance of future prosperity and happiness. In all the important issues the negro would be led by natural impulse to forward the ends of the government, and by making his influence, as part of the voting body, tell upon the legislation of the States, render the interference of the national authority less necessary.

As the most difficult of the pending questions are intimately connected with the status of the negro in southern society, it is obvious that a correct solution can be more easily obtained if he has a voice in the matter. In the right to vote he would find the best permanent protection against oppressive class-legislation, as well as against individual persecution. The relations between the white and black races, even if improved by the gradual wearing off of the present animosities, are likely to remain long under the troubling influence of prejudice. It is a notorious fact that the rights of a man of some political power are far less exposed to violation than those of one who is, in matters of public interest, completely subject to the will of others. . . .

In discussing the matter of negro suffrage I deemed it my duty to confine myself strictly to the practical aspects of the subject. I have, therefore, not touched its moral merits nor discussed the question whether the national government is competent to enlarge the elective franchise in the States lately in rebellion by its own act; I deem it proper, however, to offer a few remarks on the assertion frequently put forth, that the franchise is likely to be extended to the colored man by the voluntary action of the southern whites themselves. My observation leads me to a contrary opinion. Aside from a very few enlightened men, I found but one class of people in favor of the enfranchisement of the blacks: it was the class of Unionists who found themselves politically ostracised and looked upon the enfranchisement of the loyal negroes as the salvation of the whole loyal element. But their numbers and influence are sadly insufficient to secure such a result. The masses are strongly opposed to colored suffrage; anybody that dares to advocate it is stigmatized as a dangerous fanatic; nor do I deem it probable that in the ordinary course of things prejudices will wear off to such an extent as to make it a popular measure. . . .

DEPORTATION OF THE FREEDMEN

. . . [T]he true problem remains, not how to remove the colored man from his present field of labor, but how to make him, where he is, a true freeman and an intelligent and useful citizen. The means are simple: protection by the government until his political and social status enables him to protect himself, offering to his legitimate ambition the stimulant of a perfectly fair chance in life, and granting to him the rights which in every just organization of society are coupled with corresponding duties.

CONCLUSION

I may sum up all I have said in a few words. If nothing were necessary but to restore the machinery of government in the States lately in rebellion in point of form, the movements made to that end by the people of the south might be considered satisfactory. But if it is required that the southern people should also accommodate themselves to the results of the war in point of spirit, those movements fall far short of what must be insisted upon. . . .

Questions

1. Is Schurz optimistic or pessimistic about the likelihood of substantive reconstruction in the South? Explain.

2. Why do southern views of Union soldiers matter?
3. Why does Schurz support suffrage for the former slaves?

The Mississippi Black Codes (1865)

As Carl Schurz reported, after the Civil War whites in the South sought a system of race relations in which African-Americans would be in a clearly subordinate position and would constitute a readily accessible and controllable work force.

Immediately after the war, southern whites wrote or revised vagrancy laws and the old slave codes as a means of establishing the system of race relations they wanted. Below are the Black Codes passed by the Mississippi legislature, one of the South's most famous attempts to codify race relations.

The Mississippi codes gave blacks rights they had not had before and clearly acknowledged that chattel slavery was dead. The codes recognized the right of African-Americans to own property, though not in incorporated towns or cities. (Before the Civil War there were black property owners in the state and even a few black slaveholders, but their legal standing was unclear.) The 1865 codes also recognized marriages between blacks as legal.

1. CIVIL RIGHTS OF FREEDMEN IN MISSISSIPPI

. . . That all freedmen, free negroes, and mulattoes may sue and be sued . . . may acquire personal property . . . and may dispose of the same in the same manner and to the same extent that white persons may: [but no] freedman, free negro, or mulatto . . . [shall] rent or lease any lands or tenements except in incorporated cities or towns, in which places the corporate authorities shall control the same. . . .

All freedmen, free negroes, or mulattoes who do now and have herebefore lived and cohabited together as husband and wife shall be taken and held in law as legally married, and the issue shall be taken and held as legitimate for all purposes; that it shall not be lawful for any freedman, free negro, or mulatto to intermarry with any white person; nor for any white person to intermarry with any freedman, free negro, or mulatto; and any person who shall so intermarry, shall be deemed guilty of felony, and on conviction thereof shall be confined in the State penitentiary for life; and those shall be deemed freedmen, free negroes, and mulattoes who are of pure negro blood, and those descended from a negro to the third generation, inclusive, though one ancestor in each generation may have been a white person. . . .

[F]reedmen, free negroes, and mulattoes are now by law competent witnesses . . . in civil cases [and in criminal cases where they are the victims]. . . .

All contracts for labor made with freedmen, free negroes, and mulattoes for a longer period than one month shall be in writing, and in duplicate. . . . and said contracts shall be taken and held as entire contracts, and if the laborer shall quit the service of the employer before the expiration of his term of service, without good cause, he shall forfeit his wages for that year up to the time of quitting.

. . . Every civil officer shall, and every person may, arrest and carry back to his or her legal employer any freedman, free negro, or mulatto who shall have quit the service of his or her employer before the expiration of his or her term of service without good cause; and said officer and person shall be entitled to receive for arresting and carrying back every deserting employe aforesaid the sum of five dollars. . . .

. . . If any person shall persuade or attempt to persuade, entice, or cause any freedman, free negro, or mulatto to desert from the legal employment of any person before the expiration of his or her term of service, or shall knowingly employ any such deserting freedman, free negro, or mulatto, or shall knowingly give or sell to any such deserting freedman, free negro, or mulatto, any food, raiment, or other thing, he or she shall be guilty of a misdemeanor. . . .

2. MISSISSIPPI APPRENTICE LAW

. . . It shall be the duty of all sheriffs, justices of the peace, and other civil officers of the several counties in this State, to report to the probate courts of their respective counties semi-annually, at the January and July terms of said courts, all freedmen, free negroes, and mulattoes, under the age of eighteen, in their respective counties, beats or districts, who are orphans, or whose parent or parents have not the means or who refuse to provide for and support said minors; . . . the clerk of said court to apprentice said minors to some competent and suitable person, on such terms as the court may direct, having a particular care to the interest of said minor: *Provided,* that the former owner of said minors shall have the preference when, in the opinion of the court, he or she shall be a suitable person for that purpose. . . .

. . . In the management and control of said apprentice, said master or mistress shall have the power to inflict such moderate corporal chastisement as a father or guardian is allowed to inflict on his or her child or ward at common law: *Provided,* that in no case shall cruel or inhuman punishment be inflicted. . . .

3. MISSISSIPPI VAGRANT LAW

. . . That all rogues and vagabonds, idle and dissipated persons, beggars, jugglers, or persons practicing unlawful games or plays, runaways, common drunkards, common night-walkers, pilferers, lewd, wanton, or lascivious persons, in speech or behavior, common railers and brawlers, persons who neglect their calling or employment, misspend what they earn, or do not provide for the support of themselves or their families, or dependents, and all other idle and disorderly persons, including all who neglect all lawful business, habitually misspend their time by frequenting houses of ill-fame, gaming-houses, or tippling shops, shall be deemed and considered vagrants, under the provisions of this act, and upon conviction thereof shall be fined not exceeding one hundred dollars . . . and be imprisoned at the discretion of the court, not exceeding ten days.

. . . All freedmen, free negroes and mulattoes in this State, over the age of eighteen years, found on the second Monday in January, 1866, or thereafter, with no lawful employment or business, or found unlawfully assembling themselves together, either in the day or night time, and all white persons so assembling themselves with freedmen, free negroes or mulattoes, or usually associating with freedmen, free negroes or mulattoes, on terms of equality, or living in adultery or fornication with a freed woman, free negro or mulatto, shall be deemed vagrants, and on conviction thereof shall be fined in a sum not exceeding, in the case of a freedman, free negro or mulatto, fifty dollars, and a white man two hundred dollars, and imprisoned at the discretion of the court, the free negro not exceeding ten days, and the white man not exceeding six months. . . .

4. PENAL LAWS OF MISSISSIPPI

. . . That no freedman, free negro or mulatto, not in the military service of the United States government, and not licensed so to do by the board of police of his or her county, shall keep or carry fire-arms of any kind, or any ammunition, dirk or bowie knife. . . .

. . . Any freedman, free negro, or mulatto committing riots, routs, affrays, trespasses, malicious mischief, cruel treatment to animals, seditious speeches, insulting gestures, language, or acts, or assaults on any person, disturbance of the peace, exercising the function of a minister of the Gospel without a license from some regularly organized church, vending spirituous or intoxicating liquors, or committing any other misdemeanor, the punishment of which is not specifically provided for by law, shall, upon conviction thereof in the county court, be fined not less than ten dollars, and not more than one hundred dollars, and may be imprisoned at the discretion of the court, not exceeding thirty days. . . .

. . . If any freedman, free negro, or mulatto, convicted of any of the misdemeanors provided against in this act, shall fail or refuse for the space of five days, after conviction, to pay the fine and costs imposed, such person shall be hired out by the sheriff or other officer, at public outcry, to any white person who will pay said fine and all costs, and take said convict for the shortest time.

Questions

1. What is the significance of tracing black heritage back three generations?
2. What abuses are inherent in the apprentice law?
3. What civil liberties do the vagrancy and penal provisions violate?

Thaddeus Stevens on Black Suffrage and Land Redistribution (1867)

The Radical Republicans, including Congressman Thaddeus Stevens (1792–1868), believed that besides the vote, freedmen would need an economic basis for establishing their newly defined lives (see text p. 428). Below are excerpts from remarks made by Stevens and from a bill in which he proposed a drastic altering of southern society.

ON BLACK SUFFRAGE

Unless the rebel States, before admission, should be made republican in spirit, and placed under the guardianship of loyal men, all our blood and treasure will have been spent in vain. I waive now the question of punishment which, if we are wise, will still be inflicted by moderate confiscations. . . . Impartial suffrage, both in electing the delegates and ratifying their proceedings, is now the fixed rule. There is more reason why colored voters should be admitted in the rebel States than in the Territories. In the States they form the great mass of the loyal men. Possibly with their aid loyal governments may be established in most of those States. Without it all are sure to be ruled by traitors; and loyal men, black and white, will be oppressed, exiled, or murdered. There are several good reasons for the passage of this bill. In the first place, it is just. I am now confining my argument to negro suffrage in the rebel States. Have not loyal blacks quite as good a right to choose rulers and make laws as rebel whites? In the second place, it is a necessity in order to protect the loyal white men in the seceded States. The white Union men are in a great minority in each of those States. With them the blacks would act in a body; and it is believed that in each of said States, except one, the two united would form a majority, control the States, and protect themselves. Now they are the victims of daily murder. . . .

Another good reason is, it would insure the ascendency of the Union party. . . . I believe . . . that on the continued ascendency of that party depends the safety of this great nation. If impartial suffrage is excluded in the rebel States, then every one of them is sure to send a solid rebel representative delegation to Congress, and cast a solid rebel electoral vote. They, with their kindred Copperheads of the North, would always elect the President and control Congress. While slavery sat upon her defiant throne, and insulted and intimidated the trembling North, the South frequently divided on questions of policy between Whigs and Democrats, and gave victory alternately to the sections. Now, you must divide them between loyalists, without regard to color, and disloyalists, or you will be the perpetual vassals of the free-trade, irritated, revengeful South. . . . I am for negro suffrage in every rebel State. If it be just, it should not be denied; if it be necessary, it should be adopted; if it be a punishment to traitors, they deserve it.

BILL ON LAND REDISTRIBUTION

Whereas it is due to justice, as an example to future times, that some proper punishment should be inflicted on the people who constituted the "confederate States of America," both because they, declaring an unjust war against the United States for the purpose of destroying republican liberty and permanently establishing slavery, as well as for the cruel and barbarous manner in which they conducted said war, in violation of all the laws of civilized warfare, and also to compel them to make some compensation for the damages and expenditures caused by said war: Therefore,

Be it enacted by the Senate and House of Representatives of the United States of America in Congress assembled, That all the public lands belonging to the ten States that formed the government of the so-called "confederate States of America" shall be forfeited by said States and become forthwith vested in the United States. . . .

That out of the lands thus seized and confiscated the slaves who have been liberated by the operations of the war and the amendment to the Constitution or otherwise, who resided in said "confederate States" on the 4th day of March, A.D. 1861, or since, shall have distributed to them as follows, namely: to each male person who is the head of a family, forty acres; to each adult male, whether the head of a family or not, forty acres; to each widow who is the head of a family, forty acres—to be held by them in fee-simple, but to be inalienable for the next ten years after they become seized thereof. . . .

That out of the balance of the property thus seized and confiscated there shall be raised, in the manner hereinafter provided, a sum equal to fifty dollars, for each homestead, to be applied by the trustees hereinafter mentioned toward the erection of buildings on the said homesteads for the use of said slaves; and the further sum of $500,000,000, which shall be appropriated as follows, to wit: $200,000,000 shall be invested in United States six per cent securities; and the interest thereof shall be semi-annually added to the pensions allowed by law to pensioners who have become so by reason of the late war; $300,000,000, or so much thereof as may be needed, shall be appropriated to pay damages done to loyal citizens by the civil or military operations of the government lately called the "confederate States of America." . . .

That in order that just discrimination may be made, the property of no one shall be seized whose whole estate on the 4th day of March, A.D. 1865, was not worth more than $5,000, to be valued by the said commission, unless he shall have voluntarily become an officer or employé in the military or civil service of the "confederate States of America," or in the civil or military service of some one of said States. . . .

Questions

1. Why does Stevens endorse black suffrage?
2. How does he justify land redistribution?
3. What does the legislation propose to do? What would make northerners—otherwise hostile to former Confederates—uncomfortable with its passage?

Thomas Nast, The Rise and Fall of Northern Support for Reconstruction (1868, 1874)

Evidence of broad northern support for the Republican program could be found in many places other than the ballot box. Illustrations from Harper's Weekly, *for example, "This Is a White Man's Government," reflected popular attitudes in the North during the late 1860s.*

However, northern support for Reconstruction began to erode as early as 1868. For various reasons Republican state governments in the South got a very bad reputation in the North. Also, northern willingness to use force to keep Republican governments in office in the South, even when threatened by violence, intimidation, and fraud, was exhausted by 1874, the year the second Harper's Weekly *illustration shown here appeared.*

Both cartoons are by the renowned Thomas Nast. The first is packed with allusions. Depicted from left to right are an Irish immigrant; the former Confederate general and Ku Klux Klan leader Nathan Bedford Forrest; and an unscrupulous businessman. Together, the three figures are crushing an African-American Civil War veteran; note his Union jacket and cap, as well as the saber and American flag. In addition there are references to the 1863 Draft Riot; Forrest's involvement in an 1864 massacre of black soldiers at Fort Pillow; and a burning southern school.

The second Nast cartoon shows something else entirely—how much and how quickly public attitudes had changed.

Questions

1. How does the first cartoon play on emotions? on prejudice?
2. How does the depiction of white politicians in the second cartoon convey Nast's view of Reconstruction?
3. As cultural documents, what do these cartoons say about the prevailing attitudes toward non-WASPs?

COLORED RULE IN A RECONSTRUCTED (?) STATE.—[See Page 242.]

(THE MEMBERS CALL EACH OTHER THIEVES, LIARS, RASCALS, AND COWARDS.)

COLUMBIA. "You are Aping the lowest Whites. If you disgrace your Race in this way you had better take Back Seats."

Albion W. Tourgee, *A Fool's Errand.*
By One of the Fools (1879)

An Ohio native, Albion Winegar Tourgee (1838–1905) was working as a schoolteacher in New York at the onset of the Civil War. In April 1861, Tourgee joined the 27th New York Regiment and was wounded at the first Battle of Bull Run. He returned to the army in July 1862 as a lieutenant in the 105th Ohio Regiment. Captured in 1863 at Murfeesboro, Tourgee returned to Ohio through a prisoner exchange. He rejoined his regiment to fight at Chickamauga, Lookout Mountain, and Missionary Ridge. Twice charged with insubordination, Tourgee resigned his commission in December 1863 and studied law in Ohio.

By the fall of 1865 he had relocated as a "carpetbagger" (see text p. 432) to Greensboro, North Carolina. In 1868, thanks to the electoral rule imposed under radical Reconstruction, Tourgee won election to the state superior court. He served there for six years, finding ample opportunity to defend the rights of freedmen and denounce the atrocities of the Ku Klux Klan.

When his tenure on the court ended, Tourgee was appointed by President Grant as pension agent at Raleigh; the former judge continued his battle with the Klan and with Redeemer Democrats (see text pp. 436–37). By the summer of 1879, Tourgee had had enough and moved north with his family; eventually they settled in Mayville, New York.

In this selection from his novel A Fool's Errand, *Tourgee describes his experiences during Reconstruction through the character of Colonel Comfort Servosse, "the Fool."*

It was in the winter of 1868–69 . . . when it was said that already Reconstruction had been an approved success, [and] the traces of the war been blotted out . . . a little company of colored men came to the Fool one day; and one of them, who acted as spokesman said,—

"What's dis we hear, Mars Kunnel [Master Colonel], bout de Klux?"

"The what?" he asked.

"De Klux—de Ku-Kluckers dey calls demselves."

"Oh! The Ku-Klux, Ku-Klux-Klan . . . you mean."

"Yes: dem folks what rides about at night a-pesterin' pore colored people, an' pretendin' tu be jes from hell, or some of de battle-fields ob ole Virginny."

"Oh, that's all gammon [humbug]! There is nothing in the world in it,— nothing at all. . . ."

"You don't think dey's ghostses, nor nothin' ob dat sort?" asked another.

"Think! I know they are not."

"So do I," growled one of their number who had not spoken before, in a tone . . . that . . . drew the eyes of the Fool upon him at once.

"So your mind's made up on that point too, is it Bob?" he asked laughingly.

"I know dey's not ghosts, Kunnel. I wish ter God dey was!" was the reply.

"Why, what do you mean, Bob?" asked the colonel in surprise.

"Will you jes help me take off my shirt, Jim?" said Bob . . . as he turned to one of those with him. . . .

"What d'ye tink ob dat, Kunnel?"

"My God!" exclaimed the Fool, starting back in surprise and horror. "What does this mean, Bob?"

"Seen de Kluckers, sah," was the grimly-laconic answer.

The sight which presented itself to the Fool's eyes was truly terrible. . . . The whole back was livid and swollen, bruised as if it had been brayed in a mortar. Apparently, after having cut the flesh with closely-laid welts and furrows, sloping downward from the left side towards the right, with the peculiar skill . . . which could only be obtained through the abundant opportunity for severe . . . flagellation which prevailed under . . . slavery, the operator had changed his position, and scientifically cross-checked the whole. . . . "Nobody but an ole oberseer ebber dun dat, Kunnel." . . . When his clothing had been resumed, he sat down and poured into the wondering ears of the Fool this story:—

BOB'S EXPERIENCE.

"Yer see, I'se a blacksmith at Burke's Cross-Roads. I've been thar ever sence a few days arter I heer ob de surrender. I rented an ole house dar, an' put up a sort of shop . . . an' went to work. . . .

"Long a while back—p'raps five er six month—I refused ter du some work fer Michael Anson or his boy, 'cause they'd run up quite a score at de shop, an' allers put me off when I wanted pay. . . . Folks said I waz gettin' too smart fer a nigger, an' sech like; but I kep' right on; tole em I waz a free man . . . an' I didn't propose ter do any man's work fer noffin'. Most everybody hed somefin' ter say about it; but it didn't seem ter hurt my trade very much. . . . When ther come an election, I sed my say, did my own votin', an' tole de other colored people dey waz free, an' hed a right ter du de same. Thet's bad doctrine up in our country. . . . Dey don't mind 'bout . . . our votin', so long ez we votes ez day tell us. Dat' dare idea uv liberty fer a nigger.

"Well, here a few weeks ago, I foun' a board stuck up on my shop one mornin', wid dese words on it:—

"'BOB MARTIN,—You're gettin' too dam smart! The white folks round Burke's Cross-Roads don't want any sech smart niggers round thar. You'd better git, er you'll hev a call from the

'K.K.K.'"

... [Y]esterday ... my ole 'ooman ... tuk part ob de chillen into bed wid her; an' de rest crawled in wid me. . . . I kinder remember hearin' de dog bark, but I didn't mind it; an', de fust ting I knew, de do' was bust in. . . . Dar was 'bout tirty of 'em standin' dar in de moonlight, all dressed in black gowns thet come down to ther boots, an' some sort of high hat on, dat come down ober der faces. . . . Den dey tied me tu a tree, an' done what you've seen. Dey tuk my wife an' oldes' gal out of de house, tore de close right about off 'em, an' abused 'em shockin' afore my eyes. After tarin' tings up a heap in de house, dey rode off, tellin' me dey reckoned I's larn to be 'spectful to white folks hereafter. . . .

"Why have you not complained of this outrage to the authorities?" . . . asked [the Fool] after a moment.

"I tole Squire Haskins an' Judge Thompson what I hev tole you," answered Bob.

"And what did they say?"

"Dat dey couldn't do noffin' unless I could sw'ar to the parties." . . .

There was a moment's silence. Then the colored man asked,—

"Isn't dere no one else, Kunnel, dat could do any ting? Can't de President or Congress do somefin'? De gov'ment sot us free, an' it 'pears like it oughtn't to let our old masters impose on us in no sech way now. . . . We ain't cowards. We showed dat in de wah. I'se seen darkeys go whar de white troops wa'n't anxious to foller 'em, mor'n once."

"Where was that, Bob?"

"Wal, at Fo't Wagner, for one."

"How did you know about that?"

"How did I know 'bout dat? Bress yer soul, Kunnel, I was dar!"

Questions

1. What is the Fool's initial assessment of Reconstruction? What makes him change his mind?

2. How does the KKK seek to terrorize the black population?

3. Why would Tourgee portray himself fictionally the way he does?

Charles Sumner, "Republicanism vs. Grantism" (1872)

Charles Sumner had come to the United States Senate during the first wave of antislavery's political insurgency across the North (see Chapter 14, "The Crime against Kansas"). Throughout the Civil War and Reconstruction, Sumner was among the most vehement and politically powerful radical Republicans. But during the Grant administration Sumner frequently opposed the president, as when he denounced Grant's efforts to acquire Santo Domingo (the present-day Dominican Republic) as a territory of the United States.

Grant loyalists retaliated in 1872 by deposing Sumner as chairman of the Foreign Relations Committee. With a remarkable number of former radical Republicans, Sumner cast his lot with the Liberal Republicans who opposed Grant's reelection by supporting the Democratic candidate, Horace Greeley. This break in party ranks—specifically the defection of radicals to the Liberal Republican platform of sectional reconciliation—marked the beginning of the end of Reconstruction. Here Sumner takes to the floor of the Senate to denounce "Grantism."

Mr. President,—I have no hesitation in declaring myself a member of the Republican Party, and one of the straitest of the sect. I doubt if any Senator can point to earlier or more constant service in its behalf. I began at the beginning, and from that early day have never failed to sustain its candidates and to advance its principles. . . .

Turning back to its birth, I recall a speech of my own at a State Convention in Massachusetts, as early as September 7, 1854, where I vindicated its principles and announced its name in these words: "as *Republicans* we go forth to encounter the *Oligarches* of Slavery." . . . The Republican Party was necessary and permanent, and always on an ascending plane. For such a party there was no death, but higher life and nobler aims; and this was the party to which I gave my vows. But, alas, how changed! Once country was the object, and not a man; once principle was inscribed on the victorious banners, and not a name only.

THE REPUBLICAN PARTY SEIZED BY THE PRESIDENT

It is not difficult to indicate when this disastrous change . . . became not merely manifest, but painfully conspicuous . . . suddenly and without any warning through the public press or any expression from public opinion, the President elected by the Republican Party precipitated upon the country an ill-considered and ill-omened scheme for the annexation of a portion of the island of San Domingo. . . .

PRESIDENTIAL PRETENSIONS

. . . [t]he Presidential office has been used to advance his own family on a scale of nepotism dwarfing everything of the kind in our history . . . and . . . all these assumptions have matured in a *personal government,* semi-military in character and breathing the military spirit,—being a species of Caesarism or *personalism,* abhorrent to republican institutions. . . . [T]he chosen head of the Republic is known chiefly for Presidential pretensions, utterly indefensible in character, derogatory to the country, and of evil influence, making personal objects a primary pursuit, so that . . . he is a bad example, through whom republican institutions suffer and the people learn to do wrong. . . .

PERSONAL GOVERNMENT UNREPUBLICAN

Personal Government is autocratic. It is the One-Man Power elevated above all else, and is therefore in direct conflict with republican government, whose consummate form is tripartite . . . each independent and coequal. . . .

A government of laws and not of men is the object of republican government; nay, more, it is the distinctive essence without which it becomes a tyranny. Therefore personal government in all its forms, and especially when it seeks to sway the action of any other branch or overturn its constitutional negative, is hostile to the first principles of republican institutions, and an unquestionable outrage. That our President has offended in this way is unhappily too apparent.

THE PRESIDENT AS CIVILIAN

To comprehend the personal government that has been installed over us we must know its author. His picture is the necessary frontispiece,—not as soldier, let it be borne in mind, but as civilian. . . .

To appreciate his peculiar character as a civilian it is important to know his triumphs as a soldier, for the one is the natural complement of the other. The successful soldier is rarely changed to the successful civilian. There seems to be an incompatibility between the two. . . . One always a soldier cannot late in life become a statesman. . . . Washington and Jackson were civilians as well as soldiers. . . .

THE GREAT PRESIDENTIAL QUARRELER

Any presentment of the President would be imperfect which did not show how this ungovernable personality breaks forth in quarrel, making him the great Presidential quarreler of our history. . . . With the arrogance of arms he resents any impediment in his path,—as when, in the spring of 1870, without allusion to himself, I felt it my duty to oppose his San Domingo contrivance. . . .

DUTY OF THE REPUBLICAN PARTY

And now the question of Duty is distinctly presented to the Republican Party. . . . Do the Presidential pretensions merit the sanction of the party? Can Republicans, without departing from all obligations, whether of party or patriotism, recognize our ambitious Caesar as a proper representative? . . . Therefore with unspeakable interest will the country watch the National Convention at Philadelphia. It may be an assembly (and such is my hope) where ideas and principles are above all personal pretensions, and the unity of the party is symbolized in the candidate; or it may add another to Presidential rings, being an expansion of the military ring at the Executive Mansion, the senatorial ring in the [Senate] Chamber, and the political ring in the customhouses of New York and New Orleans. A National Convention which is a Republican ring cannot represent the Republican Party. . . . I wait the determination of the National Convention. . . . Not without anxiety do I wait, but with the earnest hope that the Convention will bring the Republican Party into ancient harmony, saving it especially from the suicidal folly of an issue on the personal pretensions of one man.

Questions

1. What are Sumner's harshest charges against President Grant?
2. In demeaning the political abilities of the "successful soldier," what is Sumner ignoring in Grant's rise to power?
3. What does Sumner fear will come to dominate the Republican presidential convention?

Connections Questions

1. Using the Mississippi Black Codes as a measure, how accurate is Carl Schurz's report ("Report on Conditions") on conditions in the South?
2. How do the two cartoons by Thomas Nast engage a reader? To what extent, if any, does the message conveyed differ from that in a written source?
3. Imagine yourself a member of Congress in the 1860s. Would you vote for Thaddeus Stevens's bill ("Thaddeus Stevens on Black Suffrage") after reading the report by Carl Schurz ("Report on Conditions")? Why or why not?

ACKNOWLEDGMENTS

CHAPTER 1

Bernal Díaz del Castillo. "Discovery and Conquest of Mexico." Excerpts from *The Discovery and Conquest of Mexico, 1517–1521* by Bernal Díaz del Castillo, translated by A.P. Maudslay, pp. 102–105, 119, 156–157. Copyright © 1956 by Farrar, Straus & Cudahy. Copyright renewed © 1984 by Farrar, Straus & Giroux, Inc.

Daniel Richter. "Iroquis and Penobscot Myths of Creation." Taken from *The Ordeal of the Longhouse: The Peoples of the Iroquois League in the Era of European Colonization* by Daniel Richter. Published for the Institute of Early American History and Culture. Copyright © 1992 by the University of North Carolina Press. Used by permission of the publisher.

"Raoul Glaber, Account of Famine." Taken from *The Ancient World to Louis XIV* in *The Western Tradition,* by Eugen Weber. Published by D.C. Heath (1990), 4e. vol. 1, pp. 250–251.

John Hales. "Objections Against Enclosure (1548)." Taken from *Ecclesiastical Memorials* (London 1721), vol. 2, Appendix of Documents, Document Q as published in *Renaissance and Reformation, 1300–1648.* Copyright © 1963 Macmillan. Reprinted with the permission of Macmillan, a division of Simon & Schuster.

"The Separatists State Their Case." Excerpt taken from "The Points of Difference Between Congregationalism and the Church of England (1603)" in *The Creeds and Platforms of Congregationalism* (Boston 1893) by Williston Walker; reprinted by Pilgrim Press, 1960.

Richard Hakluyt. "A Discourse Concerning Western Planting (1584)." Taken from *Documentary History of the State of Maine* (Collections of the Maine Historical Society 1869–1916), vol. 2, pp. 152–161 by Charles Deane, et al.

CHAPTER 2

"A Franciscan Monk Refutes Las Casas (1555)." Excerpts taken from *Letters and People of the Spanish Indies: Sixteenth Century* by James Lockhart and Enrique Otte, eds. Copyright © 1976 Cambridge University Press, pp. 220–222, 236, 239. Originally published in Madrid, 1864. Reprinted with permission of Cambridge University Press.

John Smith, "A True Relation of . . . Virginia." Taken from Vol. 7 of *English Colonial Documents: American Colonial Documents to 1776* by Merrill Jensen, ed., pp. 132–136. Methuen Books, London. Original source: John Smith, *A True Relation of such occurrences and accidents of noate as hath happened in Virginia since the first planting of that Collony, which is now resident in the South part thereof, till the last return from thence* (London, 1608). Reprinted by permission of Routledge (UK).

Nathaniel Bacon, "Manifesto Concerning the Troubles in Virginia (1676). Taken from *The Virginia Magazine of History and Biography*, 1 (1894), pp. 56–61.

"The Examination of Anne Hutchinson (1637)." Taken from *History of the Colony and Province of Massachusetts Bay* (Boston, 1767).

"The Mayflower Compact." Taken from *The Federal and State Constitutions . . . of the United States* by Francis N. Thorpe, ed. vol. 3, p. 1841 (1909). U.S. Government Printing Office, Washington, D.C.

"Metacom's War: A Puritan Explanation (1675)." Taken from *Records of the Governor and Company of the Massachusetts Bay (1853–1854)* by Nathaniel B. Shurtleff, ed., vol. 5, pp. 59–64.

CHAPTER 3

William Penn, "Preface to the Frame of Government for Pennsylvania (1682)." Taken from *Minutes of the Provincial Council of Pennsylvania* (Philadelphia and Harrisburg, 1852–1853), vol. 1, pp. 29–32.

James Albert Ukawsaw Gronniosaw, "An African Prince Sold into Slavery." Taken from *A Narrative of the Most Remarkable Particulars in the Life of James Albert Ukawsaw Gronniosaw, An African Prince* (Bath, circa 1780), pp. 7–17.

"An Act for the Better Order and Government of Negroes and Slaves." Taken from *Statutes at Large of South Carolina, 1836–1841* by Thomas Cooper and David J. McCord, eds., vol. 7, pp. 352–357.

"Early Protests against Slavery: The Mennonites (1688)." Taken from *Source Book and Bibliographical Guide for American Church History* (1921); reprint edited by P.G. Mode. Published by J.S. Canner, 1964, pp. 552–553.

"Conflicts Between Masters and Slaves: Maryland in the Mid-Seventeenth Century (1658)." Taken from *The Archives of Maryland–Proceedings of the Provincial Court*, vol. XLI, pp. 190–191 (Land Records) S, PCR, 147, MSA S 552–1. Published by the Maryland Historical Society, 1922. Reprinted courtesy of the Maryland State Archives.

Excerpts taken from Phillis Wheatley, *Poems on Various Subjects, Religious and Moral*, pp. 18, 74. (London: A. Bell, 1993).

CHAPTER 4

Excerpt taken from Benjamin Wadsworth, *The Well-Ordered Family, or Relative Duties*, pp. 22–47. (Boston, 1712).

"Esther Edward Burr, Letter on the Birth of Her Son." Taken from *Early American Women: Documentary History, 1600–1900* by Nancy Woloch, ed. pp. 52–53. Wadsworth, 1992.

Peter Kalm. "A Description of Philadelphia." Taken from *Travels in North America,* trans. by John Reinhold Forester (London, 1770), vol. 1, pp. 36–45, 58–60.

Cadwallader Colden. "State of the Province of New York (1765)." Taken from *Collections of the New York Historical Society (1878),* vol. 10, pp. 68–69.

George Whitefield. Excerpts taken from *A Continuation of the Reverend Mr. Whitefield's Journal,* pp. 14–21 (Philadelphia, 1940).

Excerpts taken from *Enthusiasm Describ'd and Caution'd Against,* pp. 3–7, by Charles Chauncy. (Boston, 1742).

Excerpt taken from "To The INHABITANTS of the Province of North Carolina," Salisbury, North Carolina, September 14, 1769, in *Some Eighteenth Century Tracts Concerning North Carolina* by William K. Boyd, ed., pp. 301–304. (Raleigh, N.C.: Edwards & Broughton Company, 1927).

CHAPTER 5

"Account of a Crowd Action (1765)". A letter from Thomas Hutchinson to Richard Jackson, dated August 30, 1765. Published in *Massachusetts Archives,* vol. 26, pp. 146–147.

"New York Merchant Boycott Agreement (1765)." Taken from the *Pennsylvania Gazette,* November 7, 1765.

"Norfolk Sons of Liberty Pronouncement (1766)." Taken from the *Pennsylvania Gazette,* April 17, 1766.

"Declarations" of the Stamp Act Congress (1765). Taken from *Proceedings of the Congress of New York (1766),* pp. 15–16.

"The Boycott Agreements of Women in Boston (1770)." Taken from *Boston Evening-Post,* February 12, 1770, *Boston-Gazette,* February 19, 1770, as reprinted in *Pennsylvania Gazette,* March 8, 1770.

"Joseph Galloway, Plan of Union (1774)." Taken from *Journals of the Continental Congress* by W.C. Ford, ed., vol. 1, pp. 49–51. (Washington, D.C.: U.S. Government Printing Office, 1904).

CHAPTER 6

"The Dangers of Race War within a War for Independence (1775)." Taken from the *Pennsylvania Evening Post,* December 14, 1775.

Thomas Paine. Excerpt taken from *Common Sense: Addressed to the Inhabitants of America . . . A New Edition* (1776).

"Thomas Jefferson Attacks the King on the Issue of Slavery (1776)." Taken from *The Papers Of Thomas Jefferson* by Julian P. Boyd, ed., vol. 1, p. 426. Copyright © 1950 by Princeton University Press. Reprinted by permission of Princeton University Press.

"The Importance of the American Victory at Trenton (1776–1777)." Taken from *The Journal of Nicholas Cresswell,* by Nicholas Cresswell, pp. 176, 179–180. Published by Dial Press, 1924.

"Sarah Osborn, Account of Life with the Army." Taken from *The Revolution Remembered: Eyewitness Accounts of the War for Independence* by John C. Dann, ed., pp. 242–250. Published by the University of Chicago Press, 1980. Original source: Sarah Osborn's application for a pension, Record Group 1.5 of the Records of Veterans Administration, National Archives.

"Charles Herbert, Prisoner of War Diary (1847)." Taken from *A Relic of the Revolution . . . by Charles H. Herbert* edited by Richard Livsey, pp. 67–173.

"Abigail Adams, Boston Women Support Price Control (1777)." Taken from *Letters of Mrs. Adams, the Wife of John Adams,* 4th edition, edited by Charles E. Adams, (Boston, 1848), pp. 84–85.

"Virginia Statute of Religious Freedom (1786)." Taken from *The Statutes at Large of Virginia,* vol. 12, pp. 84–86, edited by William W. Hening.

CHAPTER 7

"Virginia Declaration of Rights (1776)." Taken from *The Federal and State Constitutions . . . of the United States* edited by Francis N. Thorpe, vol. 7, pp. 3812–3814. (Washington, D.C.: U.S. Government Printing Office, 1909).

"Abigail and John Adams Debate the Rights of Women (1776)." Taken from the *Adams Family Correspondence,* edited by L. H. Butterfield, vol. 1, pp. 370, 382–383, 402–403; vol. 2, p. 94. Copyright © 1963 by the Massachusetts Historical Society. Reprinted by permission of the publisher, Harvard University Press.

"James Madison, *The Federalist,* No. 10 (1787)." Taken from the *New York Daily Advertiser,* November 22, 1787.

"Alexander Hamilton, Report on Public Credit (1790)." Taken from *The Papers of Alexander Hamilton* edited by Harold C. Syrett, vol. 6, pp. 65–71, 106. Copyright © 1962 Columbia University Press. Reprinted by permission of Columbia University Press.

"George Washington, Farewell Address (1796)." Taken from *A Compilation of the Messages and Papers of the Presidents* edited by James D. Richardson, vol. 1, pp. 205–216. (Washington, D.C.: U.S. Government Printing Office, 1896–1899).

"The Sedition Act (1798)." Taken from *Statutes at Large,* vol. 1, pp. 596–597.

"Thomas Jefferson, First Inaugural Address (1801)." Taken from *A Compilation of the Messages and Papers of the Presidents* edited by James D. Richardson, vol. 1, pp. 309–312. (Washington, D.C.: U.S. Government Printing Office, 1913).

CHAPTER 8

"Thomas Jefferson, Message to Congress (1803)." Taken from *A Compilation of the Messages and Papers of the Presidents* edited by James D. Richardson, vol. 1, pp. 352–353. (Washington, D.C.: U.S. Government Printing Office, 1908).

"Noah M. Ludlow, From New York to Kentucky in 1815." Taken from *Dramatic Life as I found It* by Noah M. Ludlow. Published by G.I. Jones and Company, 1880, pp. 5–14, 17–21, 76–78.

"Journals of the Lewis and Clark Expedition (1805)." Taken from *Original Journals of the Lewis and Clark Expedition, 1804–1806,* edited by Reuben Gold Thwaites. First published by Dodd, Mead and Company, 1904–1905; facsimile reprint published by Arno Press, 1969, vol. 1, pp. 359–360.

"William Henry Harrison, Speech to Tecumseh and the Propher (1811)" and "Report to the Secretary of War (1814)." Taken from *Life of Tecumseh* by Benjamin Drake. Published by E. Morgan & Co., 1841. Facsimile reprint, Arno Press and The New York Times, 1969.

"Richard Mentor Johnson, The Benefits of Slavery in Missouri." Taken from *Annals of Congress of the United States, 1789–1824,* 16th Congress, 1st session, pp. 345–359. (Washington, D.C.: U.S. Government Printing Office, 1819–1820).

"Charles Ball, Life on a South Carolina Cotton and Rice Plantation." Taken from *Slavery in the United States: A Narrative of the Life and Adventures of Charles Ball, A Black Man* by Isaac Fisher. (New York: John S. Taylor, 1837), pp. 164–167, 187.

CHAPTER 9

Taken from *A Statement of the Arts and Manufactures of the United States of America, for the Year 1810: Digested and Prepared by Tench Coxe, Esquire of Philadelphia.* Published by A. Cornman, 1814.

"Martin Van Buren, Against Unrestricted Male Suffrage (1821)." Taken from *The Votes and Speeches of Martin Van Buren . . . In the Convention of the State of New York (Assembled to Amend the Constitution in 1821).* Published by T. Weed, 1840, pp. 15–17.

Excerpt taken from *The Mother's Book* by Lydia Maria Child. (Boston: Carter and Hendee, 1831).

"On the Writing of American History." (1805). Taken from *History of the Rise, Progress, and Termination of the American Revolution* by Mrs. Mercy Warren, Boston, 1805. Facsimile reprint AMS Press, 1970, pp. iii–viii.

Excerpt from *The Duty of Christian Freemen to Elect Christian Rulers* by Ezra Stiles Ely, Published by W.F. Gettes, 1828, pp. 6–14.

Excerpt taken from *Essays Literary, Moral, and Philosophical* by Benjamin Rush (Philadelphia, 1798). Reprinted by Union College Press, 1988, Schenectady, NY, pp. 44–54.

CHAPTER 10

"Jacob Pussey, A Textile Manufacturer Discusses His Enterprise (1832)." Excerpt taken from *Documents Relative to the Manufactures in the United States* (1833), vol. 3, pp. 800–802, 224–226. Also from *Reprints of Economic Classics* by Augustus M. Kelly (1969), vol. 2, pp. 663–666, 224–225.

"A Mill Worker Describes Her Work and Life (1844)." Excerpt taken from *The Lowell Offering*, June and August 1844, pp. 169–172, 237–240. Also from *Looking for America: The People's History*, 2e, edited by Stanley L. Kutler. Published by W.W. Norton & Company (1979), vol. 1, pp. 260–265.

Excerpt taken from *Society in America* by Harriet Martineau. Published by Saunders and Orley (London, 1837). Reprinted by AMS Press (New York, 1966), vol. 2, pp. 355–358.

"A Railroad Journey South (1838)." Excerpts taken from *Records of Later Life* by Frances Kemble (London, 1882), vol. 1, pp. 170–172, 174, 178–179, 181–183.

Excerpt taken from *The Autobiography of Benjamin Franklin* (1818). Reprint published by (New York: Airmont Publishing, 1965), pp. 79–86.

"On Conversion (1821)." Taken from *The Autobiography of Charles G. Finney*, condensed and edited by Helen Wessel, pp. 13–25. Copyright © 1977. Reprinted by permission of Bethany House Publishers (Minneapolis). All rights reserved.

"Beginning of the Temperance Movement (1812)." Excerpt taken from *The Autobiography of Lyman Beecher* edited by Barbara M. Cross. Harvard University Press (Cambridge, Mass.): vol. 1, pp. 179–182. Copyright © 1961 by the President and Fellows of Harvard College. Reprinted by permission of the publisher.

CHAPTER 11

"Henry Clay, Speech on the Tariff (1824)." Taken from *Annals of Congress of the United States, 1789–1824*, 18th Congress, 1st session (1824), pp. 1962–2001. (Washington, D.C., U.S. Government Printing Office).

"Amos Kendall, The Beginnings of Grass Roots Democracy (1830)." Taken from *Francis P. Blair Papers*. Copyright © Princeton University Press. Reprinted by permission of Princeton University Press.

"Opposition to Banks and Monopoly (c.1832)." Excerpt taken from *A Collection of the Political Writings of William Leggett* edited by Theodore Sedgwick, Jr. (New York, 1840), vol. 1, pp. 97–101.

"Seth Luther, Address to the Working Men of New England (1832)." Taken from *The Globe,* May 13, 1832 (Washington, D.C.)

"*People v. Cooper.*" Excerpt taken from *A Documentary History of American Industrial Society* edited by John R. Commons et al. (New York, Russell & Russell, 1958), vol. 4, pp. 277–312. Reprinted with the permission of Scribner, a division of Simon & Schuster.

CHAPTER 12

Excerpt taken from *Walden, or Life in the Woods and On the Duty of Civil Disobedience* by Henry David Thoreau. Boston, 1854; reprint NAL, Penguin, 1960.

Excerpt taken from *The Blithedale Romance* by Nathaniel Hawthorne. (Boston, 1852).

"Rebecca Cox Jackson, On the Shakers." Excerpt taken from *Gifts of Power: The Writings of Rebecca Jackson, Black Visionary, Shaker Eldress* edited by Jean McMahon Humez. Published by the University of Massachusetts Press, 1981, pp. 220–221. Courtesy of The Western Reserve Historical Society, Cleveland, Ohio.

"Breaking Out of Women's 'Separate Sphere' (1838)." Excerpt taken from *Letters to Catharine E. Beecher, in Reply to an Essay on Slavery and Abolitionism, Addressed to A.E. Grimke* by A.E. Grimke. (Boston, 1838; facsimile reprint Arno Press, New York, 1969), pp. 103–113.

"Seneca Falls Resolutions (1948)." Excerpts taken from *History of Women Suffrage* by Elizabeth Cady Stanton, Susan B. Anthony, and Matilda Joslyn Gage. (1881–1922; reprinted by Arno Press and *The New York Times,* 1969), vol. 1, pp. 70–73.

"Commencement of *The Liberator* (1831)." Excerpt taken from *Liberator,* January 1, 1831, in *Selections from the Writings and Speeches of William Lloyd Garrison* by William Lloyd Garrison. (New American Library, 1969), pp. 62–63.

Excerpt from *American Slavery as It Is: Testimony of a Thousand Witnesses* by Theodore Dwight Weld. (New York, 1839; reprint Arno Press, 1968), pp. 60–63.

CHAPTER 13

"Slave Management on a Mississippi Plantation (1852)." Excerpt taken from *A Journal in the Back Country* by Frederick Law Olmsted. (New York, Manson Brothers, 1860; reprint, Williamstown, Mass.: Corner House Publishers, 1972), pp. 72–83.

"The Virtues of Slavery, The Impossibility of Emancipation. (1831)." Excerpt taken from *Dew's Review* by Thomas R. Dew.

"Memories of a Slave Childhood." Excerpts taken from *Unwritten History of Slavery: Autobiographical Accounts of Negro Ex-Slaves* by O.S. Egypt, J. Masuoka, and C.S. Johnson. Social Science Source Documents No. 1 (Fisk University, Social Science Institute, 1946), pp. 113–117, 276–279. Reprinted by permission of Fisk University-Special Collections. Also excerpted from *The Female Experience: An American Documentary* edited by Gerda Lerner. (Indianapolis: Bobbs-Merrill, 1977), pp. 11–14.

CHAPTER 14

Excerpt taken from *Union and Freedom, without Compromise, Speech of Mr. Chase of Ohio, On Mr. Clay's Compromise Resolutions* by Salmon P. Chase. (Washington, D.C.: Buell and Blanchard, 1850).

"The Fugitive Slave Act of 1850." Taken from *Statutes at Large,* vol. 9, pp. 462ff.

"The Rescue of a Slave (1855)." Excerpt taken from *The Underground Railroad* by William Still. (Philadelphia, 1872), pp. 86–87.

"The Crime against Kansas (1856)." Excerpt taken from *Charles Sumner: His Complete Works* (Lee and Shepard, 1900; reprint, New York: Negro University Press edition, 1969), vol. 5, pp. 125–126.

Excerpt taken from *Dred Scott v. Sanford,* 19, 393 (1857).

"The Lincoln-Douglas Debates (1858)." Taken from *Political Speeches and Debates of Abraham Lincoln and Stephen A. Douglas, 1854–1861* edited by Alonzo T. Jones. (Battle Creek, Mich., 1895).

"A German Immigrant in Philadelphia (1885)." Excerpt taken from *Speeches, Correspondence, and Political Papers of Carl Schurz* (Carl Schurz to Gottfried Kinkel), edited by Frederic Bancroft. (New York, 1913), vol. 1, pp. 17–20.

"The American 'Know Nothing' Party Platform (1856)." Excerpt taken from *National Party Platforms, 1840–1976* by Donald Bruce Johnson and Kirk H. Porter. (University of Illinois Press, 1978), 22–23.

Excerpt taken from *Uncle Tom's Cabin; or Life among the Lowly* by Harriet Beecher Stowe. (Boston, John P. Jewett & Company, 1852; reprint, New York: Bantam Books edition, 1981), pp. 283–294.

"Defending Slavery to the British Minister in Washington." Excerpt taken from *The Papers of John C. Calhoun* (John C. Calhoun to Richard Pakenham, 18th April, 1844), edited by Clyde N. Wilson.

"The Trial of John Brown (1859)." Excerpt taken from *The Life, Trial and Execution of Captain John Brown . . .* (New York: R.M. DeWitt, 1859), pp. 94–95.

CHAPTER 15

"The New York City Draft Riots (1963)." Excerpt taken from *What Answer?* by Anna Elizabeth Dickinson (Boston, 1868), pp. 242–259.

"The Work of the United States Sanitary Commission (1864)." Excerpts taken from *The Philanthropic Results of the War in America: Collected from Official and Other Authentic Sources, by an American Citizen* [Linus P. Brockett]. (New York: Sheldon & Co., 1864), pp. 32–41, 89–91.

Excerpt taken from *My Diary North and South* by William Howard Russell. (London, 1863); reprinted, edited by Eugene H. Berwanger, New York: Knopf, 1988), pp. 257–277.

"A Soldier's Letter to His Wife (1862)." Taken from *A Gentleman and an Officer: A Social and Military History of James B. Griffin's Civil War* edited by Orville Vernon Burton and Judith N. McArthur. (New York: Oxford University Press, 1996). Reprinted by permission of Jack L. Gunter, direct descendent of James B. Griffin (Farmer's Branch, Texas).

"The Gettysburg Address (1863)." Taken from *The Collected Works of Abraham Lincoln,* edited by Roy P. Basler et al. (New Brunswick, N.J.: Rutgers University Press, 1953), vol. 7, p. 23.

"Black Soldiers in Missouri Bring Families to Freedom (1864)." Excerpt taken from *Freedom: A Documentary History of Emancipation, 1861–1867,* edited by Ira Berlin et al., series 1, vol. 1, pp. 479, 483–485. Assistant Provost Marshal J.P. Lewis, telegram to Assistant Adjutant General J. Rainsford, 6 March 1864; and Sam Bowmen to Dear Wife, 10 May 1864, National Archives, Washington, D.C.

CHAPTER 16

"Carl Schurz, Report on Conditions in the South." U.S. Congress, Senate, 39th Cong. 1st session (1865). Excerpts taken from Doc. No. 2, pp. 1–5, 8, 36–39, 41–44.

"The Mississippi Black Codes (1865)." Excerpts taken from *Laws of Mississippi* (1865), pp. 82 ff.

"Thaddeus Stevens on Black Suffrage and Land Redistribution (1867)." Excerpt taken from *Congressional Globe,* January 3, 1867, p. 252; March 19, 1867, p. 203.

"The Rise and Fall of Northern Support for Reconstruction (1868, 1874)." Cartoons by Thomas Nast, "This is a White Man's Government," from *Harper's Weekly,* September 5, 1868 and "Colored Rule in a Reconstructed State," from *Harper's Weekly,* March 14, 1874. Art courtesy of Research Libraries, New York Public Library.

Excerpt taken from *A Fool's Errand, By One of the Fools* [Albion W. Tourgee]. (New York: Fords, Howard, & Hulbert, 1878), pp. 182–192.

"Republicanism vs. Grantism (1872)." Excerpt taken from *Charles Sumner: His Complete Works* (Lee and Shepard, 1900; reprint New York: Negro University Press, 1969), vol. 20, pp. 83–171.